New Patterns of Democracy in India

SECOND EDITION

New Patterns
of Democracy
in India

VERA MICHELES DEAN

HARVARD UNIVERSITY PRESS
CAMBRIDGE, MASSACHUSETTS, 1969

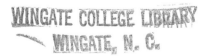

To my friends in India
both Indians and Americans
who shared their thoughts with me

Preface to the Second Edition

A decade after publication of this book in 1959, when we can look at independent India in greater perspective than was possible at that time, it seems appropriate to reassess the conclusions I had then reached after a ten-year acquaintance with India as writer and teacher. The decision to update my book appears particularly desirable at this time, when India, more than two decades after achieving independence as a nation, is soberly weighing both its past struggles and its future goals. With this purpose in mind, I have added a new chapter which summarizes the main trends of development in India since 1959 and attempts to forecast India's future developments; have updated the bibliography; and have made minor corrections in the text.

As I look back over the past decade, I realize even more deeply than I did in 1959 why I felt immediately at home the first time I visited India in 1950. For, although I have traveled widely in Europe, Asia, the Middle East, and Latin America since 1919, when I came to the United States as a young girl from what was then darkest and revolution-torn Russia, and have happily made my home here ever since, it was in India that I had the unforgettable experience of feeling as if by some miracle I had returned to the scenes of my childhood. There I rediscovered those contrasts of extreme poverty and great wealth, of exciting intellectual controversy about the basic issues of existence, of the interweaving of great ideals and their as yet limited fulfillment which nurtured my thinking in Russia during the fateful period 1903–1919.

It did not seem strange to me that Mahatma Gandhi and Leo Tolstoy, coming from two far-separated points, both geographically and intellectually, found that they shared common ideals and goals, as witnessed by their correspondence, which I had the pleasure of seeing at Tolstoy's home, Yasnaya Polyana, when I visited it in 1964. Nor did this affinity between the Indian and Russian minds — not only among intellectuals, but also among peasants — puzzle me once I began to be more and more steeped in the many-faceted life of independent India.

And yet, of course, India, although today still far behind the technological development achieved by Russia in the half-century 1918–1968, is far ahead in its determination to develop democratic institutions within a vast, only recently united nation of over five hundred million people, widely different in religions, languages, and ways of life. The U.S.S.R. is far ahead of India in terms of industrial development and astronautical feats. But it is far behind in terms of respect for human values and concern for human rights. Each can learn from the other — to the benefit of both. And meanwhile, of course, India is in the exceptional position, achieved by its consistently maintained policy of non-alignment in world affairs, of being able to draw also on the rich experience of highly developed Western nations — not only its former ruler, Britain, but also the United States — with respect both to political democracy and to non-Communist methods of social and economic development. If a synthesis of the varied basic values of the twentieth century is to be found anywhere in the non-Western world, it is in India that it emerges today.

As a non-Westerner by origin (for I place Russia under the rubric of non-Western), and a Westerner by training and allegiance, I have found India an ever stimulating source of ideas and experiences. For the inspiration I have thus gained, I am particularly indebted to the many friends I have made in India over the years, and most of all to A. D. Gorwala, distinguished civil servant in the period of British rule, and, since independence, editor and publisher of the magazine *Opinion*; H. M. Patel, former Under-Secretary both of Defense and of Finance in the government of India; G. L. Mehta, distinguished statesman and diplomat, India's former ambassador to the United States, and now the recognized leader of all Indians who seek to industrialize their country; Sunil Roy, former gifted and enterprising Consul-General of India in New York, one of India's best diplomats, now Director of Tourism; Durga Das, enterprising journalist, director of the *India News and Feature Alliance*, a syndicate which distributes material on foreign and domestic affairs to some eighty newspapers, English and vernacular, which I have served for a number of years as United Nations correspondent; Dr. D. R. Gadgil, deputy chairman of the Planning Commission since 1967, a distinguished scholar in the field of economics; and his predecessor in that post, Asoka Mehta, former Socialist leader.

Among the many Americans who have devotedly helped the development of India in various capacities, I would like to single out particularly Chester Bowles, ever energetic, imaginative, and hard-working diplomat-statesman who has inspired so many Indians and Americans to persist in the exhilarating tasks of aiding India within the framework of its own aspirations; and Douglas Ensminger, president of the Ford Foundation in India, whose unfailing concern for the Indian people and unremitting efforts to blaze new trails in the great task of their economic and social development inspired and sustained the concern about India's welfare which those of us who have had the honor to know him and work with him have experienced.

New York   Vera Micheles Dean
November 14, 1968

Preface to the First Edition

The first time I went to India, and to Asia, in October 1950, I was warned by some of my friends that I should be prepared to see and hear many things that would be wholly alien to me. Brought up in European traditions, and educated in universities of the United States where I have spent all my adult life, I braced myself to meet the impact of the unknown and perhaps unknowable.

Yet from the first moment I felt entirely at home in India. True, the landscape, the people, the street scenes, with cows peaceably ambling along thoroughfares and the colorful crowding of bazaars, were new to the eye, but the spirit infusing what I saw and heard was peculiarly, even poignantly, familiar. I felt as if I were reliving experiences I had had before — as if the sights and sounds of India were a transparency through which I could see anew a past laid aside long ago. Irrational as it might seem, I suddenly saw a new meaning in the Hindu concept of transmigration of souls.

And then one day I realized that I did not need to go so far afield for an explanation. For what I relived in India was my childhood experience of Russia. Here, again, were "dark villages" struggling under the burdens of age-old poverty. Here were cities, disfigured by wretched slums, in the throes of the early stages of industrialization. Here were intellectuals, aware of their nation's problems, suffering from a guilt feeling about the wretchedness of the poor in town and countryside, yet slow to action, and talking like characters in Chekhov's *Cherry Orchard*.

But there was also a striking difference in this familiar picture. For here was a country which, through a conjunction of its religious beliefs, the leadership of men like the Hindu

Asoka and the Muslim Akbar, and the blending of India's ancient traditions with the ideas and practices of British liberalism, was absorbed in the development of a society that differed profoundly from that of Russia. Here was an economically underdeveloped country, still wrestling with the limitations on social mobility imposed by the caste system, but intent on forging new patterns of democracy in political, economic, and social relations.

If India fails, then the communism of Russia, and even more of China, will be regarded by other underdeveloped countries as the only answer to their problems. If it succeeds, then India's way may become a guideline to other areas of the non-Western world. Thus the new patterns India is evolving have become of paramount significance to all the world, both Communist and non-Communist. But, irrespective of whether India succeeds or fails as compared with Communist China — for where is the yardstick to measure success or failure? — the West has a stake in India's democracy in and of itself.

Vera Micheles Dean

New York,
June 15, 1959

Contents

Illustrations

"The nations of the world are moving toward freedom and democracy from different starting points in history. It is logical that they should try to build their present and their future on the elements of their usable past. The history of India and the history of the United States, to give one example, have very few things in common. But they do share a common hope for a better life in a more widespread freedom. This important point of resemblance is most reassuring, and it should suffice."

Carlos P. Romulo
Friend to Friend (John Day)

"The most explosive element thrown into the Asian drama is the principle of universal suffrage which all these countries in South and Southeast Asia have accepted, almost as if it was something natural that they should, and which, in addition, India has had the determination to give life and reality to in election after election . . .

"It is for the political leaders to turn this tremendously explosive power of adult suffrage, released for the first time in history in an underdeveloped country, into a concerted and constructive effort towards rapid economic development of an ever more integrated nation. To proceed slowly in this situation would for a democracy be suicidal. Of this I am deeply convinced."

Gunnar Myrdal
United Asia
Special Number, "An Evaluation on the Second Five Year Plan," Number Four, 1958.

New Patterns of Democracy in India

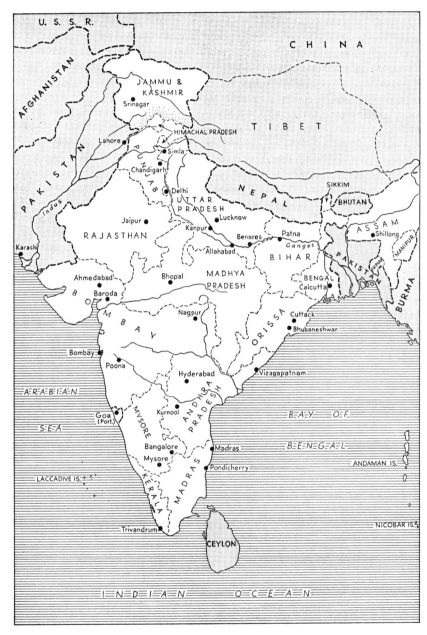

INDIA, 1959

Chapter 1

Profile of India

The monsoon season, with its sudden daily downpours and brief intervals of clearing when the cloud-burdened sky is suddenly irradiated with fresh-washed azure and gold, has a dual psychological effect on the Indian people.

The seemingly ceaseless rain, beneficent as it is for India's urgently needed crops, can also wreak havoc as rising rivers flood the countryside and sweep away homes. The immobilization of physical activity encourages at worst passivity, and, at best, a spirit of contemplation. But, when the sun breaks through, spirits rise. The prospect of a good harvest stirs hope. People who had just been taking refuge in doorways or huddling under the huge black umbrellas which give a funereal air to monsoon-swept streets come out to enjoy the respite; and the landscape suddenly blooms with the women's colorful saris.

A decade after independence India is in a monsoon mood. It feels neither the elation of 1947, when-with the departure of the British it looked confidently to its future as a free nation, nor the sense of expectation generated by the launching of the first Five-Year Plan in 1951.

Years of profound change and often painful readjustment have left their imprint on India. It is now realized that independence from foreign rule marked not the end but the beginning of the new nation's struggle for freedom. The political revolution which united India against Britain is seen as the first stage of a long and arduous process which must bring an economic and social revolution if India is to garner the fruits of its efforts and not see them swept away in a torrent of internal conflicts.

India's mood today is sober — among some who know the seriousness of its problems even somber. There is a sense of pessimism, of frustration, as the myriad difficulties of building a united nation and modernizing an archaic economy emerge in all their starkness, no longer veiled in the glamorous haze of nationalist hopes.

If we are to understand India today, we must see it as a country where the ancient past accumulated during several thousand years of known history lives side by side with the all-permeating ferment of the present and reaches ahead to shape the future. In India it would be an impossible task to separate the elements of continuity from the elements of change. For the two are inextricably woven together to form the seamless fabric of Indian existence.

This unselfconscious interweaving, at a given moment in history, of past, present, and future, is perhaps the most outstanding aspect of the way of life of a country which, until it achieved independence from Britain in 1947, had been peculiarly indifferent to historical recording of its millennial development. Happy nations, the saying goes, have no history. India has passed through dark valleys of strife and misery as well as reached pinnacles of glory. What it has lacked is not history but historians.

To a non-Indian, however, the most noticeable characteristic in every field of Indian activity — whether it is philosophy or economics, labor problems or politics or foreign policy — is the constant attempt to reconcile conflicting views or actions, to discover a workable compromise, to avoid seeing the human situation in terms of all black or all white, and instead to paint the canvas in various shades of gray. As India's philosopher Vice-President Sarvapalli Radakrishnan has put it: Why look at things in terms of this or that? Why not try to have both this *and* that?

Nor is this point of view, which is deeply rooted in Hindu religion and philosophy, prevalent solely among Hindus. It has also come to affect the thinking and attitudes of the Muslims, who conquered India in what was the West's Middle Ages and ruled it for three centuries, yet have been so deeply imbued with the Hindu state of mind that India's Islam, represented by the forty million Muslims who chose to remain there after the 1947 partition of the subcontinent, is regarded as the most mellow and progressive in the Islamic world. It is not an accident that the Mogul ruler Akbar in the sixteenth century, a contemporary of Queen Elizabeth, sought to reconcile Islam not only with Hinduism but also with Judaism and Christianity (as it was brought by the Jesuits to the Portuguese colony of Goa) in a synthetic religion of his own devising, very much as the Hindu emperor Asoka, nearly three centuries before Christ, absorbed Buddhism, the reform movement of Hinduism, into the Hindu faith, to such an extent that today there are but a few Buddhists left in India. The absorption by Hinduism of Buddhism, which had sought to reform it but was eclipsed by the Brahminical reaction, was a feat that would have had a parallel in the Western world if Catholicism had succeeded in absorbing Protestantism and had thereby reduced it to a minority religious group.

Nor is this spirt of reconciliation limited to the old well-established religions of India. Zoroastrians, Jews, and Christians also reflect this spirit. And in the political field even the Communists have been uniquely affected by Indian conditions. For in the one state, Kerala, where in 1957 they achieved minority control of the government with the aid of five independents, they govern only by accepting the need to rule under constitutional democratic procedures.

When Americans visit India they are apt to be struck, first of all, by its great poverty and its technological backwardness. This is not surprising, because we put so much emphasis on technology that we are apt to regard good plumbing or chrome-decorated cars as symbols of a high culture.

Measured by such a yardstick, India may seem to us culturally backward. It is essential, however, that we should not confuse technological underdevelopment in the twentieth century with lack of culture. For India, whose known history goes back several thousand years, has had many periods of cultural achievement which would be regarded as great in the history of any nation. Particularly impressive is the fact that heights of achievement in the arts, in science, in administration, were reached both under the Hindus and under the Muslims. The age of the Hindu Emperor Asoka (around 300 B.C.) who became a convert to and a missionary of Buddhism was matched in glory by the age of Akbar, the Mogul ruler who reigned about the time of Queen Elizabeth of England. Moreover, the two cultures of the Hindus and the Muslims, springing from two of the great faiths of mankind, Hinduism and Islam, became closely interwoven, with each deeply affected by the other. The result, as the Marquess of Zetland has said, is that a striking characteristic of India's cultural legacy is its infinite variety.

One can see this variety in the Hindu temples of Ellora, carved out of rock, some of which have the majesty and serenity of Greek temples; and in the pure simplicity and dignity of the Muslim mausoleum the Taj Mahal, as contrasted with some of the often over-ornate Hindu temples of South India. One can see it in the Ajanta paintings, the work of Buddhist monks who unfurled colorful tales of Indian life on the walls of the cells they had built in caves; and in the beautifully detailed Rajput paintings, inspired by Persian art, but as time went on increasingly devoted to contemporary subjects. One can see this variety in the work of India's most famous literary figure, Kalidasa, court poet and playwright in what is known as the Golden Age of Hinduism. Kalidasa has been compared to Shakespeare for his best-known play, *Shakuntala*, with its tender scenes of royal love and the sense of humor of its court jester, which inspired Goethe, and to Shelley for his lyric poems, the best-known of which is *The Cloud Messenger*. But one also sees this variety in the eloquent poetry of Sir Mohammed Iqbal, a Muslim poet and an earnest Muslim nationalist who died in 1938, and in the poetry of Rabindranath Tagore, the Hindu who in his little book on *Nationalism* rose above the confines of nationhood to plead for an international community.

But even those who think of culture as connected with plumbing can gain new insight into India's cultural achievements by studying the archeological finds made in 1922, when a British archeologist discovered the remains of a great prehistoric city at Mohenjo-daro, dating back probably to 2500 or 3000 B.C.

As H. G. Rawlinson has said in *India: A Cultural History*, "The town is well laid out. Its streets are at right angles, running due north and south and east and west. The main street, which is 33 feet wide, has been traced for over half a mile and is unpaved. The side roads are about half this width. The buildings are of burnt brick set in mud mortar. No stone is used and the absence of any kind of ornamentation is conspicuous. The windows and doors open upon the main street, and it was probable that some were several storeys high, with flat roofs. An unusual feature of the houses is the presence of bathrooms, and also of an elaborate drainage system, greatly in advance of anything known in later India. For this purpose, pottery drain pipes and receptacles were laid down, communicating with the street drain or gutter. No temple has been discovered, but a large public bath, 39 feet by 23, has been unearthed. This bath, which was rendered water-tight, is provided with steps leading down to the water, a promenade, and compartments for the bathers. Ingenious arrangements for filling and emptying it are provided. Just to the south of the bathroom is a large building, over two hundred feet long and one hundred feet wide, which may have been the royal palace."

Many centuries later, about A.D. 400, the Chinese scholar Fa Hsien gave a striking picture of India as a peaceful, prosperous country. Speaking of the capital of that time, Pataliputra, he tells us of the splendid car-processions held every month, when images of the Buddha were carried around, and the occasion was marked with games and music and the offering of incense and flowers, and of the excellent charitable arrangements. "The nobles and householders have founded hospitals within the city, to which the poor of all countries, the destitute, crippled and diseased, may repair. They receive every kind of requisite help gratuitously. Physicians inspect their diseases and, according to their cases, order them food and drink, medicine or decoctions, everything in fact which may contribute to their ease. When cured, they depart at their convenience." And Fa Hsien writes in glowing terms of the justice, clemency, and efficiency of the government.

Another Chinese scholar, Huien Tsang, spoke well of the personal habits of the Hindus. "They are very particular in their personal cleanliness. All wash before eating: they never use food left over from a former meal. Wooden and stone vessels must be destroyed after use: metal ones must be well polished and rubbed. After eating they cleanse their mouth with a willow stick, and wash their hands and mouths."

And if we think that Americans are responsible for all scientific inventions in human history, then let us look at this summary of scientific achievement in the sixth century, again by Rawlinson in his *Cultural History* of India:

"Universities for secular and religious studies flourished at Nalanda and other centres of learning. Medical science was widely studied, and Sanskrit medical treatises were the basis of much of the later Arabian learning which reached Europe in the Middle Ages. Dissection was practiced, and students were trained in 'holding the lancet, in cutting, marking and piercing with it, in extracting darts, in cleansing wounds, in causing them to dry up, the application of ointments and in the administration of emetics, purges and oily enemas.' " In astronomy, much was due to the Alexandrian Greeks, to whom the Indians freely acknowledged their indebtedness. "The Greeks are barbarians," says the Hindu astronomer, Varahamihira, as quoted by Rawlinson, "but the science of astronomy originated with them, and for this they must be reverenced like gods." Hindu astronomers had discovered that the heavenly bodies were spherical, and shone by reflected light; they were aware of the diurnal motion of the earth on its axis and had calculated its diameter. Brahmagupta (A.D. 628) anticipated Newton by declaring that "all things fall to the earth by a law of nature, for it is the nature of the earth to attract and keep things." The Vaisesika school of physicists propounded the atomic theory. In mathematics "the theorem of Pythagoras was understood, a value was calculated for π, a table of sines given, and a rule laid down for the solution of simple equations."

Today, free India is once again seeking to blend the cultural values of many traditions — this time of the traditions of East and West. Side by side with the villager's bullock cart India builds atomic reactors. Side by side with the Ajanta Cave paintings, and the beautifully intricate yet serene traditional Indian dance, young Indians experiment with French impressionist painting techniques and listen to American jazz. Inevitably, in this transition period, there are clashes between intellectual and artistic loyalties and a tendency to imitate Western models instead of drawing on the rich heritage of India's own cultural past.

But two of India's most impressive qualities are the absorptiveness of Hinduism, and its emphasis on the individual as the decisive factor in every field of endeavor. Now that the creative forces of India are no longer diverted, as they were under British rule, to the struggle for independence from

Britain, the Indians may experience a cultural renaissance expressing their ideas, their tastes, and their aspirations. As Buddha put it in his deathbed message to his disciples: "Be ye lamps unto yourselves. Be a refuge to yourselves. Hold fast to the truth as to a lamp. Look not for refuge to anyone besides yourselves."

India's gift for fitting new ideas into old molds, for taming the conqueror by making him part of the ongoing process of its history, serves it well in the modern era of seismic transformations which have shaken and rent asunder some other nations at a comparable level of economic and social development. The resiliency of its intellectual and social fabric makes it less susceptible to the shocks which have caused profound convulsions in more rigid societies, such as Russia, China, Japan, or the Arab nations.

In a society hospitable to many faiths and intolerant of none, polytheism, the personalization of plants and animals reminiscent of Greek, Roman, and Teuton mythology, and the consultation of astrologers about specially propitious days survive side by side in the twentieth century with the sophisticated agnosticism of a Nehru and the rationalism of the distinguished nuclear physicist Homi Babha. Great dams at Bhakra and in the Damodar Valley, nuclear reactors, experiments with solar heat can coexist with cow-worship and the saucers of milk which women who hope to have children leave for the sacred cobras. In such a society there is little danger of the vacuums of faith which in other lands followed the destruction of ancient beliefs before they could be replaced by new ideologies. One set of ideas need not be sharply divided from another. Instead, each tends to shade off into the next. Thus, lines which might elsewhere become impassable demarcations are blurred into indistinctness.

This, critics of India say, may eventually prove dangerous, if the lines between Mr. Nehru's moderate parliamentary socialism and the ruthless plans of the totalitarian Communists should be blurred beyond differentiation. Meanwhile, however, the philosophy of "this *and* that" rather than of a divisive choice between "this and that" has served India effectively in the turbulent decade since it achieved independence in 1947, only to see the subcontinent partitioned into two nations — India and Pakistan — with the resulting bloody tragedy of Hindu-Muslim riots, when millions of refugees streamed across new borders, raw materials were cut off from factories, and families were forced to accept bitter separation.

In this decade India has carried out five major tasks which in 1947 seemed insuperable, and would have tried the mettle of far more stable and technologically developed nations.

First, in spite of the fact that the new state of Pakistan carved out of the Indian subcontinent was squarely based on religion, with the Koran made the cornerstone of its 1956 constitution (abrogated in 1958), in contrast to India, which was committed to being a secular state, a reconciliation has been achieved, by and large, between the 340 million Hindus and the 40 million Muslims within the Republic of India.

Second, India's leaders have created a unified country out of the two separate segments into which it had been divided under British rule — British India and 562 princely states, of which all but one, Kashmir, still a bone of contention between India and Pakistan, have been absorbed into the Republic of India with a minimum of conflict. This has involved the acceptance by Indian princes not only of a new national order for the country but of a new economic and social order comparable to the changes brought about by the French Revolution in the status of the *ancien régime* of monarchy and aristocracy in 1789. Yet these changes have been carried out without the revolutionary upheaval which shook France to its depths, and whose imprint on French society is still visible today. In contrast to France, India's monarchical-feudal order was brought to an end almost overnight (1947–48), largely through the blandishments and threats of a great statesman, Sardar Vallabhbhai Patel, free India's first Deputy Prime Minister and Minister for States. True, force was used in the states of Junagadh and Hyderabad, but on balance India's *ancien régime* slipped from the scene with remarkably little friction.

Third, close to 400 million people speaking fourteen major languages, some dominant in areas the size of France, Germany, or Italy, have been knit into a single nation which has achieved a sense of national consciousness previously unknown in the subcontinent's history. When we consider the immense difficulties, which are still far from being surmounted, of creating the united Europe dreamed of for centuries, we may some day regard Mr. Nehru as a modern Charlemagne.

Fourth, in a country where 80 per cent of the population lives in primitive villages comparable to those of premedieval Europe, the Indians are developing a mixed voluntary economy, directed by the central government under a series of five-year plans, but most of which — notably agriculture and all but a small percentage of industry — is controlled by private owners. This is in marked contrast to state ownership of resources and industrial enterprises in Russia and Communist China.

For the modernization of this ancient economy, which the British, who after 1858 completely controlled British India, and in the princely states controlled defense, communications, and foreign policy, had done relatively little to change, India's leaders have mobilized the resources of twentieth-century science and technology — from new fertilizer plants to atomic energy for peacetime uses, from solar energy to study of Japan's achievements in rice-growing, Scandinavia's know-how in operating small industries, and American experience with agricultural extension work. And, with their traditional predilection for finding a workable mixture of "this and that," while still retaining the British influence which has permeated Indian schools and colleges, they are seeking a formula for the greatly needed reorganization of their educational system by blending the values they regard as most useful in both American and Russian education — particularly in the fields of science and technology — into a system adapted to Indian needs.

Fifth, in spite of the country's economic and social backwardness, in spite of 85 per cent illiteracy and the persistence of the caste system, India has succeeded in establishing and operating the greatest democracy in the non-Western world. Confounding the belief of political scientists that literacy is necessary for the successful operation of a democratic government, India has held two general elections, in 1951–52 and in 1957, in which, outside observers agreed, voters who could not read and write showed common sense and discrimination in choosing representatives to the House of the People, the lower house of the Parliament, whose practices are modeled on those of Britain's House of Commons, the Mother of Parliaments.

It is true that India has not yet achieved the two-party system familiar to Britain and the United States. The Congress party, headed by Mr. Nehru, who is both Premier and Foreign Minister and leader of the party, still occupies the center of the stage, challenged only by the Communists (and this with, for them, unwonted politeness). The Socialists, who could have become an important opposition party, have for the most part, chosen to eschew open party conflicts which they regard as unseemly in a period of national strain and stress, frequently concentrating their energies on nonpartisan activities and on cooperating in government projects — as when Asoka Mehta served as chairman of the Food Grains Committee in 1957. But Mr. Nehru, in spite of his tremendous influence and prestige, has been careful to observe the practices of parliamentary government. And, by symbolizing, in his own thought and actions, the reconciliation of conflicts among his people, he has acted not only as leader, but also as sounding board, spokesman, and conscience of the newly unified nation.

This political achievement is the result, in turn, of a synthesis, probably unique in history, between the traditions of two widely separated peoples — the English and the Indians — who, much as they differ in other regards, share the qualities of respect for the dignity of the individual, the responsibility of the ruler for the welfare of the ruled, and the capacity for administration of multilingual and multiracial societies. In this case, too, the Indians, instead of rejecting the contribution made by their Western colonial ruler, have absorbed it into their own political order. By promptly effecting a reconciliation with the British the moment they had won independence, and voluntarily joining the Commonwealth, the Indians enriched their own life for today and tomorrow by a creative blending of the values of East and West.

And sixth, India has taken the view that independence, which Americans eloquently urged when the Indians lived under British rule, means not only political and economic independence but also freedom to choose its own course in world affairs. It has steadfastly opposed the thesis, propounded by the United States during the cold war, that every nation must make a choice in world affairs between "this *or* that," between democracy and communism.

Instead, India has clearly demonstrated its determination to uphold democracy by voluntarily joining Britain in the Commonwealth — a fact we often overlook when we complain that the Indians are not sufficiently dedicated to democracy — yet has refused to join the military bloc headed by the United States and has insisted on its right to deal as it sees fit with its neighbors to the north — Communist Russia and Communist China, and to accept from them, in what the economist Wilfred Malenbaum describes as a "unique" involvement by East and West, such aid as it deems necessary for the fulfillment of its economic plans. At the same time it has increasingly supported the United Nations, which it regards as the proper forum for the great debates of our time on the pros and cons of nuclear tests, of disarmament, of prospects for the coexistence of different systems girded for battle with the weapons of clashing ideologies.

In world affairs, as within its own borders, India has persevered in seeking to achieve reconciliation through compromise. That it has failed to attain this aim in the controversial case of Kashmir only proves that the Indians are no more invulnerable than other human beings to the appeals of what they regard as national interest. In this respect India, like the rest of us, has not yet been able to make the admittedly difficult transition from the nation-state to the role of a fully functioning member of the world community.

India's philosophy of "this and that," however, does not mean a philosophy of "getting the best of both worlds," on the one hand, or of "hunting with the hounds and running with the hares," on the other. What it means is a continuing effort to practice a philosophy of tolerance, compromise, and synthesis — even if this is not always successful in practice.

But, do all these achievements of the post-independence years add up to what we in the West call democracy? Is India headed for communism? Or is it developing its own patterns of democracy, based on its historical traditions and the fusion of its ideas and practices with those of the British under whose rule it lived for over three centuries? Before judging India's past record and future prospects, let us consider whether and in what measure it possesses the ingredients of democracy.

Chapter 2

Ingredients of Democracy: Land and Resources

Citizens of the Western democracies in the twentieth century seldom realize that they are the fortunate inheritors of institutions and practices for which their forefathers battled and toiled for several hundred years. Like heirs of great wealth, they are apt to take their special advantages for granted, without recognizing that they have been endowed, with no exertion on their part, with privileges which millions of other people outside the Atlantic community have seldom if ever enjoyed.

Assuming, all too often, that freedom of the individual, equality before the law, governments responsible to the voters, and a high and still rising standard of living based on modern technology are the rule rather than the exception, they are surprised or even shocked not to find among the peoples of many of the underdeveloped non-Western countries practices which they regard as fixtures in a democratic society. At first sight, they are inclined to blame what seems to them an incredible sign of backwardness on the inadequacy or the evil intent of local rulers.

Seldom do Western visitors to non-Western lands pause to ask themselves how the democracy to which they are accustomed was molded over the years, and whether the ingredients that went into its making exist today or can be produced tomorrow in countries like India and Indonesia, Pakistan and Ghana.

Yet it should be clear by now that democracy as we know

it in the United States and Britain, in Canada, and France, and the Scandinavian countries is a potent mixture distilled over centuries which may not be easily duplicated under different political, economic, social, and ideological conditions. It is significant that the democratic institutions of the countries bordering on the Atlantic Ocean have not, even in the second half of the twentieth century, become rooted in some parts of Central Europe or in the countries of the Mediterranean, notably Spain and Portugal, whose leaders contend that democracy is unsuited and even dangerous for their peoples.

While the Atlantic democracies differ markedly from each other, they have several features in common. First, their access to the sea brought them early in their history into contact with peoples of other lands and other continents — contact which encouraged emigration, trade, and the exchange of ideas.

Second, at the end of the Middle Ages, when Western Europe was exposed to the intellectual ferment of the Renaissance and the Reformation, and sought in science the key to the Industrial Revolution, these countries had relatively small populations — 5 million in England and 20 million in France. And, even so, having discovered and conquered territories overseas, these countries found outlets for their population in the New World and in Australia.

Third, these countries, through their seafarers and traders, were able to obtain in Asia, Africa, the Middle East, and the Western Hemisphere, raw materials for their nascent industries and markets for their manufactured goods. Thus as a result of three lucky breaks — emigration, import of raw materials, and industrialization which permitted more effective use of the land and encouraged the movement of population from farms to towns, with a resulting decline in the birth-rate, the Western nations succeeded in disproving the prophecy of the English cleric Thomas Malthus at the

turn of the eighteenth century that Europe's population
would outrun its food resources unless it adopted preventive
checks like war or pestilence, or positive checks on the rate
of birth.

And, fourth, with the growth of trade and banking, and
the flowering of the professions in urban centers, the Western
nations developed an educated, politically conscious, and
civically responsible middle class either through a series of
revolutions, as in France and England, or through revolt
against colonial rule and, later, against slavery, as in the
United States. This middle class, equipped with education,
gradually forged a society which has both stability and a
capacity for continuing change. Stability has had as its bed-
rock a consensus, often arrived at only after civil strife, about
the basic premises of a democratic society which, whatever
may be the divergences between political parties or economic
and social groups, are sufficiently respected to be held above
the electoral battle. At the same time, adaptation to economic and social changes has made it possible for the democracies to broaden political suffrage continuously so as to
include the increasingly powerful industrial workers, and to
provide rising living standards for ever larger groups of
the population.

It can be argued that the peoples of the Atlantic area
possess unique gifts for human relations which have made
possible the creation and survival of democratic institutions,
in spite of two world wars and financial disasters. Yet it is
difficult to escape the conclusion that even the most politically
gifted people might not have made a success of the difficult
art of reconciling divergent individuals and groups which is
characteristic of democracy, had they not been endowed with
certain material advantages.

What are the chances that India, which upon achieving
independence unhesitatingly chose democracy as its national
way of life, may already possess or can hope to acquire the

ingredients which in the West proved necessary for the fulfillment of democratic ideals?

The Indian government, in its endeavor to reorganize the vast subcontinent, truncated at the outset by the partition of India and Pakistan, has had to take stock of its assets and liabilities before undertaking the economic development of the nation under a series of five-year plans. This stocktaking is not calculated to cheer hardheaded administrators. Contrary to the impression created in the early years of the East India Company, when English traders first came into contact with glamorous maharajahs, India is far from possessing fabulous wealth. The geological survey now under way may reveal as yet unknown resources, but, on the basis of information now available, nature cannot be said to have been kind to India.

A considerable portion of the country, bordered in the north by the snow-capped Himalayas, a strategic barrier to conquest today as in the days of the British, and surrounded on three sides by sea, is arid or semiarid. India's three great rivers — the Ganges, the Brahmaputra, and the Indus — have their headwaters in the Himalayas, and the bulk of the population is concentrated on the rich soil along their banks. While India as a whole is not overpopulated, there is an overpopulation problem in these riverside areas, particularly in West Bengal, one of the most productive agricultural regions of the country, which is irrigated by the Ganges, sacred to devout Hindus, that flows across the country, emptying into the Bay of Bengal.

Not only does India lack good arable land sufficient for its population of close to 400 million, but its forests, which according to the epic *Ramayana*, had once flourished in the south, have been cut down over the centuries for fuel. Deforestation has created a serious problem of soil erosion, and has made it necessary for the Indians to find alternative sources of fuel. Since coal deposits are limited, the peasants use cow dung for cooking, and one of the most striking aspects of an Indian village are the cakes of dung shaped by women and plastered on the walls of their houses to dry in the sun. The use of cow dung for fuel, in turn, has deprived the already exhausted soil of an ancient country of the natural fertilizer needed to replenish its vitality.

Nor is the climate favorable to agriculture, which is still the mainstay of the country's economy. Periods of intense heat and aridity are broken by the monsoon rains which arrive twice a year — in mid-June from the southwest, bringing heavy rains over most of India, and in September from the northeast, bringing rain to the southeastern coast, but not to the rest of the country. The vital importance of these rains was once expressed by a British viceroy who said that the annual budget of India was determined by the monsoons.

The monsoon rains, which in July and August fall practically every day for varying periods of time, are both a blessing and a curse. They are a blessing because without them the crops would shrivel and India's already limited food resources would be gravely diminished. But they are also a curse because they frequently wash away the crops, precipitate floods that cause incalculable damage, and often sweep away entire villages. The monsoon season, during which the peasants cannot work in the fields and are driven indoors, also brings unemployment or underemployment to the villagers, who at best eke out a meager living for themselves and their families. The tragedies that violent fluctuations of rain and alternations between drought and torrential downpour bring to the impoverished Indian countryside, have been poignantly told in Kamala Markandaya's novel of village life, *Nectar in a Sieve*.

In spite of these difficulties, overpessimism about India's agricultural potential is unjustified. Side by side with the intense heat, the aridity, the monsoon rains which sometimes bring floods, India has a climate which can produce crops all year round — two or perhaps even three a year — if intensive Japanese-style cultivation is widely adopted. According to experts, there is no real evidence that, given modern and effective agricultural practices, India needs to be an agriculturally hopeless nation.

Some observers, however, ask: is it possible that India, following the example of the Western nations five hundred years ago, may be able to turn to industry, and thus draw away from the land into urban communities the millions who are now dependent on primitive farming for their livelihood? The answer to this question will depend not only on the actual resources of raw materials India possesses at the present time, but on the ratio between its resources and its population. This ratio, both actual and potential, does not bode well for India. A conservative estimate of the population growth of the subcontinent, taking India and Pakistan together, indicates that the present population of about 400 million may reach 840 million by 2050, or over 200 million more than the present population of mainland China, which is already pressing hard on the food resources of that country in spite of its greater productivity per unit of land.

As has already been pointed out, India as a whole does not suffer from overpopulation. But 69 per cent of the people are concentrated in the river-irrigated sections of the country, which constitute only 32 per cent of the territory. The problem, thus, is not of over-all overpopulation, but of a high degree of density in relatively limited arable areas.

Nor can it be said that India's population is increasing at a more rapid rate than that of other regions of the world (some Latin American countries have a higher rate of increase). The difficulty is that the increase comes on top of an already vast population. Around 300 B.C. India had a population of between 100 and 140 million, which remained relatively stable. By 1600, at the height of the Mogul empire, India, apparently as a result of wars, banditry, epidemics, and famines, had only about 125 million people, at that time approximately the population of Europe which had 100 million in 1650.

When the British came, however, in the early sixteenth century, their impact on India was similar to the early impact of the Industrial Revolution on Europe. In an agrarian, non-mechanized society, such as that of India, children are an asset, since they are needed as extra hands for working the land. Between 1871 and 1941, the rate of increase was 0.60 per cent a year, which was lower than in Europe during a comparable period. But in 1921–1941 the increase suddenly shot up steeply to 1.2 per cent, which meant the addition of 83 million people, or about half the total present population of the United States.

There were three main reasons for this sudden population growth under British rule. First, the British introduced law and order — through the East India Company which also acted as a political and administrative agent, and then through the British Crown, which took over administration after the Mutiny of 1857. Under the new regime of law and order, wars and banditry sharply declined.

Second, the British took measures to reduce the famines due to the unpredictable monsoon rains and compounded by inadequate means of transportation, which left some parts of the subcontinent to starve while others had ample sources of food. The British built an extensive network of railways which, while originally designed to serve the strategic needs of the British armed forces in India, were also used to move food and other necessities of life. Before the British came, it is estimated that 15 million people had died in Bengal during one great famine. This was due not to lack of food, but to poor distribution facilities. The British, faced by the same problems, reduced the incidence of famines by improving distribution. During World War II there was a serious shortage of food in some areas, but this was mainly due to the fact that the railways were strained to the breaking point by the need to move troops and strategic materials in preparation for an anticipated invasion of the country by the Japanese. The British also built storage facilities for grain, and continued to expand irrigation systems. Today about 20 per cent of the area under cultivation is irrigated.

And, third, the British took measures to control epidemic diseases. At first India experienced a greater incidence of diseases as the people of a formerly insulated country came in contact with the British and other Europeans — a situation similar to that of Alaska, where a high incidence of TB among Eskimos was noted after the arrival of Americans. But strict public health measures which were soon introduced greatly reduced cholera through water control, adequate sewage systems, properly cooked food, and so on. The incidence of smallpox was cut down by vaccination. The most stubborn diseases proved to be dysentery, malaria, and bubonic plague, which must be controlled on a community, rather than on an individual, basis.

Through these various measures, the British reduced the mortality rate and prolonged life in India. Admirable as these measures were, and necessary as they would be in any modern community, they had the unanticipated effect of producing what is called a "population explosion." The British, like other colonial as well as native rulers of underdeveloped countries, with the best intentions in the world, decreased the death-rate, but paid no heed to Malthus' warning of the dire fate that awaits countries whose population growth outruns their food resources. Having removed what Malthus would have described as positive checks — wars, epidemics, banditry — the British, and the Indians serving in their administration, failed to introduce preventive checks. They did not realize, what is painfully evident today to the leaders of independent India as well as of other underdeveloped nations faced with comparable problems, that famine prevention and public health measures must go hand in hand with the adoption of planned parenthood and the development of industries which might relieve population pressure on the land and facilitate the modernization and higher productivity of agriculture.

Faced with a population burden such as never confronted the Western nations when they started to industrialize, India cannot count on some of the remedies which the Western nations, with their small populations, were able to use. India cannot hope to find outlets overseas for substantial numbers of its population, not only because the areas of the world suitable for human habitation are already settled, but also because some of the countries which could use additional immigrants impose color bars, notably South Africa and Australia. Nor can it hope to obtain, as the Western nations did, new sources of cheap raw materials to supplement its own natural resources. Nor can it plan to purchase foreign raw materials or manufactured goods abroad to speed its industrialization unless it obtains foreign currency in considerable amounts for years, and probably decades, to come, since like most underdeveloped countries it does not yet possess a sufficient range of exportable items which it could sell advantageously in world markets in competition with the more advanced industrial nations.

Within its own borders India has coal and iron ore. These, together with manganese, make it possible for it to develop a steel production which, although modest as compared with that of Japan and China, not to speak of the Western industrial nations and the U.S.S.R., is expected to reach 6,-000,000 tons at the end of the Second Five-Year Plan in 1961. India's iron ore is of high quality, and some of it is being exported, principally to Japan. Its coal resources, with the important exception of metallurgical coal, are regarded as adequate, but expansion of transportation facilities is required for their most effective utilization. India, however, has the advantage of possessing important sources of materials necessary for atomic energy — thorium and monazite sands — and it hopes to develop atomic energy for peacetime purposes, to offset its lack of other fuels — wood, metallurgical coal, and oil which it must import from abroad, being even more dependent on the oil resources of the Middle East than Western Europe. India has mica and graphite which, together with manganese and iron ore, are among its principal exports, but needs, in addition to oil, nitrates, copper, tin, and, above all, food — which in spite of three years of favorable monsoon rains, was still in short supply in 1957 and 1958.

Important as is heavy industry — the production of machines to build other machines and to produce manufactured goods — India's top priorities have been an increase in food, the output of antibiotics to check diseases, particularly malaria, which debilitates its population, and cotton to clothe its people.

Thus, at the time when India achieved independence, it lacked some of the important ingredients that seem to have made democracy workable in Western Europe: a numerically small population, outlets for emigration, adequate resources of food and raw materials supplemented by imports from overseas territories, and favorable prospects for effecting an orderly transition from a backward agrarian economy to an economy combining modernized agriculture with diversified industry.

But material resources are only one of the factors in the building of democracy. What about the human material of India — the traditions, beliefs, and skills of its people?

Chapter 3

Ingredients of Democracy: People and Ideas

A favorable geographic position, a moderate and stable climate that makes human existence bearable, agricultural and industrial resources in a workable ratio to the population not only existing but potential — these factors in a combination that can provide at least adequate food and modest amenities for all citizens are important ingredients of a democratic society. But these are material factors, some of which, notably climate, may be difficult to control, while others, like supplies of food and industrial raw materials, may be increased by imports from abroad, by modernization of production techniques, and by new or as yet unanticipated scientific discoveries.

Effective action to alter material factors, however, ultimately depends on the effectiveness of human beings — on their willingness and their capacity to change existing conditions. Some democratic thinkers, particularly in the United States, are inclined to believe that the destiny of any given society depends on the "will of the people" or, to put it in current American idiom, on "group thinking" or "group dynamics." Yet the experience, not only of the underdeveloped non-Western nations but also of the advanced nations of the West, notably the United States, Britain, and France, demonstrates that even worldwide mechanization has not eliminated the importance of leadership. The significance and influence of the "charismatic personality" — the individual who believes or is believed by others, or most often both, to be one who is specially designated by the deity or by fate to play a decisive role at a decisive moment in his people's history, is not limited to Asia, the Middle East, and Africa, with Nehru, Sukarno, U Nu, Nasser, or Nkrumah. Nor is Russia unique in its "cult of personality," be it Stalin or Khrushchev. The West, too, as late as the middle of the twentieth century, has turned for guidance to, or found a father image in such varied personalities as Hitler and Winston Churchill, Franklin D. Roosevelt and Mussolini, General de Gaulle, Adenauer and Salazar.

These and other men have been significant not merely because they had the courage to take risks and the readiness to make decisions in times of stress when others were fearful and indecisive. They have moved men and women to action because, whether they actually put this into words or not, they aroused memories of a glorious past that had long lain dormant, and symbolized ideas which their people believed in but had ceased to implement. They were like poets who, consciously or unconsciously, reflect the deep-seated emotions and beliefs of their contemporaries and thus, through individual affirmation, give voice to collective aspirations.

Such leaders derive their strength and make their contribution to the times in which they live because, and not in spite of, the traditions of their peoples. They may, and often do, bring new ideas and practices from other lands and cultures into their own, but they do so because, unlike foreign rulers, no matter how effective and selfless these may be, they are regarded by the people, and so regard themselves, as an integral part of their community. It is only because, whether intellectually or instinctively, they are aware of the needs and potentialities of their people, that they are able to infuse ancient customs with new meaning, to stir a stagnant society into constructive action, to adapt and remold human material formed over centuries or even millennia, to the demands of the nuclear age.

Foreign intervention may tamper with, but can never permanently cut, this umbilical cord which links leaders to the peoples from whom they have sprung. And the achievements, or failures, of every society must be judged not by what it might have become had it been made in the image of a foreign land, no matter how politically mature or technologically advanced, but by what it is today within the context of its own particular past experience.

It is tempting to assume that the democratic patterns we see in independent India are due solely, or primarily, to the guidance it received from its British rulers during the three centuries when first the East India Company, then the British Crown, played an increasingly influential part in the political, economic, and educational formation of the Indian people. Nor is it easy for the Westerner to avoid the temptation of regarding India as a depressingly backward country, and dismiss such features of its life as are indubitably democratic on the ground that they are merely leftovers from the British regime or will prove transitory in a nation which has many reasons for moving toward authoritarianism.

Yet, both the Hindu majority and the Muslim minority within the Republic of India have long possessed the ingredients of democracy, even if these have taken forms different from those of the democracy with which we in the West are familiar.

The Hindus, traditionally, have believed in the concept of the secular state — long before Henry VIII separated the state from the Catholic Church and created his own national religious institutions, or the French proclaimed separation of church and state in 1901, or the Russians, rejecting religion as "the opium of the people," broke the tie that had previously existed between the Russian tsardom and the Russian Orthodox Church. Nor do the Hindus look to a religious hierarchy for spiritual, let alone political, guidance. Their worship is individual, not collective. In their view, the

Muslim conquerors of the fifteenth century were irrational and mentally immature in demanding that all Hindus should be converted to one faith alone — Islam. Many Hindus, however, were converted, some for reasons of convenience or personal gain, others (many of the lower castes and outcastes) because Islam's brotherhood ideal offered a welcome contrast to Hindu casteism. The result is that many of the people now listed as Muslims in India are descendants of converted Hindus.

But, while India was never a theocracy, its religious and social values were so closely intertwined at the level of individual and group behavior that the more "free" or "liberal" atmosphere which in the West is associated with the separation of church and state did not develop except in some outstanding instances. And, while India did not have a spiritual hierarchy comparable to that of the Catholic Church — that is, an integrated, disciplined structure — the Brahmins exercised a powerful authority, and Hindu tradition acted on society as a coercive and limiting force. Custom and tradition were pervasive, and only a few exceptional individuals rose to the level of making conscious choices between theological paths; for the rest of the Hindus the theological path, as well as the path of life and secular morality, was strictly prescribed. However, in Hinduism the possibilities of paths to salvation were more varied than in Islam, and in this respect Hinduism was less monolithic.

By contrast, the Muslims — and this is a fundamental cleavage between the two religions, and for that reason also between India and Pakistan — think in terms of a state based on religion. The Koran is the cornerstone of Muslim systems of government, as was made clear in the now defunct constitution adopted by Pakistan in 1956. By contrast to Hinduism, which passed through a period when Buddhism challenged its polytheistic beliefs, its caste system, and its accepted way of life as determined by the Brahmins, only to be absorbed into Hinduism, Islam, although divided between two sects, the Sunnis and the Shiites, has not experienced a comparable reformation, let alone a fundamental reformation like that of Catholic Christianity by the Protestants. Yet, in contrast to India with its caste system, which still persists, in spite of the outspoken opposition of Nehru and his supporters and of the prohibitions of the 1950 Constitution, Islam affirms its belief in a socially democratic system, with every man equal to every other man — with the notable exception of non-Muslim "infidels." The Muslims in India have held to this concept and have practiced it, although they have not remained altogether unaffected by the Hindu caste system, and have even formed castes of their own.

Hinduism is an exceptionally inclusive and absorptive religion, which recognizes diversity of belief and is tolerant of diversity. Everyone, according to the Hindus, is partly right and partly wrong. Nothing is all black or all white; there are many shades of gray.

Hinduism has lasted for thousands of years, surviving Muslim conquest and attempted conversion, as well as attempts at Buddhist reformation and the injection of Christian ideas under British rule, because it is or can be "all things to all men."

The range of acceptance is very wide. Hinduism can satisfy those who want to worship the forces of nature and a variety of animals — cows, cobras, monkeys — because they believe that the godhead is immanent in all things. It can also satisfy the intellectual sophisticates who envision a supreme being, representing a godhead made manifest in human form, such as the god Krishna who appears on earth to encourage the fighting spirit of the warrior Arjuna in the *Bhagavad-Gita*, a stirring portion of one of India's great epics, the *Mahabharata*. Unlike the Muslims, who do not permit representation of God, or of his prophet Mohammed, the Hindus portray their gods realistically, as earthly men and women, in the Buddhist paintings of the Ajanta caves and the sculptures of Ellora and Orissa — so realistically indeed that Westerners have regarded them in some instances as disturbingly explicit. The Hindus, however, look at gods and goddesses with something of the carefree spirit of intercourse between deities and mankind which we find in Greek and Roman mythology where, too, the forces of nature took human form, in nymphs and other supernatural beings, and gods descended upon earth to enjoy human satisfactions, as when Zeus took the form of a swan to visit Leda. Nor are the Hindu gods above enjoying a drink of *soma,* an intoxicating liquor of which they partook on their Olympus, according to ancient Hindu legends, just as men did on earth.

Unlike the Muslims, the Hindus are not missionary-minded — with the exception of the Buddhists, who after initial successes in forming monastic orders for men and women, and sending high-born missionaries to neighboring Ceylon, Burma, and China, now form only one per cent of the total population of India. The Hindus do not recruit converts. They absorb them into their own many-faceted and continuously changing faith.

By contrast, the Muslims are strict monotheists. Mohammed, in A.D. 800, was inspired by the desire to purify Arabic thought which in his opinion had been made impure by its adoption of polytheistic ideas, and of beliefs derived from Judaism and Christianity. While the Hindus make a cult of diversity, the Muslims make a cult of uniformity. To them, those who are not with Islam are against it, are infidels against whom it is proper to take up the sword in a holy war (*jihad*). Yet the Muslims too have shown a capacity for absorption — if not of ideas then of spiritual leaders of other faiths. In their huge roster of prophets they have included Abraham, Jesus Christ, and the Angel Gabriel.

At first glance it may seem that Hindus and Muslims are very different in their attitude toward religion. The Hindus tend to be inward-looking. Their religion urges them to take time for contemplation and, after having perceived their faults, to seek self-improvement. The Hindu, whether sitting on the doorstep of his village hut or meditating on the bank of the sacred river Ganges in Benares or praying in the temple, worships and thinks by himself. By contrast, Muslims seem more like Westerners, not only because they eat meat, which many devout Hindus do not touch, limiting themselves to vegetarian fare, but because they are outward-looking in their faith, and worship as a group at prescribed hours of the day at the call of the *muezzin*.

Yet both these faiths, which in many respects seem far apart, have similar prescriptions for the salvation of the individual. While the Hindu often appears to be a fatalist, accepting uncomplainingly the disasters inflicted on him by nature or the deity, this seeming fatalism may be due more to physical debility and traditional hopelessness about the impossibility of changing his status in life and the poverty of the country as a whole. In the *Bhagavad-Gita*, however, Lord Krishna tells Arjuna that man must act, and if he performs the right deed then he may hope to achieve salvation (*moksha*). Contrary to the assumption often held in the West that the Hindus, by emphasizing contemplation, may fail to be sufficiently concerned with deeds, the *Bhagavad-Gita*, in pellucid terms, points out that thought and action are inseparable, as Krishna tells Arjuna:

> But thou, want not! ask not! Find full reward
> Of doing right in right! Let right deeds be
> Thy motive, not the fruit which comes from them.
> And live in action! Labour! Make thine acts
> Thy piety, casting all self aside,
> Contemning gain and merit; equable
> In good or evil: equability
> Is Yog, is piety! Yet, the right act
> Is less, far less, than the right-thinking mind.
> Seek refuge in thy soul; have there thy heaven!

Scorn them that follow virtue for her gifts!
The mind of pure devotion — even here —
Casts equally aside good deeds and bad,
Passing above them. Unto pure devotion
Devote thyself; with perfect meditation
Comes perfect act.

According to Hindu belief, everyone is reborn. The only question is whether one will move upward or downward in the hierarchy of caste or, for that matter, in the hierarchy of living species (a man might be reborn as a snake, or cow, or other animal). Whether rebirth is interpreted to mean physical reappearance after death in a new form, human or animal, perhaps in a higher or lower caste than before, or as the spiritual rebirth of the individual upon performance of the right deeds, it holds out a material incentive to achievement which contradicts the assumption that fatalism is an ineradicable element of Hinduism. The scope of the achievement, however, is severely limited. Men are reborn if they strive to do right as defined by the station of life to which they have been born, that is, their caste.

However, for the Hindu who is weary of successive rebirths, what we might call weary of ever striving, there is a possibility, through extraordinary striving, to reach the highest form of salvation (*moksha*), to be freed from the wheel of Karma or rebirth altogether. The Hindu thinks in terms of consciously inducing a state of detachment and contemplation through the use of four or five yogas or disciplines, of which the *Raja Yoga*, which involves body control and is best known to Westerners, is only one (the discipline Gandhi emphasized is the *Karma Yoga*). In effect, those who practice yoga — and Prime Minister Nehru is one of them — find in self-discipline a temporary surcease from the anxieties and troubles that beset all human beings, and an opportunity to clarify their thoughts for the next stage of life's struggle. While Christians think of nonconsciousness as induced by physical suspension of life, with afterlife as reward or punishment, Hinduism offers two kinds of rewards to the believer and particularly to the well-doer. These are either *moksha* (salvation) by doing the right thing (a Hindu concept), or the complete suspension of human endeavor through *nirvana* (nonconsciousness, a Buddhist concept), when "the strife is o'er." Many Hindu texts imply, however, the *moksha* is limited to twice-born, or higher castes, or even to Brahmins.

The Muslims, by contrast, believe in concrete material rewards for good and evil. The good (but apparently only those of the masculine sex) can hope to reach heaven where they will enjoy perpetual bliss, being waited on by lovely houris. The evil may expect to be thrust into a hell which has its Satan (Shaitan) and demons who will torment him. Yet the Muslim, like the Hindu, is not a fatalist. While he believes that he must accept the will of Allah, he is taught that Allah is not only stern but also merciful. The devout Muslim, like the devout Hindu, can improve his future prospects by good works, such as the giving of alms to the poor; by contributions to religious and educational foundations, which in Muslim countries are the recipients of great wealth from the rich; and, if at all possible, by making at least one pilgrimage to the sacred city of Mecca. The devout Hindu, for his part, hopes to see Benares, the holiest Hindu city, before he dies. Both faiths, in spite of their differences, hold up an activist ideal during the individual's lifetime, and emphasize the importance not only of worship, but also of good works.

Where Hindus and Muslims appear to differ most sharply is in their attitude toward the use of force. The Brahmins have traditionally stressed nonviolence (*ahimsa*) toward both men and beasts. The injunction against the killing of human beings and animals and the eating of meat, engraved in a rock edict proclaimed in the third century before Christ, by the Hindu Emperor Asoka who adopted the Buddhist faith, has made a profound imprint on the Indian mind. The devout

Hindu refuses to kill cows, even though they may perish from lack of care and feeding and become a menace on public thoroughfares; or the sacred cobras, even if they inflict fatal bites on men, women, or children; or monkeys, held sacred in memory of the aid they gave prince Rama, hero of the epic Ramayana, in his efforts to find and bring home his wife, Sita, who had been made captive by the demon-king and held on the island of Lanka (now Ceylon) — in spite of the fact that the monkeys are believed to eat up annually about one-thirtieth of India's limited supply of food grains. And one reformist sect, the Jains, are so careful not to commit violence that they enjoin care in breathing, for fear that insects might be inhaled along with air. It should be pointed out, however, that for the fighting castes, the Kshatriyas, fighting is a duty. And the ideal of nonviolence has never been especially strong among the peasants, who are the majority of the population, and are farther from the reach of Brahminical influence.

In spite of the belief in nonviolence, which has inspired the attitude of independent India in world affairs, it would be contrary to the facts to contend that the Hindus never resort to force. When their interests were at stake, they fought each other during the turbulent centuries when princely state was ranged against princely state, with a resulting condition of anarchy and violence that was brought to an end only with the coming of the British. And, at the time of partition, passions inflamed among both Hindus and Muslims by the violent rending asunder of the subcontinent led to acts of frightful cruelty on both sides.

The Muslims, for their part, make no secret of their belief that force can and should be used to defend Islam and its institutions against unbelievers, be they the Western Crusaders of the Middle Ages or the Hindus who oppose Pakistan and hold on to Kashmir today. Yet the Muslims living in India, perhaps because of the impact made on them by Hindu ideas and practices, are today in the forefront of the world's

Islamic peoples in their support of religious, social, and educational reforms. India nurtured two well-known Muslim philosophers, Syed Ahmad Khan (1817–1898), and Sir Mohammed Iqbal (1875–1938).

Syed Ahmad Khan contended that every individual has the natural right to interpret the Koran and the Sunna (commentaries on the Koran), and to rethink his religion for himself. He went even further, and said that Christianity and Islam are both good religions, although Islam is better. He believed that there could be a reconciliation between Islam and other faiths, and was convinced that Muslims must study the modern world, including the physical sciences. He reasoned that, since the world has been created by God, it is the duty of man to study the world He created. In accordance with these ideas Syed Ahmad Khan in the 1870's founded the Muslim university of Aligarh.

Sir Mohammed Iqbal, who was also a well-known poet, wrote *The Reconstruction of Religious Thought in Islam*. He said that the name of Allah was given to God for convenience and that actually God is the essence of man all around in the universe. He also emphasized the right of every man to make his own religious interpretations. Everyone, and not only Muslims, he contended, must rethink his faith in the light of modern conditions.

In contrast to their advocacy of a modernized Islam both Sir Syed Ahmad Khan and Iqbal found it impossible to accept the permanent integration of Muslims in a predominantly Hindu society. Syed Ahmad Khan became one of the supporters of the idea of a Muslim League, which was founded in 1906 and, subsequently, under the leadership of Jinnah, developed into the core of the separate Muslim state of Pakistan, the idea of which was originated by Iqbal. In a long poem entitled *Shikwa* (Complaint) Iqbal drew a picture of the degraded condition of the Muslims of his time as compared with the past when their sway extended from Spain to Indonesia, and asked God what He meant by overthrowing the only Faithful.

In spite of this religious chauvinism, the modernizing heritage of Syed Ahmad Khan and Iqbal may bear important fruit in independent India if the two groups can achieve, not only coexistence, but in some spheres also active cooperation and commingling. The dilemma for the Muslims is that if they go too far in cooperating with the Hindus, their distinctive way of life may be undermined. Yet, if they do not participate fully in the building of the new nation, they run the danger of remaining an isolated segment of the population which might be left behind as the Hindus move toward a modernized society and an industrialized economy.

The emphasis of Hinduism on individual responsibility and on doing the right deeds, its opposition to collectivism in religion and to the religious state, and its capacity to absorb other beliefs and to reconcile conflicting ideas, if effectively applied in practical politics, constitute solid ingredients of modern democracy. So do the Muslims' emphasis on social equality and their concern for the welfare of their coreligionaries expressed through charitable contributions. In what might otherwise be regarded as a harmonious approach to a democratic society, the principal discordant note seems to be supplied by the caste system, which today remains an important feature of the Hindu way of life.

The caste system, however, is regarded by Hindu reformers as not being an integral element of the Hindu religion. True, it has been interwoven with Hinduism in two respects: First, the top caste of Brahmins, who originally were priests, consisted of those who had knowledge of the sacred lore of Hinduism; and second, the individual may hope to move into a higher caste than the one into which he was born by doing the right deeds which lead to his rebirth. And Gandhi regarded the caste system, albeit reformed, as the proper structure for society.

Basically, however, the caste system had its origins in differences of color (*varna*, the Hindu term), or race (caste comes from the Portuguese word *casta* or race, which means high breed). Successive waves of invasions from Central Asia brought into India peoples of diverse colors. The earliest invaders known to history were the Dravidians, short, squat and dark, who found on the land primitive aborigines black in color, and were themselves succeeded by the light-colored, blue-eyed, tall Aryans, who apparently installed the caste system as we know it today.

The system consisted of four main castes and of a fifth group, the outcastes, also called pariahs or outsiders, or untouchables. The four castes were both social and economic categories: Brahmins, who in the early days were priests, and wise men or teachers (*gurus*), and today provide some of the leading administrators, intellectuals, and professional men, among them Jawaharlal Nehru: Kshatriyas, the warriors, to whom Buddha belonged before he forswore the luxury of his father's court and became a humble preacher of *The Middle Path* and the most outstanding missionary in India's religious history; the Vaisyas, merchants and landowners, the caste within which Gandhi was born; and the Sudras, who include peasants, craftsmen, and workers.

India's caste system is in many respects similar to the social structure of medieval Europe, with its princes, its feudal lords, its merchants, and, at the bottom, its peasants, craftsmen, and workers. In the Middle Ages, however, Christianity made it possible for the most lowly to attain exalted rank in the religious hierarchy through study and devotions. Nor did the medieval system have a specified category of outcastes, although it had thousands of dispossessed and underprivileged people. Moreover, while Europe's caste system gradually disintegrated under the impact of the Industrial Revolution, yielding ground to what became the class struggle between workers and employers, India's caste system has persisted relatively unchanged into the middle of the twentieth century, where it seems a striking anachronism in the midst of a society that is striving to industrialize.

There are two main reasons for this persistence. First, the caste system served as a cement for the widely diversified society of a vast subcontinent with at least fourteen major languages which was racked again and again throughout its long and turbulent history by wars between rival princes. The caste system provided an element of order and stability under conditions of flux. There was a place for everyone, determined at birth, and everyone knew his place in the social scheme, which also meant that he knew the occupation he was to pursue. This hierarchical structure survived successive waves of invasions as well as the imposition of British rule because it continued to exist in a backward agrarian society that remained static until the twentieth century. And, second, within each caste, as well as within the subcastes which are estimated to number 3,000, there was equality between fellow caste members, rich and poor, successful and unsuccessful. Each caste had its own caste council, which settled problems within the caste group, and provided a form of social security for indigent or unfortunate members, looking after widows and orphans, for example.

The British have been criticized for not overthrowing the caste system after they had assumed control of India in 1858. Yet it is difficult to see how the British could have undertaken to abolish a social structure that was firmly embedded in the life of the country without provoking a tremendous public outcry and even revolt. Only the Indians themselves could successfully challenge the premises on which the caste system was based. This Gandhi and his followers did not do, although thirty years before independence they did challenge untouchability. Gandhi campaigned vigorously to end untouchability, contending that the outcastes should be called Harijans, or "children of God," and should have equal rights with the castes. His campaign on behalf of the outcastes sparked a social revolution which is still under way, and which in scope and significance equals his campaign of passive resistance and nonviolent noncooperation for independence from Britain.

The scope and significance of this revolution can best be understood if we bear in mind that in the past the untouchables were barred from using village wells, sharing food with other castes or even preparing it for them, associating with them in any activity, attending school with them, or entering Hindu temples. Even their mere presence in the vicinity of touchable castes was not permitted, and they had to live in a specially allotted section of the village, in what we might describe as a ghetto. In short, in American terms, they could not be integrated with the rest of the population, or, to use the South African phrase, they were condemned to *apartheid*, to "apartness" from the rest of the population. This exclusion of the untouchables was based on the contention that, since they performed unclean tasks such as tanning, scavenging, and so on — tasks which in the dim historic past had been arbitrarily assigned to them by other castes — they were unclean, and any contact between them and other groups would result in pollution, which would require elaborate rites of purification.

Today, the 1950 Constitution prohibits discrimination of any kind on grounds of color, race, or creed, thus implementing Gandhi's ideals of integration, as well as the liberal and socialist concepts which were held by an important segment of the Congress party. In spite of this prohibition, untouchability still exists, just as in the United States the mere passing of laws against racial inequality has not yet brought about equality. More powerful than legal prescriptions, however, is the impact on the caste system of industrialization.

For industrialization, as was the case in Europe's Middle Ages, breaks up the static framework of the primitive village and creates a new mobility, as more and more villagers move to towns and take up jobs in industry, where the test of an individual is not his membership in this or that caste, but his capacity to perform skilled tasks. The two most effective weapons against untouchability are the village bus, invariably overcrowded, where untouchability is impossible to maintain; and the factory cafeteria, where the management offers cheap and nutritious meals at modest prices that draw workers of various castes, who eventually begin to wonder why, if they can work side by side on the assembly line, they cannot eat side by side, even if the meal is not prepared by hands belonging to their own particular caste.

With the spread of industrialization, the caste system may be expected to disintegrate slowly. But even its critics are inclined to favor gradualness in its abolition, so that a dangerous social vacuum may not develop, and ask themselves whether the caste will not be succeeded, as in Europe, by the class system, with some of the disruptive struggles between workers and employers which have already occurred in some factories, notably at the Tata steel works in 1958 between rival unions. But whatever the future may bring, there is no reason to believe that the dissolution of the caste system would weaken Hinduism as a religion and a philosophy.

But if the caste system, in the past, has been an obstacle to democratization (although, within the context of India's traditions and circumstances, no greater an obstacle than segregation of our Negro fellow citizens has been in a social and economic order we regard as democratic), the political and administrative ideals and practices of both Hindus and Muslims in India at peak periods of India's history can be regarded as valuable preparation for modern democracy. Under three dynasties — the Maurya dynasty (322–185 B.C.), the Gupta dynasty (A.D. 320–450), and the Mogul ruler Akbar (1556–1605) — India displayed a statesmanship, a concern for cultural values, and a spirit of reconciliation between conflicting faiths and ideas that were a match for any Western nation.

The Maurya dynasty was founded by Chandragupta who, according to legend, was found by shepherds on the bank of a stream where he had been left by his mother, a fairy. The administrative system he established, as described in the *Arthasastra* of Kautilya, his chief minister, shows that the area of India he controlled was divided into five provinces, with the central province governed by the Emperor and the others by four viceroys. Under the viceroys there was a carefully graded bureaucracy in which we can see the prototype of India's modern civil service, established by the British. While the Emperor was the absolute ruler, he governed with the advice of a Council of Ministers; was readily accessible to the people, in the manner of France's Louis IX who received petitioners under the shade of a tree; and was the final court of appeal in all cases. The criminal code was harsh, but delinquent judges could be tried and removed. And in the capital city, Pataliputra, there were six boards of administrators for industry, markets, weights and measures, the recording of vital statistics, the welfare of visiting foreigners, and the collection of taxes. All agricultural land was the property of the Crown, and cultivators paid a tax in the form of one-sixth to one-quarter of the year's produce. Foreign and domestic trade were encouraged.

Chandragupta's grandson, the Emperor Asoka, left an indelible imprint on Indian thought. Asoka, a Hindu, during the war against the neighboring Kalingas which he waged early in his reign was deeply shocked by the terrible carnage and devastation he witnessed, and was converted to Buddhism, becoming determined henceforth to govern according to the rules of law and piety laid down by Buddha (565–483 B.C.). Buddha, like Mahavir (or Jina) who was the founder of Jainism, was a "radical." Both challenged the Vedas, the sacred books of Hinduism, and the position of the Brahmins.

They both wrote and spoke in a vernacular language under-standable to the common people, Prakrit instead of the San-skrit used by the Brahmins. Both Buddhism and Jainism call to mind the Protestant reformation. Like the Protestants, who were Catholics disillusioned by what they regarded as the defects of Catholicism, Buddhism and Jainism were sects of Hinduism.

Buddhism and Jainism, however, continued to use some of the concepts of Hinduism, notably the significance of the individual's deeds which determine his future, and the belief that right conduct and right knowledge help to attain salva-tion. The Buddhists, however, introduced the concept of egalitarianism, which directly challenged the caste system and the privileged position of the Brahmins as expounders of Hinduism. Their egalitarianism had a strong appeal for the merchant class (just as Protestantism attracted the merchant class of Europe), which contributed generously to the Bud-dhists. Unlike the Hindus, the Buddhists believed in mission-ary work, in conversion, not only at home but also through foreign missions in Burma, Siam, China, Ceylon, and Japan. They founded monastic orders of men and women, who en-gaged not only in missionary activities but also in education.

Having accepted Buddhism, Asoka accepted nonviolence as a guiding principle of life. He never waged war again, and became a lay monk, as did some of the other members of his family. He erected a pillar on the spot where Buddha was supposed to have been born, as well as on other sites, and called himself the father of his people.

Asoka embodied his ideas about the duties and responsi-bilities of the ruler in a series of edicts which were engraved on rocks and on iron pillars. In his edict on "The Sacredness of Life" he said that at his court "no animal may be slaugh-tered for sacrifice, nor shall any merry-making be held." He provided "healing arrangements for men and healing arrange-ments for beasts. Medicinal herbs also, both medicinal herbs for men and medicinal herbs for beasts, wheresoever lacking, have been everywhere both imported and planted. Roots, also fruits, wheresoever lacking, have been everywhere imported and planted. On the roads, too, wells have been dug and trees planted for the enjoyment of man and beast." "The living," he said, "must not be fed with the living."

Asoka enjoined his collaborators to observe Buddha's Law of Piety, and to look after the welfare and the happiness of their subordinates, of servants and masters, of Brahmins and the wealthy, the helpless and the aged. In his edict on "Toleration," he urged "reverence to men of all sects, whether ascetics or householders." The root of the matter, he said, is "restraint of speech, to wit, a man must not do reverence to his own sect or disparage that of another without reason. Depreciation should be for specific reasons only, because the sects of other people all deserve reverence for one reason or another.

"By thus acting a man exalts his own sect and at the same time does service to the sects of other people. By acting contrariwise a man hurts his own sect, and does disservice to the sects of other people. For he who does reverence to his own sect while disparaging the sects of others wholly from attachment to his own, with intent to enhance the splendor of his own sect, in reality by such conduct inflicts the severest injury on his own sect."

Asoka constantly stressed the special duties of an elite of governors concerned with the welfare of the people, in a manner reminiscent of Plato's *Republic*. During his reign not only was administration strengthened and improved but education was widespread, as noted by the Syrian envoy Megasthenes who commented on the high moral character of the Indian people and on the number and variety of their professors and doctors.

By contrast to Asoka, the greatest ruler of the Gupta dynasty, Samudragupta, known as the Hindu Napoleon, was a military and a militant man. But he was also a poet, a musician (he is pictured playing the *vina*, or with a lute on his knees), and a patron of the arts comparable to the Medici. The Gupta period was known as "The Golden Age of Hinduism," because literature and the arts flourished at Samudragupta's court. A Chinese visitor, Fa Hsien, who came to India to study Buddhism, left an interesting account of this period, and was very impressed by the prosperity and culture of the country. This period saw the flowering of the epic (*Kavya*), for which the court poet Harisena was particularly famous. Sanskrit, until then the language of the sacred books of Hinduism, was developed into a classical literary language. Lyric poetry flourished, particularly under Chandragupta II (who died in 415 B.C.). Books came into common use, usually written on birch bark, or palm leaves which served as paper, with ink used for writing. Astronomy and mathematics also flourished, and an Indian astronomer was supposed to have originally evolved the law of gravity. Medicine and surgery were taught and practiced. Art and sculpture achieved a high level.

But of all the artists of the Gupta dynasty, the most famous, and according to contemporary accounts, the most attractive, was Kalidasa, who excelled both in lyric poetry, for example his poem *Cloud Messenger* in which a husband separated by unfortunate fate from his wife sends her a loving message by way of a cloud; and in playwriting, particularly his masterpiece *Shakuntala*, which influenced Goethe. Kalidasa, who has been described variously as India's Shelley, Milton, or Tennyson, has a great gift for picturing nature — his descriptions of flowers and animals are both vivid and moving. At the same time, he has a sensitive perception of human emotions, as in his descriptions of the sad state of the King, overwrought by his sudden discovery that he had ill-treated the woman he had loved and married in the hermit's retreat he had visited in the forest. The ideas of nonviolence toward animals stressed by Asoka are reflected in *Shakuntala*, where the King, upon entering the hermitage, relinquishes his bow and arrows and abandons hunting, which until then he had been enjoying, out of respect for a holy place.

The political, administrative, and cultural achievements of Hinduism suffered an eclipse after the "Golden Age" for a period of three to four hundred years which were marked by strife between various princely houses, and India lost its sense of unity. Economic life continued to be prosperous, but the Indian political structure was seriously weakened. As one of India's few historians, K. M. Panikkar, has said: "There was no sense of India. . . Patriotism was wholly absent." India, which for many centuries had had close contacts with other lands, from Syria to China, became isolated from the rest of the world, and in an era when the great seapowers of Europe had not yet emerged, felt relatively safe from foreign invasion.

The Muslim incursions from Central Asia, often accompanied by plunder, and sometimes by slaughter of Hindus, whom the Muslims regarded as infidels, started about the year 1000 and continued until 1525, when the Muslim leader Babar reached Delhi and established the Mogul Empire. Babar's own humane and tolerant attitude toward Hindus and their beliefs set the tone for future cooperation between conquerors and conquered in a multiracial and multilingual society.

The Muslims, however, contrary to the practice of their coreligionaries in the Arab lands, did not try to wage a holy war against the Hindus, "infidels" though they were from their point of view. For one thing, the Muslims, accustomed to a nomad way of life, and trained at an earlier time for military prowess, found that many Hindus were nonmilitant and devoted themselves to the settled life of agriculturalists. The Muslims needed the Hindus as cultivators of the land. Then, too, the Muslims had had no experience in trade, and relied on the Hindus for their talents as merchants. And the Hindus were useful also for government service, since they spoke the languages of the people. For example, important administrative posts under Akbar were held by Hindus, and several of the top generals were Hindu Maharajahs. The Muslims took the top administrative jobs, for themselves, but they recognized the educational and administrative qualifications of the Hindus.

Thus, by and large the Muslims left the caste system alone, and it survived intact. And, while the Muslims destroyed Hindu temples, they seldom put the infidels to the sword. Instead, they used a poll tax imposed on non-Muslims, as well as the lure of jobs in administration, as levers to persuade the Hindus to accept Islam. In fact, Muslims unconsciously strengthened Hinduism, for religion became a rallying point for a people forced to live under the rule of foreign invaders of another faith. The Hindus, for the most part, did not turn to the faith of their Muslim conquerors, and remained true to the beliefs and practices of Hinduism. Many Hindus, amid the turmoil of invasions, adopted mysticism as expressed in the Bhakti philosophy, turning their thoughts more and more inward. They also studied and practiced the vernacular languages, earlier fostered by the Buddhists and Jains, and showed an increased desire that religion and literature should not remain a monopoly of the Brahmins. The Hindu religion and the Sanskrit language (as contrasted with Urdu) became two unifying elements for the future reconstruction of a united India. But Urdu, too, was an Indian language. Urdu (the Turki word for camp) developed in India in and around the camp of Babar and other Moguls from a combination of the Persian, with admixture of Turki words, used by Mogul soldiers and the Hindustani used by the Indian people. And Urdu became a unifying element for the Muslims of India.

The Muslims, moreover, made two important contributions to the democratization of Hinduism. They promoted their belief in the equality of men, who in their view should be judged not by the group or station into which they are born, but on the basis of their own individual skills. And they introduced Muslim law, based on the Koran, which at that time was often more advanced than Indian law.

The coexistence of Hindus and Muslims under the Moguls produced a society which was divided into two sectors: the Muslim sector, organized on vertical lines, and kept mobile by the concept of equality; and the Hindu sector, organized on horizontal lines through the static caste system. These two sectors, living side by side, did not merge before 1947, and each became the core of the two national states established after partition, India and Pakistan.

It is a tantalizing question whether, given a greater degree of understanding and statesmanship on both sides, a merger of the two faiths could have been achieved, or whether basic differences, particularly in the Hindu and Muslim views of the role of religion in the state, would have made this impossible even under the most favorable circumstances. A glimpse of what might have been was given by the Mogul emperor, Akbar (1556–1605), who in many striking respects is comparable to the Hindu emperor, Asoka. Akbar, according to contemporary accounts, was a man of mellow temper and showed a vision remarkable for the ruler of any country.

His breadth of outlook was possibly affected by his early experience, for he had spent his childhood outside of India, in Persia, where his father had been forced to take refuge as a result of dynastic rivalries. Akbar, a Muslim, not only married a Hindu princess, which in that time was an extraordinary action for a Muslim, but also wives of other faiths, including a Christian. Each of his wives, in his magnificent palace at Fatephur Sikri, near Agra, had her own courtyard, with her own religious edifice, where she could practice her own faith.

In his palace Akbar also built a Hall of Worship, to which he invited Hindus, Jains, Zoroastrians, Christians, and Jews, as well as Muslims, for religious discussions, suggesting topics and taking part in debates. He also invited Jesuit priests from the Portuguese colony of Goa, but eventually broke off with them because of their intolerance toward the Hindus, an intolerance which was alien to his nature.

Akbar appointed Hindus to high posts in his administration, and chose a Hindu, Raja Todar Mal, as Prime Minister, who devised an administrative system which persisted into the twentieth century. The empire was divided into fifteen provinces (*Subas*), each of which was divided into districts (*Sarkars*). Each district was governed by a Sarkadar, a great noble or a member of the imperial family, who had under him a carefully graded body of officials paid out of the treasury, not through land assignments as in the past, so as to avoid extortion. Civil cases between Muslims were adjudicated according to Muslim law. Hindu disputes were settled by village councils (*panchayats*) and caste councils.

The Emperor was an absolute monarch, acting as supreme head both of the civil administration and of the armed forces. He exercised personal rule, but was concerned with the welfare of the people, again very much like Asoka. He checked the powers of the nobles, and tried to give just government, preventing extortion and misappropriations of money.

At heart, Akbar was a mystic, who was always trying to discover the hidden Truth, and in this search he experimented with one creed after another. He was deeply influenced by the philosopher and poet, Kabir, who was an exponent of doctrines similar to those taught by the Sufis in Persia who were also mystics. He disliked rigid Muslim orthodoxy. Toward the end of his life he wanted to find a common creed which would embrace all the religions of his Empire. In 1579 he issued the Infallibility Edict declaring that the Emperor had the right to decide "for the benefit of the nation, and as a political expedient," any religious question about which there was a conflict of opinion. That same year, under the influence of a bold thinker, Shaikh Mubarak and his two sons, Abdul Fazl and Shaikh Faizi, he recited a prayer in the Great Mosque at Fatephur Sikri, composed for him by Faizi, one of the most learned men of his age and at that time the poet laureate.

In 1582 Akbar promulgated an eclectic creed of his own, *Din Ilahi* or *Divine Monotheism*. Candidates for admission to this new faith were required to abjure Islam altogether and surrender to Akbar as their spiritual guide, or God's representative on earth. This creed, however, shocked orthodox Muslims and attracted few adherents.

The Muslims in India were concerned not only with religion, but also with the arts, particularly architecture. They built magnificent edifices, notably the Taj Mahal in Agra, and showed great talent for poetry; Akbar, in particular, encouraged literature not only among Muslims, but also among Hindus.

Akbar's greatest contribution, however, was that to an extent unmatched, and not even attempted again in India until after partition, he undertook and achieved a reconciliation between Muslims and Hindus. He removed discriminatory measures imposed by former Muslim rulers, notably the poll tax on non-Muslims and the pilgrims' tax levied on Hindus who visited holy places such as Benares. It was Akbar's dream to create a national state where Muslims and Hindus would live as equals. And he dreamed also of establishing a national monarchy, possibly similar to what Henry VIII had accomplished in England. Akbar made the first conscious attempt in India to formulate the concept of the secular state, and in this respect is regarded both as the creator of modern India, and as the leader who achieved a reconciliation between and a synthesis of Islam, Hinduism, and Christianity. Disillusioned with what he regarded as the narrowness of orthodox Islam, he displayed a passion for spiritual certainty, and toward the end of his life promulgated an eclectic monotheistic creed, which, however, disappeared once he had passed from the scene.

After Akbar's death his ideals of Muslim-Hindu unity in one national state faded away, as the Mogul empire, once more rent by dynastic strife, gradually disintegrated, loosening its hold on the subcontinent. The door was thus left open for the incursions of the Western seapowers, Britain and France, the Netherlands and Portugal, which struggled with each other to gain the prize they thought India would prove to be.

In this contest Britain, which had defeated the Spanish Armada in 1588, proved superior to its rivals. By the 1760's Clive, who had come out to India as a young writer for the East India Company of British merchants, had decisively defeated the French and their Indian allies at the battle of Plassey in 1757, and had established a British-controlled administration which operated side by side with the local rulers of Bengal, Bihar, and Orissa, with Clive as first Governor of Bengal at the age of 35. Britain's preponderant naval power assured its victory over the Portuguese, Dutch, and French, and the only non-British settlements that remained in India after 1763 were Goa, still held by Portugal today, and Pondicherry and Chandernagore, which the French ruled until Premier Pierre .Mendès-France relinquished them in 1954.

Chapter 4

The Building of a Nation

When the East India Company, chartered in 1600, started its operations in India, establishing factories in Calcutta and Madras, the subcontinent which had known a high degree of unity under the Mauryas, the Guptas, and the Moguls in the times of Akbar, was in a state of dangerous political fragmentation, not unlike Europe after the death of Charlemagne. Rival princes jousted with each other for power and prestige and, as the struggle between the Western nations seeking the wealth of the Indies sharpened, lent their support to one or the other of the contending sides. Political and military strife undermined administration, jeopardized economic development, and caused stagnation in cultural activities. Had this process continued, India might have suffered the same fate as China in the nineteenth century, when the great powers, intent on obtaining markets and railway concessions, used gunboat diplomacy to achieve their ends, with little or no concern for the interests and welfare of the Chinese people, whom they regarded with contempt, expressing surprise when Chinese leaders who opposed their incursions displayed what Westerners described with hostility as "anti-foreign" sentiment.

India was spared China's ordeal by the success of the East India Company in defeating the attempts of Britain's rivals — France, the Netherlands, and Portugal — to share the trade opportunities which they all envisioned in the subcontinent. The Company's success, it is generally admitted, was due not only to Britain's naval superiority but also to the fact that it operated under a system of free enterprise and

decentralization as contrasted with the mercantilist philosophy of France's Prime Minister, Colbert, who established
the French East India Company in 1664 as a government-
controlled undertaking.

While the French in India had to wait for orders from
Paris, which not only took a long time in reaching them but
were framed by men with no trading experience, the English
were able to make decisions on the spot and to adapt their
policies to local circumstances, knowing that the test of their
endeavors would not be compliance with governmental rules
in London but success measured in monetary terms. When
they found that trade could not be effectively carried on under
conditions of local disorder, corruption, extortion, and disruption of communications as a result of military skirmishes
between princes, the East India Company administrators did
not hesitate to wage war on those Indian rulers who challenged its plans, as Clive did at Plassey, or to make compacts
with friendly princes, as if the Company were itself a sovereign state. When Clive, who by that time had been honored
with the title of Lord Clive of Plassey, returned to India in
1765, to deal with new disorders he said, with what turned
out to be a prophetic sense, "tomorrow the whole Mogul
power is in our grasp." Yet two years later, at the peak of
what he could not but consider merited glory, when he returned to England after establishing a Society of Trade
which had a monopoly in betel leaf, salt, and opium, he met
with strong public criticism, and was brought before the
House of Commons, where he said he was treated like a
sheep-stealer rather than like a man who had built an empire.
He was so deeply shocked by this sudden turn in his fortunes
that after brooding on his downfall, he committed suicide in
1774 at the age of fifty.

The career of his successor, Warren Hastings, was as spectacular and as fraught with sharp contrasts between heights
of success and depths of failure. In the wake of a terrible

famine that swept India in 1770 — "the scene shocks humanity too much to bear description," said one official — Warren Hastings was sent to India as Governor of Bengal, the richest agricultural area of India. He was then 40 years old, having risen, like Clive, to the top from the lowly post of writer for the Company, which he had taken at the age of 18. Hastings was primarily not a soldier but a student and administrator. A Persian scholar, he learned Urdu, Bengali, and Arabic, and was deeply interested in the history, art, and culture of India.

Hastings did not think well of the double government system established by Clive, with East India Company administrators operating side by side with local governments, and decided that the Company should rule alone. He settled in Calcutta, which he made the capital of Bengal.

By that time the British government realized that, as Clive had so recently predicted, it was winning a great empire in India through the efforts of the East India Company, and in 1773 the government of Lord North put through Parliament an act regulating the Company's activities in India. This act provided for a civil and military government in the provinces of Bihar, Bengal, and Orissa, and Hastings, as Governor-General, became head of the government, assisted by four councilors. The governor-general and the councilors also had the power to supervise Madras and Bombay, where the Company also had trading centers.

The act, in addition, established a supreme court, consisting of a supreme justice and three other judges, which was to deal with all cases involving British subjects in the three provinces. Most important of all for the future development of British rule in India, the directors of the Company were to submit copies of all their correspondence to the government, and every six months were to account for their activities to Parliament. Thus was started the process of transition by which a merchant company with no responsibilities to the government except for the requirement of obtaining its charter was gradually shorn of the political, administrative, and military functions it had assumed, not from choice but from the necessity of maintaining conditions of order favorable to trade, and was increasingly made responsible to the legislature, which in turn was responsible to the British people.

A further step in this evolution was taken by Prime Minister William Pitt who in 1784 introduced the India Act. Under this act Indian affairs were placed under a committee of three senior directors of the East India Company, which in turn was to be supervised by a Board of Control whose members were appointed by the Crown. The office of President of the Board of Control was the forerunner of what eventually became in the nineteenth century the office of the Secretary of State for India. Hastings, who had already experienced many clashes about his authority with the Supreme Court, was alarmed by the India Act, and returned to Britain, where a storm of criticism awaited him. His enemies — Pitt, Fox, and particularly Edmund Burke — who had increasingly condemned Hastings' activities, notably his alleged mistreatment of Indian rulers that was said to include torture and extortion for purposes of personal enrichment — obtained his impeachment by the House of Commons. When he was brought to the bar of the House, amid scenes of colorful splendor vividly described by the historian Macaulay in his essay, *Warren Hastings,* he was subjected to the most eloquent denunciation by Burke of which this distinguished and often vitriolic orator was capable. Although Hastings was finally acquitted, he retired from political life with a sense of grim failure.

Yet, in retrospect, Hastings laid the basis for orderly and just rule by the British through three principal contributions. First, he contended that power should always be accompanied by a sense of responsibility, in this respect continuing the philosophy of the Hindu Asoka and the Muslim Akbar. Second, he urged the officials and employees of the East India Company to observe principles of good conduct in their relations with the Indians, declaring that it was in the interests of Britain, as well as India, that the peasants should be assured orderly rule, justice, and freedom from outside attack. And, most significant of all for a future understanding between the British and the Indians, he respected the traditions and culture of the subcontinent. He based a new civil and penal code on Indian customs, arranged for translations of ancient Hindu books by Indian scholars, thereby introducing the treasures of Indian literature to Europe, and in many other ways sought to preserve and promote India's cultural values, which the Indians themselves had tended to neglect during the turbulent centuries of disintegration of the Mogul empire. Thoughtful Indians, among them Raja Ram Mohan Roy, and even Dadabhay Naoroji, who first used the word *Swaraj* (self-rule) to describe India's goal, recognized the benefits of British rule for India. In fact, when Naoroji attacked Indian rulers, he did it in a book entitled *Poverty and Un-British Rule in India.*

The experience of Clive and Hastings epitomized two basic problems of Britain's relationship with India for nearly three hundred and fifty years. On the one hand, the British could and repeatedly did, claim that their arrival in the subcontinent, although admittedly inspired by motives of private profit-making, had the twofold result of safeguarding India from invasions by other powers while restoring law and order within the continent, and of serving the strategic and economic interests of Britain and the empire it built around the world during that period. On the other hand, both British critics of this relationship and Indian nationalists could and repeatedly did contend that, however true these claims might be, the price paid for the achievements first of the East India Company and subsequently of the British Crown, which in

1857 took over the administrative functions the Company had previously exercised, was too high, both in moral terms and in economic terms.

British critics — Burke among them — again and again were conscience-stricken at what they heard about the ruthlessness of Company-appointed administrators toward the Indians, their contempt for people of color, their enrichment through methods which would have been condemned in Britain, such as bribery, extortion, and torture of persons from whom funds were sought, as well as the sale of opium, and the violation of Christian principles which the British working in India claimed to support and propagate. What troubled British critics most was the use of a double standard of moral conduct — depending on whether a man acted in Britain or in India. The Indian nationalists, who could heartily subscribe to the views of British critics, increasingly argued, as the struggle for independence from Britain gained momentum after 1858, that the presence of the British, whatever its advantages for India, was an obstacle to the modernization and development which the subcontinent might have been able to experience in the absence of foreign rule, no matter how benevolent.

This clash between two aspects of British rule — what seemed good and useful to merchants and administrators, and what seemed evil and ineffectual to British critics and to Indian nationalists — is a familiar feature of the colonial relationship between a Western nation and a non-Western people. Colonialism, whatever its initial motivation — whether military or political or economic or ideological — is bound to have the appearance of the Roman god Janus with two faces looking in opposite directions. The colonizer genuinely believes, or rationalizes its actions into believing, that it is conferring benefits on the colonized people, from whom it expects at least gratitude and at most uncritical cooperation in the policies it regards as necessary.

The colonial people, for its part, even when, as proved to be the case in India, it acknowledges its indebtedness to the colonizing power in some respects, resents and by all means at its disposal opposes the foreign ruler and is willing to risk the possible dangers of disorder and misrule as a result of independence, on the ground that "good government is not a substitute for self-government." What makes the argument between the two invariably confused, and when resistance is allowed to reach the stage of armed uprising, dangerous for both, is that the colonizing power does not regard it necessary to observe, in its colonial possessions, the moral rules of conduct to which it would be held at home, justifying this double standard by arguments such as that its overseas subjects are either backward or inferior, and therefore unprepared for self-government. Meanwhile, the colonial peoples, having been repeatedly told of the superior advantages of democracy and Christianity as contrasted with their authoritarian regimes and their own faiths, are led to expect from the Western ruler higher standards of relations between human beings than those to which they have been traditionally accustomed.

Here too a two-faced picture emerges — with the colonial power showing at home the noble mien of respect for representative government, for individual liberty, for free enterprise, and for the equality of man; and in the colonial possession the less appealing features of administrators, traders, and even educators and missionaries. These, for whatever reason, believe it proper to restrict political liberties, to limit free speech, to extol the advantages of what amounts to benevolent dictatorship by the colonial power, to discourage the growth of economic activities which might compete with those of the metropolitan country, and to discriminate against the natives in social life. They inculcate religious and educational values which, however suitable they may be in the West, are often ill-adapted, and in any case often opposed, to the needs of the non-Western lands, and often arouse deep-seated opposition to values imposed by the outsiders, which in turn nurtures nationalism and anti-Westernism.

It is in this context of mixed experience with Western colonialism — or, to use the Indian formula of "this and that" rather than "this or that" — that the impact of British rule on India must be judged and the alternatives that might have occurred had the British never come to India must be evaluated.

On the credit side of the ledger, an outside observer would have to put down at least five major contributions made by Britain.

First, the British, through the East India Company, checked the political and economic disintegration of the subcontinent that had set in as a result of the breakdown of administrative control by the Mogul empire with its capital in Delhi.

Second, after eliminating their Western competitors for influence and control in India, they henceforth protected the subcontinent against intervention or incursion from outside — not only by the West, but in the nineteenth century also by the Russian Empire under the Tsars.

Third, they introduced order and security in the areas over which they had control, eventually extending this control over the entire subcontinent, which the British Crown, after 1858, administered in two separate sectors — British India, ruled directly from London, and 562 princely states, where the local rulers remained in power, but made bilateral pacts with the British Crown.

Fourth, they introduced the rule of law, familiar to the English people, with equal treatment for individuals, irrespective of color, race, or religion.

And, fifth, in contrast to the Dutch in Indonesia and the French in Indo-China, they gave an opportunity, after 1858, to a small but significant number of Indians of high intellectual quality to be trained for civil service, at home and in English universities, and entrusted them with high-level jobs, thereby preparing a select group for the administrative tasks they might have to perform in an independent country.

In a subcontinent menaced by chaos, the British gradually constructed the skeleton of a unified area where they instilled, within limits they themselves determined, some of the basic principles of law and government which they had evolved in their own society.

What the British had not yet done by 1947, when they decided it was wise to withdraw from India before their task, as they had previously seen it, had been completed, was to clothe this skeleton with adequate flesh and to articulate it in all the parts necessary for a modern state. Whether or not they would have succeeded in completing this task had they found it possible to remain in India for a further, undefined period of time must remain one of the unanswerable questions of history, but it seems doubtful that they could have done so, given the growing strength and impatience of Indian nationalism.

Assuming that the British, by 1947, had gone as far as they could, an outside observer would have to set down a major charge on the debit side of the ledger, which must be broken down into several separate items. This major charge is that the British, once they had introduced order and security against outside attack, the rule of law, and a core Indian civil service — all of which were necessary for the safe operation of British administration in India — they either did little to change the patterns of Indian life or, when they changed these patterns, gave little thought to the consequences of their actions. They thus created serious problems for the future, which were left as a harsh inheritance for independent India.

The British abolished certain practices which they found repugnant to Western customs, such as suttee, infanticide, and thuggee (banditry), but they carefully avoided tampering with the caste system, choosing, like their Mogul predecessors, to leave it alone. While it is understandable that the British preferred not to challenge head-on a social and economic system deeply entrenched in Hindu life, the result was that the political structure they slowly erected in India stood apart from, and did not merge with the Hindu structure. It has remained for the government of the Republic of India to start dismantling the caste system and to forge a political, social, and economic framework within which new human relations could be developed without undue shock to public order and to the sensitivities of the people.

Meanwhile, the changes the British did make had far-reaching consequences which they either did not or could not foresee at the time, but whose impact is now having serious results for India. First, as already indicated, by reducing the death rate through public health measures and increased internal security without taking steps to decrease the birthrate the British, like other colonial rulers, unwittingly set the stage for an explosive growth of population which has proved a tremendous obstacle to India's economic development.

Second, under the governorship of Lord Cornwallis (1786–1798) the British, through the "Permanent Settlement," created a new group of middlemen, the *zamindars* (holders of land), who had previously served as tax collectors for the British, and now were made landlords. They had the obligation to pay the Company a fixed or "permanent" sum on taxes which they collected, keeping the rest for themselves. This "Permanent Settlement" which, Lord Cornwallis believed, would introduce in India the way of life of England's landed gentry, proved to have an effect the British had not anticipated. For one thing, since the zamindars had to pay a fixed sum in perpetuity, whatever the amount of the taxes they collected, the Company, and ultimately the British government, was deprived of additional revenue in days of prosperity. For another, whenever the zamindars were unable to pay the sum set for them, they lost their land, with a consequently disruptive effect on land ownership. The most serious and disastrous effect of the zamindari system, however, was its effect on the peasants, who were left pretty much at the mercy of the zamindars. The peasant had to pay heavier rents, often risk or lose his land to the zamindar, owe the zamindars forced labor duty, and so on. The social effect of creating a landed and often absentee landlord class, which has political repercussions in India today, is another very important and direct effect of the zamindari system of former days.

Third, the British introduced in India the system of education they found desirable in Britain, as proposed in the *Minute on Education* drawn up in 1835 by Macaulay, who regarded Indian ideas and literature as barbaric ("a single shelf of a good European library," he said, "was worth the whole native literature of India and Arabia"), and believed that the English should bring light to "the children of darkness." English was made the medium of instruction in institutions of higher learning. This in itself proved useful to India when it achieved independence, although only 10 to 15 per cent of the Indian population speak English today, and the teaching of English has markedly deteriorated since 1947. But the question which now confronts India is whether British education, based until 1945 on the concept of training an elite in exclusive schools and colleges, Eton and Harrow, Oxford and Cambridge, primarily in the humanities with little emphasis on science and technology, was suited for Indian needs. In India, with a vast and growing population, the masses must receive at least a modicum of education if they are to create a democratic society and to satisfy their newly aroused aspirations for advancement; and urgent tasks of modernizing agriculture and creating new industries call for more and more young men and women trained in modern technical skills rather than for those who seek white-collar jobs as government clerks or as writers.

Fourth, while the British continued the construction of irrigation facilities and built communications — railways, posts and telegraphs, and telephones, all of which were necessary for their civilian and military administration — they did little to encourage the development of India's economy and in some important respects actually discouraged it. From the point of view of the Indians, the lack of British initiative in the economic sphere seemed to be an evil design to destroy their opportunities for ultimate independence and to keep them in thrall to the British Empire. It must be borne in mind, however, that the British at that time, and until the rise of socialism in Britain during the 1930's, were firm believers in free enterprise, free trade, *laissez faire*, and an unplanned economy. They could thus justify to themselves their lack of alacrity in examining India's potential resources and devising methods for their most effective use.

At the same time, it is clear that the British saw in India a source of cotton for their Lancashire mills, then the most advanced in the world, and as an outlet for their finished cotton goods. Their economic policy was calculated to achieve both objectives. By abolishing India's customs tariff in 1882, and refusing to establish another tariff until 1923, after World War I, they made it impossible for India either to keep out British cotton goods, or to establish under at least temporary protection, some of those "infant" industries which other countries had created at a comparable stage of economic development, to replace their heavy dependence on cotton. Although a revenue tariff of 5 per cent was imposed on imports in 1894, the Lancashire cotton interests protested against it. British goods were therefore admitted at 3½ per cent but, to offset this, a countervailing excise duty of 3½ per cent was imposed on goods made out of cloth produced in India which competed with that made in Lancashire — an instance of Britain's capacity to combine its belief in *laissez faire* with a measure of planning. Meanwhile, by insisting on importation of their cotton goods into India on preferential terms, the British caused the decline of cottage industries in the villages, which had provided a subsidiary source of employment and income for the peasants.

Britain's refusal to recognize the double problem its cotton goods policy was creating for India aroused the vigorous opposition of Gandhi, who urged his supporters to symbolize their resistance by devoting some time each day to work at the spinning wheel, and to refuse to wear garments made of British-manufactured cloth, using instead homemade goods (*swadeshi*, or made in one's own country) produced by the cottage industries. Here, again, the British failed to see the consequences and interconnectedness of their policies. A population rapidly increasing as a result of lower death rates but unchecked by lower birth rates needed employment, yet the British government did not face the need to encourage corresponding growth in productivity.

The peasants either had to find increased employment in handicrafts in the villages, or seek work in newly created industries as peasants had once done in Western Europe at the end of the Middle Ages. But the British showed little inclination to diversify the Indian economy by the creation of new industries which might have competed with those of the metropolitan country — although they did provide technicians to improve the productivity of India's cotton mills. When the well-known and highly respected Parsee industrialist, J. R. Tata, decided to build the first (and until after independence the only) steel mill in India, and sought capital in Britain, the president of the Federation of British Industries, expressing profound disbelief in the capacity of the Indians to create such an enterprise, is said to have exclaimed: "I'll eat every ton of steel they make!" Although this gentleman was presumably spared the ordeal of eating

1,200,000 tons of steel a year — the eventual output of the Tata mill — the required capital had to be raised in the United States.

The net result of Britain's lack of economic policy, or the use of economic policy to discourage local initiative, is that independent India found it had to modernize and reorganize its primarily backward agrarian economy and, at the same time, do what it could toward diversifying its production through the creation of essential industries, among them an antibiotics plant, three fertilizer factories, a locomotive works, and three new steel mills, before it could hope to make a start on the output of consumer goods sufficient to fill even the minimal needs of the population. Moreover, it had to undertake this gigantic task with only a handful of scientists, technical experts, and responsible entrepreneurs, since the British had not encouraged technological education or a climate favorable to the emergence of enterprising business-men, as distinguished from speculators in commodities who are characteristic of underdeveloped countries, and in India deal largely in such commodities as sugar, cotton, or jute.

And fifth, but perhaps most unfortunate for India's immediate future, foreign rule impeded the country's social and cultural development. At this time in its history India, having made contact through Britain with the West after centuries of isolation, could have benefited by the application of modern science and technology to modernize not only its economy but also its education, its social structure, and its political system. Yet the energies and creative faculties of its intelligent and enterprising people were diverted for a century to the struggle for independence, which for long periods removed some of its most prominent leaders to jail and, no sooner had Britain withdrawn, to the devastating Muslim-Hindu riots which sapped the vitality of both new nations when they were most in need of strength for new undertakings and of cooperation in common problems.

Chapter 5

The Peaceful Revolution

If, as British defenders of their country's rule in India contend, this rule on balance benefited the subcontinent, how can one explain the Mutiny of 1857, which came after the significant reforms effected under the India Act, or, more important, the long-sustained and finally victorious independence movement which forced Britain's withdrawal from India in 1947?

In essence, the answer to this question has two aspects. First, no foreign ruler, particularly of a great nation with an ancient history and a distinguished civilization, can expect that, however beneficent and just may be its administration, it can remain indefinitely in power. The most it can hope for is that, after giving the people it governs such preparation as it deems possible for self-government, it will retain with the ultimately independent nation ties of mutual respect and friendship as Britain did succeed in doing with India and Pakistan after they had voluntarily joined the Commonwealth. And, second, the ideals of democracy — ideals of individual freedom, of equality, of economic and social welfare — are incompatible, over the long run, with the colonial relationship. Yet by introducing these ideals to the colonial people, the colonizing power, in effect, prepares the way for the eventual dissolution of its rule, to which these ideals are a daily challenge.

But while some Indian politicians and commentators, particularly on the occasion of the hundredth anniversary of the Mutiny in 1957, have sought to link that event to the movement for independence, the Mutiny, unlike the series of developments which brought into being the Republic of India, was a step backward and not forward in India's history. The Mutiny was not a national movement, nor did it have the fulfillment of nationalist aspirations as its objective. It represented a reaction against the British by those elements in India who felt that in one way or another, they had been injured, frustrated, or dispossessed by the social reforms introduced by the foreign ruler. Some princes resented the fact that the British, by taking over administrative functions, had limited their sovereignty, as indeed they had. Religious leaders feared that British ideas, which also included the introduction of Christianity to the Indians, would challenge and jeopardize the influence of Hinduism. The Muslims who, resenting the British "infidels," had been reluctant to study English and had consequently been unable to win civil service posts, were alarmed by what they regarded as the British preference for the Hindus.

These various emotions, which had long been smoldering, found the hundredth anniversary of the battle of Plassey, which marked Clive's victory over the French, an appropriate occasion for an explosion. The immediate — but in historical perspective least important — reason for the mutiny, which happened to align both Hindu and Muslim soldiers against their British officers, was the introduction of new cartridges for the Enfield rifles used by the British in India. These cartridges had to be encased in grease, and it was rumored that both cow fat, unacceptable to the Hindus who worship the cow, and pig fat, unacceptable to the Muslims who are forbidden to eat pork, had been used for this purpose. The soldiers' mutiny, which set off other, but so far as can be determined, either unconnected or only loosely connected incidents, in various parts of the country, led to bitter fighting in Delhi between the British officers and their mutinous soldiers beleaguered in the Red Fort, which still bears marks of the struggle, and in Lucknow. And it profoundly shocked the British, and shook their previous assumption that they were governing Hindus and Muslims not only for their benefit, but also with their acquiescence and support.

The most important result of the Mutiny was the decision to complete the transformation of British rule that had been started by Pitt in the India Act by transferring the governance of India from the East India Company to the British Crown. This decision was embodied in a proclamation by Queen Victoria, published on November 1, 1858, which was described as the Magna Carta of India. By this proclamation, the subcontinent became the Indian Empire, with the Queen as its Empress.

The Queen made three principal promises to the people of India. First, the princes who had remained loyal during the Mutiny would be safe from encroachments on their territories by the British. Second, there was to be complete freedom of religion, and the rights and customs of India — of Hindus and Muslims alike — were to be protected and respected. And, third, the Indians were to have the right to hold any administrative office.

The British thus recognized the need for a gradual adjustment in their rule of the subcontinent. From that time on, slowly but continuously, their administrators, both in London and in India, showed a realization that they were acting as trustees for the Indian people and had a responsibility to prepare them for future self-government through greater and still greater involvement in higher and higher offices of state, through the best possible education of their elite for civil service, through encouragement of a free press. When the Britisher Allan Octavian Hume urged the creation by the Indians of the Indian National Congress in 1885, he said: "Whether in the individual or the nation, all vital progress must spring from within, and it is to you, her most favored sons, that your country must look for the initiative. In vain may aliens like myself love India and her children, give time and trouble, money and thought; in vain may they struggle and sacrifice . . . They lack the essential of nationality, and the real work must be done by the people themselves." The British, however, found it difficult to recognize that the Indian nationalists, whom they themselves had groomed for independence, would not stop short of actually cutting the tie which had been forged between Britain and India during three centuries. They faced this contingency only in 1947, when the last Viceroy, Lord Mountbatten, sensed that continuation of British rule might lead to bloodshed and disaster, and so advised the Attlee government.

When the parting did come, Britain succeeded in avoiding a bloody struggle such as France experienced before it decided to relinquish Indo-China. Its departure, however, was promptly followed by the partition of the hitherto undivided Indian subcontinent between India and Pakistan.

This wrenching experience will long be analyzed by historians seeking to discover whether the partition could have been averted by greater wisdom on the part of the three parties concerned — Britain, the Indian National Congress, and the Muslim League. Did the British before they decided to withdraw from India, as some experts contend, follow a policy of "divide and rule," putting Muslims against Hindus and vice versa, and thereby preventing a harmonizing of the interests of the two groups? Did Nehru and other leaders of the Indian National Congress show lack of magnanimity toward the Muslims before independence, as argued by the late Muslim leader, Maulana Azad, Minister of Education in Nehru's post-independence cabinet? Or did fiery Muslim leaders like Mohammed Ali Jinnah, head of the Muslim League, block conciliation by their intransigent insistence on the creation of a separate state based on Islam?

Whatever may be the answers to these highly controversial questions, the harsh fact is that the subcontinent was partitioned at short notice, in the midst of bloody riots on both sides which took a toll of thousands of lives. When the fighting stopped, some five million refugees had fled from India to Pakistan, and approximately the same number from Pakistan to India, leaving most of their possessions behind. Resources, as well as people, were split between the two new nations, with jute, for example, left in Pakistan, and factories processing jute in India. The political, economic, military, and psychological wounds of this explosive partition are still open. In two respects, however, India and Pakistan promptly took similar actions. Both became republics, and both joined the Commonwealth, led by their former ruler, Britain.

The British had been slow in facing up to their ultimate departure because, after the 1858 Proclamation, they had expected to continue to rule India with the support of an elite native group, composed, in the 562 princely states, of the princes, and in British India of the Indian Civil Service, with British and Indian expert administrators within its ranks, all loyal to the British Crown. In 1858 they did not foresee the rise to power of a small but active and highly influential middle class, whose emergence was made possible by British-introduced reforms, and opportunities for study in English universities where they learned the ideas of European nationalism, as well as of English liberalism and socialism. Nor did the British foresee the growing concern the middle class felt over the economic backwardness of India, the wretched conditions of its villages and cotton mills, the status of the untouchables, the persistence of the caste system, and the discrimination on grounds of color to which they themselves were subjected in India by their British rulers, although they did not experience it as students in Britain. The British did not understand the explosive character of the ideas they had nurtured and propagated, from their own Magna Carta to the poetry of Milton and Shelley, from Lord Byron's support of the Greek independence movement in 1820 to the sympathy of British poets for Kossuth and Mazzini, from the economic theories of Bentham to those of Tawney and Laski. Nor was this surprising. For those who administered Britain in the nineteenth century and the early decades of the twentieth were not always aware of the impact these ideas would have on the English people as the middle class expanded its power at the expense of the landed gentry and the aristocracy, and industrial labor came to play an increasingly important role in the political arena.

Yet these ideas did not merely, as it then seemed, weaken Britain by undermining and eventually ending its rule over India. They also strengthened both Britain and India. For, by absorbing, through the British experience, the Western concepts of democracy, liberalism, and non-Marxist Fabian socialism, India, as it had done again and again when challenged by new thoughts and beliefs, made its own the best of Europe's political and social heritage. Armed with these ideas, India achieved a synthesis, unique in modern history, of West and East — an Anglo-Asian synthesis, which gave it an opportunity to carry out a peaceful revolution, as contrasted with the bloody and ruthless revolutions that swept at approximately the same time its great neighbors, Russia and China.

This synthesis was made possible not only by the Hindus' gift for absorptiveness, but also by the remarkable affinity between the ideas and attitudes of the English and the Indian peoples. Seldom, if ever, in history did two peoples living under different geographical and climatic conditions, and nurtured in widely contrasting traditions and philosophies, coincide to such a marked extent on the basic concepts of relations between human beings in organized society. Admiration for an elite (the witty Anglo-Indian writer Aubrey Menen points out the existence of the caste system in Britain), tempered by concern for the welfare of "man and beast" as Asoka put it; the high priority given to good government, and the emphasis placed on the responsibility of the ruler to the ruled; the toleration for all religious faiths; even the talent, which the British more than other Western colonial rulers have displayed again and again, for administering multiracial and multilingual societies — all these factors combined to create a mutual respect and understanding even at the height of the Indians' struggle to oust the British. As Gandhi repeatedly said, he had no hatred for the British, whom he greatly admired, but he believed firmly — as the British did — in freedom.

The significance, and even the existence, of India's peaceful revolution was obscured, not only for Westerners but also for many Indians, by the fact that it was interwoven with and, during the century between the Mutiny and the achievement of independence, dominated by the mounting struggle for independence from Britain. Yet, it is this interweaving of revolutionary political, economic, and social ideas with nationalist sentiment which, once independence had been won, made it possible for India to go on, with no serious interruption in rhythm, to the weaving of new patterns of democracy.

The revolution carried out by the Indians without resort to violence after the organization of the Indian National Congress in 1885 consisted of four main strands, which remain strong and significant in independent India. These four strands are nationalism; Gandhism; socialism; and communism.

For India nationalism was a new idea, inspired by the belief of European liberals in the desirability of freedom from foreign domination and of self-determination for all nations. In Europe nationalism — the sense of national identity and the longing to embody it within the form of a national state — had helped to create such important nations as England, France, and Spain in the Middle Ages; and in the nineteenth century had inspired the forging of the German Empire out of a congeries of small states, and of an independent Italy, after the ousting of the Austrians through the heroic efforts of

Mazzini and Garibaldi. It had paved the way for the ultimate breakup, after World War I, of the Austro-Hungarian Empire, challenged in the 1840's by the Poles and the Hungarians; had freed the Greeks from Ottoman rule; had turned back, in Austria and Prussia and Russia, the conquering march of Napoleon; had stirred the imagination and talents embodied in Verdi's *Aida*, Chopin's *Funeral March*, Byron's "The Isles of Greece, The Isles of Greece"; and had ultimately led Woodrow Wilson to proclaim, during World War I, the principle of "self-determination of nations," which brought freedom to Czechoslovakia, Poland, and other countries that had once been part of either the Austro-Hungarian or the Russian empires.

Yet, it was not until after World War II that the Western powers suddenly realized that the principles they had eloquently supported in Europe, when it caused the disruption and disintegration of hostile empires, could be and were being invoked against them by the colonial peoples who lived under their rule. The Atlantic Charter, the product of two statesmen — Winston Churchill and Franklin D. Roosevelt — who had extolled the values of democracy in the struggle against Nazi and Fascist totalitarianism, although drafted in universal terms, was limited in its application by Churchill, over American protests and much to the dismay of the Indians.

Valuable as the concept of nationalism was to the Indians in their struggle for independence, they were more concerned with freedom than with the assertion of a nationalist spirit which, they believed, was ill-adapted for and might even prove disruptive in India. The poet Rabindranath Tagore, in his thoughtful little book on *Nationalism*, admitted that nationalism was an important weapon in the work of the Indian National Congress, but, recognizing the diversity of India's many peoples, in terms of color, languages, religions, and so on, he thought that India would need not only a sense of national cohesion but also a high degree of tolerance to hold all its diverse peoples together in a single organized society.

Nationalism, said Tagore, with a sense of reality which is not often found among peoples striving for independence, is not necessarily liberal — it can be reactionary. And, there was a danger that, once India had become independent, each of the various linguistic groups composing the subcontinent would insist not only on cultural but also on political autonomy, with disruptive consequences for the new republic. True, there have been clashes over the use of Hindi in South India, between the Dravida Kazhagam and similar groups in Madras state and the Central Government in New Delhi, and India still faces an unresolved dispute in Bombay state about the formation of separate units for those who speak Gujerati and those who speak Marathi. In spite of these linguistic conflicts, however, India within a decade successfully adapted nationalism, which had served its cause against Britain, to the needs of a community of different language groups which is gaining a sense of national identity at home and of national dignity abroad, without resorting to the emotional excesses which often mark nationalist triumphs.

The moderation that has marked India's nationalism can be attributed not only to the absorptive qualities of Hinduism but also to the supranational views of the two principal leaders of the independence movement — Mahatma Gandhi and Jawaharlal Nehru — who were able again and again, even in periods when they might understandably have felt bitter toward both the British and toward those Muslims who favored partition, to rise above their own people's interests and see the need for understanding and reconciliation.

Gandhi, a lawyer trained in Britain, affectionately called "Gandhiji," and honored as the Mahatma (great soul) was a patriot who recognized the qualities of foreign rulers whom a lesser man might have demagogically denounced as oppressors. He was a religious leader who contended that "Hinduism is not an exclusive religion and should find room for the worship of all the prophets of the world," who drew inspiration from Jesus Christ's Sermon on the Mount, and who, at the risk of his life, defended the religious freedom of the Muslims within a predominantly Hindu state. He was a man of peace, who used nonviolent noncooperation to undermine British administration and unresistingly went to jail for his principles, inflicting far greater injury on Britain by his steadfast refusal to use force than he could have done by rallying thousands of armed followers to his cause. One of the reasons for his success was that he knew the powerful influence of the conscience of the British at home, torn between their desire to maintain the empire and their repugnance to use ruthless methods against the Indian nationalists which a Hitler or a Stalin would not have hesitated to use under comparable circumstances — and adopted the means best suited for dealing with his opponents.

He was a revolutionary who strove unremittingly to end the status of the "untouchable," arguing that untouchability was a betrayal of Hinduism, and who saw the need to improve the conditions of India's impoverished, ill, undernourished, illiterate peasants, and of workers condemned to live in crowded miserable slums of big cities under demoralizing circumstances. Yet, he associated with and accepted aid from Brahmins who did not share his desire for social equality, and from industrialists like Birla, owner of textile mills whose labor conditions must have shocked Gandhi. Nor, in his desire to improve the lot of human beings, did he favor socialism, in contrast to Nehru who had expressed Socialist views as early as the 1920's.

But, while Gandhi did not support socialism as a political movement, he fostered socialism as an ideology. True, he was not a dogmatic Socialist. He did not advocate socialism in the sense in which many Americans think of it — that is, as synonymous with state ownership. Gandhi vigorously distrusted the concentration of power and wealth in the hands of the state — but he also distrusted their concentration in the hands of a few private owners. What he urged was the "trusteeship of wealth" by those who possess it and their responsibility to the people as a whole. This concept is closely akin to socialism as it is practiced both by Nehru and by the Indian Socialists, and thus can be said to have paved the way for India's so-called "socialism."

According to Gandhi, however, the Socialists believed in violence, which he rejected, and were primarily concerned with man's material progress, while he was concerned with man's spiritual improvement through the practice of true Hinduism, which teaches the individual to spurn all desires because desires only tend to confuse him, and to become finally "With self, in self, content." He wanted to improve life in the villages instead of sending villagers to the cities to find work in urban industries, and, because of his opposition to the imports of British cotton goods, he fostered village handicrafts both as a source of employment for the peasants and as an instrument of struggle against the British. His opposition to socialism, together with his emphasis on village life, caused many to believe that Gandhi was an opponent of industrialization. There is very little unanimity among his followers, however, as to what his economic and social policies might have been had he not been struck down by an assassin in 1948. His sayings, as conveyed to his many devout disciples in his *ashram* (retreat) or on long walks in the countryside or as expressed at public meetings attended by thousands of people, were too fluid and flexible to be embodied after his death into a rigid doctrine which, in any case, would be contrary to Hindu practice. He used to say that his latest thoughts on any given topic were the ones to be followed, even if they contradicted earlier views.

While Gandhi was alive he was ready to give his opinions

on all subjects, but he felt that when he was no longer living his followers would have to think for themselves — and today not all of them by any means think alike. Some, notably his most famous disciple, Vinoba Bhave, still favor a simple way of life, emphasis on the development of villages outside large cities, improvements of village life, prohibition, the practice of handicrafts, the use of homespun goods in preference to goods made by machines, and preoccupation with spiritual rather than material concerns. Others have found no incompatibility between Gandhism and industrialization. They contend that electricity distributed by the great new Bakhra and Damodar Valley dams will make it possible for the villagers to diversify their production without leaving their rural community, and to participate actively in the modernization of the country's economy.

It is conceivable, however, that had Gandhi lived he might have found himself in conflict with Nehru, whom he regarded as his "younger brother." Nehru, also trained for the law, a graduate of Cambridge University, member of a distinguished Brahmin family from Allahabad, originally from Kashmir, was, by comparison to Gandhi, with his familiar shawl and cotton dhoti and big-framed spectacles, a man of the world, a sophisticate, and an admitted agnostic. He shared Gandhi's ardor for independence, which inspired not only him but also his father and mother and his sister, Madame Vijayalakshmi Pandit, to become Mahatma's followers, and was vigorously at his side throughout the period of difficult years of struggle with Britain. And he shared Gandhi's concern for the poor and the underprivileged.

But Nehru, compared to Gandhi who thought of the country's economy in nineteenth-century terms, had already projected his mind into the twentieth century. His philosophy of socialism, derived from his study of the works of Britain's Fabian Socialists, led him to think of social revolution not only in terms of abolishing discriminations based on race, color, and caste status, but also of transforming the country's economy in terms of a socialist democracy.

Although Nehru in his writings shows his interest in Marxism and recognizes its applicability in Russia and China, he has given no indication of using it as the touchstone for India's future. Once he became Prime Minister of independent India, he made it clear that his objective was the creation of a mixed economy, similar to that developed in Britain in the early decades of the twentieth century and consolidated by the Labour party under the leadership of Prime Minister Clement Attlee after its electoral victory in 1945. A modern economic system in an underdeveloped country, as he envisages it, should assure initiative for the government to start new enterprises that are regarded as in the public interest but would not bring profits to private investors, domestic or foreign, such as dams, irrigation projects, and other nonself-liquidating undertakings, as well as factories for the output of goods new to the country, such as antibiotics and fertilizers, steel and locomotives, some of which may eventually be sold to private owners. But there should also be ample room for private enterprise, provided the private entrepreneurs, whether domestic or foreign, take into consideration the interests of the nation as a whole, and do not waste the country's limited resources of capital, technical skills, and foreign currency on the production of what, under the harsh conditions of India's existence, must be regarded as luxury consumer goods. Actually, while India's economy is usually described as Socialist, it is estimated that, if agriculture, still the principal source of employment and income in the country, and private industry are taken together, then it can be said that 90 per cent of India's economic activity is in the hands of private owners.

While Nehru's concept and practice of socialism are now generally accepted, even by the conservatives among the business community, they are often criticized by the Socialist party, which after independence split off from Nehru's ruling Congress party. The Socialists, who at first concentrated their activities among the factory workers of big cities, are now also active in the villages, particularly since their principal leader, Jayaprakash Narayan, often regarded as Nehru's most promising successor, has forsworn the political party struggle as unsuited to India's difficult conditions, and has become a follower of Gandhi's disciple, Vinoba Bhave, in his *Bhoodan* (land-gift) movement.

While, if the Socialists were in power they would presumably go further than Nehru in socializing India's industrial enterprises and perhaps also in consolidating village lands into cooperatives, their differences with the Prime Minister seem to concern details rather than the essential philosophy of socialism. These point up the familiar gap between those who have assumed some of the responsibilities, and hence the limitations, of exercising political power, and those who are not only out of power, but after much thought, as in the case of Narayan, have decided to eschew the political arena.

The real conflict, if it comes, would be not between Nehru and the Socialist party, but between Nehru's socialism and communism. In the so far peaceful revolution under way in India, communism is a significant factor, but a factor whose ultimate effect it is as yet impossible to evaluate. Unlike the Indian nationalists, who fought for freedom from the British, the Communists stayed aloof from the struggle; during World War II, when Germany attacked Russia in 1941 and was immediately offered aid by Britain, they supported the British. This anti-nationalist position, different from that usually taken by Communists in colonial areas, gave the Communists a poor headstart in independent India. Nor has Nehru's government been hesitant in using drastic measures to suppress Communists whenever it could be proved that they were disrupting law and order — although in world affairs it has maintained a policy of neutralism between the non-Communist bloc led by the United States and its Communist neighbors, Russia and China.

However, as the Congress party, many of whose members, after devoting the best years of their life to the struggle for independence, have now grown old and weary, lost some of its fire, and the vast difficulties of transforming a primitive agrarian country into a modern state began to emerge, the Communists gained ground. The successes they have achieved, notably in the state of Kerala, where they won control of the government in 1957 by a slim margin, have been due not to popular enthusiasm for Communist ideology, or to admiration for Russia and China, whose ruthless methods are repugnant to thoughtful Indians. They have been due to the Communists' claims that they would be more active, more determined, and more efficient than the Congress party, which in many areas of the country has lost the enthusiastic support it had once enjoyed, in promoting economic development and fostering social equality. For the time being, at least, the success of the Communists seems to depend in direct ratio on the failures of the Congress party, and might be reversed if Congress could revitalize its membership, its machinery, and its program.* As of 1959 the most widely known Communist leader was the Chief Minister of Kerala, E. M. S. Namboodiripad, a high-caste Brahmin, sober of mien and manner, who was once a member of the Congress party, which he left in 1939.

India's peaceful revolution was sparked in the first instance

---

* Following widespread nonviolent demonstrations against the Communist government's school law — which both the Christian and the Hindu Nair schools regarded as a threat to their existence — and the use of force by the government, the Congress party, first in Kerala and then at the Center, demanded intervention by New Delhi. On July 31, 1959, after prolonged discussions of what was recognized as a crucial issue, it was announced that President Prasad, as authorized by the constitution, would take over the administration of Kerala, in spite of protests by the Communist Chief Minister. (*August 9, 1959. V.M.D.*)

by the desire for national independence, which in turn had been inspired by the liberal and social thought of Western Europe. Having achieved independence, India used the philosophies of Gandhism, drawn directly from Hinduism; of socialism, derived from the British Fabians and the experience of the British Labour party; and of communism based on Marxism, to weave new patterns of existence in what is today the largest political democracy in the world — a democracy which has adopted voluntary socialism as the guideline of its economic development, and which is determined to assure social welfare and justice through community action.

Chapter 6

New Political Patterns: Government by Reconciliation

The new patterns of democracy in India had been emerging since the Mutiny — but until 1947 the Indians had not participated directly in the task of making them, for lack of a responsible government of their own.

True, the process of governmental change which, to use a now familiar American phrase, had been proceeding with "all deliberate speed" since 1858, had shown considerable acceleration in the first three decades of the twentieth century, as the tide of Indian resistance mounted. The first of three important steps was taken in the Minto-Morley reforms of 1909 through the India Councils Act. This Act provided that the British Viceroy was to be responsible to the Secretary of State for India in London and to the British Parliament. The Provincial Legislative Councils were to be doubled in membership, and to have elected as well as nominated members. The Imperial Legislative Council was to be increased from 21 to 60. And Indian members were to be appointed to the Viceroy's Executive Council, to the executive councils of Bombay and Madras, and to the Council of the Secretary of State for India in London.

From the point of view of the Indians, this was an improvement, but it was far from adequate. Immediately after World War I, in which the Indians had fought at the side of the British in Europe and the Middle East, Edwin Montagu, Secretary of State for India, introduced what is known as the Montagu-Chelmsford reforms through an Act of Parliament.

The Provincial Legislative Councils were further enlarged, with a majority of members being elected. Indian Ministers were appointed in the provinces under a system known as *dyarchy* (double rule). In British India the functions of government were divided at the Provincial level into two categories — transferred subjects and reserved subjects. The transferred subjects, which were to be administered by Indian ministers responsible to provincial legislatures, were local self-government, education, agriculture, and forests. The remaining subjects, particularly law, order, and revenue, were administered by officials responsible not to the legislature but to the Governor. At the center all subjects were to be reserved. Thus security, both internal and external, and the sinews of finance, as well as control of India's contacts with the rest of the world, remained in the hands of Britain. In the case of the princely states, the Viceroy presided over the Chamber of Princes, which was formed in 1925, but the princes had authority to rule their states as they saw fit, and this they did on an authoritarian basis, without benefit of democratic methods.

Dyarchy was regarded by the British as a transitional stage on the road to Indian self-government. The lineaments of the future became discernible in the third important measure of that period, the India Act of 1935. This Act provided for greater autonomy by the governments of the provinces (a provision which was put into effect), as well as for greater autonomy at the center (this provision was not implemented). It also envisaged the establishment of a Central Indian Legislature, composed of two houses, in which the representatives of the princely states as well as of the provincial legislatures would participate. This federal legislature never came into existence. It was opposed by the princes, who refused to abandon their sovereignty, and the spread of representative institutions to their territories. It was also opposed by the Muslims, who dreaded domination by a Hindu majority, and by the Hindus, who believed that the casting vote might be in the hands of undemocratic representatives of the princes. The result was that at the outbreak of World War II India had obtained autonomy at the provincial level, but the situation at the center remained as it had been in 1919. A striking example of the way in which the British controlled India and overruled its leaders on matters of prime importance was London's decision to take India into World War II without prior consultation with Indian leaders.

Some observers believe that, had the Congress accepted the 1935 constitution and cooperated within its framework at the Center, independence would have come sooner than it did and without the disadvantages of partition. The dynamic of power would of itself have compelled the British, under the exigencies and stresses of World War II, to hand over to their Indian colleagues in government the authority that they felt they could not entrust to men untried and inexperienced.

The war, with the practically unopposed conquest by Japan, in 1941–42, of some of the richest colonies of the Western powers in Asia, made it clear beyond doubt that the West could no longer hold its possessions by force of arms. Wartime negotiations showed that the British, although willing to make further adjustments, were not yet ready to take the final, fateful step, of giving India the key to its own future.

Then, suddenly, Winston Churchill, Britain's wartime Prime Minister, was unexpectedly defeated in the first postwar general election of 1945, and the tide turned. Sir Winston had been contemptuous of Gandhi and had minced no words about his own philosophy of colonialism when he said, "I was not appointed His Majesty's Prime Minister to preside over the liquidation of the British Empire." This task was promptly shouldered by his successor as Prime Minister, Clement Attlee, who entrusted to Lord Mountbatten, India's last Viceroy, a man known for his understanding attitude

↑ A power station of the Damodar Valley Development Project

A low-cost road in India under construction ↓

↑ UN Secretary-General Hammarskjold and Prime Minister Nehru

A Communist organizer in Kerala ↓

LOOK Magazine Photo

toward the Indians, the task of exploring the next step. When Mountbatten, after consultations with Hindu and Muslim leaders, reported to Attlee in June 1947 that there was no time to lose if Britain was to leave India in an orderly way, the British government decided to advance the date of independence for the subcontinent to August 15. Lord Samuel, speaking in the House of Lords, subsequently said that "Nothing became Britain in India so much as the manner of its going." But it would have been a happier occasion both for those of the British who were reconciled to departure, and for their former subjects, had it proved possible to avoid a hurried, inadequately prepared withdrawal, and the rending experience of partition. The argument frequently made by supporters of colonialism that the grant of independence requires long and careful preparation was weakened in this instance when it became clear that in spite of decades of preparation, the final parting occurred under circumstances that neither the ruler nor the ruled had anticipated or would have willingly chosen.

The moment India achieved independence, it was faced with two demanding political tasks. First, now that India was on its own, it had to draw up the blueprint of the type of government it regarded as best suited to the country's needs. Second, it had to reorganize the National Congress into the ruling political party.

The form of government which independent India selected is that of a federal republic, a union composed in 1947 of 27 states, which by 1957 had been reduced through reorganization to 14 states and 6 territories (including Delhi), in a number of instances along linguistic lines. India's lawmakers, already acquainted with the unwritten constitution of the British, studied the American, Russian, and French constitutions, and benefited a good deal by the experience of the United States, in the drafting of the Indian constitution, one of the longest in the world, which runs 251 pages and is composed of 395 sections. But, while India could not find a British model to follow for its federal structure, it adopted not the presidential system of democracy of the United States, but the British parliamentary system.

The Indian federation, as pointed out earlier, had to weld together British India and 561 of the 562 princely states, with Kashmir the only state remaining in a special relationship to India. This meant an amalgamation of British India, which under direct British rule from London had experienced democratic practices, however limited by British control, and states which had been traditionally ruled by authoritarian princes unacquainted with representative government. This seemingly insuperable amalgamation was effected with a minimum of stress and strain — except for the states of Hyderabad and Junagadh, and of course Kashmir — largely due to the statesmanship of Vallabhbhai Patel, a close associate of Gandhi and Nehru and a man of outstanding statesmanship, who played a key role in carrying out the administrative transition from colonialism to independence with remarkable speed and harmony. Patel, who had the qualities of a high-class Tammany politician, persuaded the princes (to some this term might seem a British understatement) that it was to their advantage to join the new republic — and they did, after receiving from the government privy purses to compensate them for their loss of personal revenue.

While the structure of the republic is federal, considerable power is concentrated at the center. Flexibility is assured by the provision that the Central Government and the states have concurrent powers over economic and social planning, commerce, social security, health, and education. All the residual powers not specified in the constitution rest with the Central Government, which controls foreign policy, defense, internal security, and revenue — the subjects which the British had listed as reserved topics under the dyarchy.

The Central Government has emergency powers to act in

situations "whereby the security of India or any part of the territory thereof is threatened, whether by war or external aggression or internal disturbance (actual or potential)." In such a case the President may issue a proclamation of emergency which remains in force for two months or longer if approved by both houses of Parliament. During that period, the guarantees to individuals under the Bill of Rights may be suspended, the President may issue administrative orders for any state, and the Union Parliament may legislate on subjects normally restricted to states' actions. This provision of the constitution, which has been invoked on several occasions, during which periods a presidentially appointed government has functioned in the states affected, gives the Central Government a weapon against recalcitrant states or states which might try to subvert existing institutions — for example if the Communists in Kerala should try to introduce totalitarian methods.

So far, in practice, the President, now Rajendra Prasad, occupies a ceremonial position similar to that of the President of France before the establishment of the Fifth Republic in 1958. It is conceivable, however, that an Indian De Gaulle might some day make use of the emergency powers entrusted to the President under the Constitution to make Parliament subservient to the Executive and to curtail individual liberties. The Vice-President, at present the world-renowned philosopher Sarvapalli Radakrishnan, has played a significant consultative role because of the readiness of Prime Minister Nehru to seek his advice on controversial and difficult issues. The central role, however, has been played by the Prime Minister, whose personality has dominated the Indian political scene since Gandhi's death in 1948, but the structure of the government would, in any case, probably require a strong prime minister.

India's parliamentary system is closely modeled on that of Britain, with the elected representatives of the *Lok Sabha*

(House of the People), comparable to the House of Commons, following the practices of the British House, including a Speaker, who is addressed respectfully by the MP's; a government bench, where members of the cabinet and their aides are seated and from which they answer questions many of which are submitted in writing in advance, printed and distributed; and the opposition seated across from the government — although in view of the dominant position of the Congress party, its members occupy a much larger segment of the seats than the government party would do in London. And the elections for the House are conducted as meticulously as in Britain.

In lieu of a House of Lords, India, which has not tried to perpetuate an aristocracy composed of its princes, and therefore has no hereditary group to match the Lords, has an upper house, the *Raya Sabha* (Council of States), composed of 250 men and women elected by the state legislatures (this is a feature reminiscent of the French system), and 12 members nominated by the Prime Minister from among citizens distinguished for their achievements in administration, literature, the arts, work in civic organizations, and so on. The Council of States has incurred some of the same criticisms about ornamental desuetude made in Britain about the House of Lords.

The second task of India's political leaders was to reorient the Indian National Congress, which had served as the organ of resistance to the British, so that it could play the role of a responsible political party, and change over from critic of existing institutions to architect of new ones.

Reorganization of the party system proved more difficult than that of the state. The Congress, like other national movements in non-Western countries, had until then been a catchall for all opponents of the foreign ruler, whatever their political views — from old-line conservatives and reactionary orthodox Hindus to the most advanced Socialists, with one notable exception — the Communists who, as already has been pointed out, had remained outside the national struggle. While the Socialists soon withdrew from Congress on the ground that it was too dominated by conservatives, the Congress party still commands the largest measure of popular support, receiving 45 per cent of the total vote in the first general elections of 1951–52, and 47 per cent in the second general elections of 1957. Yet, in spite of the predominance of the Congress party, India cannot be described as a one-party state, given the liveliness of the opposition parties, the rule of the Communists in Kerala, and the growing influence of independents in politics.

Nor can the unanimous election on February 2, 1959 of Mr. Nehru's attractive 41-year-old daughter, Indira Gandhi, wife of Feroz Gandhi, a member of Parliament (not related to the Mahatma) as president of the Congress party, be interpreted as a symptom of totalitarianism. Rather, it illustrates the persisting magic of the Nehru name in the party's ranks. Mrs. Gandhi replaced U. N. Dhebar, an old party wheel horse, whose policy a group of fifteen younger party leaders of which she was a member, known as "the Ginger Group," had criticized in 1958 for its complacency. Mr. Dhebar, for his part, had accused Mr. Nehru of being intolerant to criticism from within the party.

Mrs. Gandhi has had little experience of practical politics except as a constant companion and official hostess of her father, but she and her friends in "the Ginger Group" are known to feel that the Congress party must bestir itself to greater and more constructive activity if it is to retain its influence in the country. Mrs. Gandhi to whom, when she was a teenager, Nehru, in jail, addressed letters about the rise and fall of empires which were subsequently published under the title *Glimpses of World History*, is the third-generation leader in the party, for her grandfather, the lawyer Motilal Nehru, inspired to political action by Gandhi, headed the Indian National Congress in the 1920's.

The Socialist party, which has some brilliant theoreticians, notably Jayaprakash Narayan, the party's most popular leader, and Asoka Mehta, who has written extensively on problems of party politics, has not succeeded in assuming the role of His Majesty's Opposition, which would have kept the dominant Congress party on its mettle during the arduous formative years of the new nation, but it has often offered informed and constructive criticism. The Socialist leaders have either forsworn party strife, as in the case of Jayaprakash Narayan, who has become absorbed in the Bhoodan movement, agreeing with its founder Vinoba Bhave, that India's most important problem is to defeat communism by providing land for the landless. Or else, like Asoka Mehta, they have decided that they could serve the country in its hour of stress more effectively by accepting appointments on national committees to study such urgent matters as better production and distribution of food, even if such participation might appear to condone governmental policies of which they do not approve. It is not impossible that men like Mehta might someday collaborate with the Congress party in a National government. Still another Socialist, Dr. Rammanohar Lohia, has formed a party of his own, the "left" All-India Socialist party, which refuses electoral alliances with any other party. Nor did the Socialist party appreciably strengthen its electoral position by merging, in September 1952, with the Kisan Mazdoor Praja party, led by a brilliant former Gandhi supporter, Acharya Kripalani, who had become disillusioned both with the Mahatma and with Congress.

In 1953 it had seemed for a short time that Jayaprakash Narayan, able, attractive, who had studied at the University of Wisconsin, and is one of the most liked public figures in the country, might be selected by Mr. Nehru as his successor.

But Narayan, who did not want to be tied down by previously accepted conditions if and when he should succeed Nehru, presented a fourteen-point plan which was unacceptable in some respects to the conservatives in Congress, and the negotiations about his appointment as Vice-Premier in the Nehru cabinet broke down.

The one important opposition party, the Communists (CPI), has hitherto been hampered by its past record of pro-British activities during World War II, and more recently by the conviction, voiced by Mr. Nehru and other Indian leaders, that the Communists are not free agents, but operate on orders from Moscow. After going through many internal struggles and reorganizations, the Communists, shaken in 1953 by Khrushchev's revelations of Stalin's iniquities, and cold-shouldered by the Russians during the Khrushchev-Bulganin visit in 1955, have tried to play the role of a constitutional party, ready to cooperate with all but the right-wing communal groups. Aware of the Hindu repugnance for violence, the Communists have stressed their determination to take and exercise power by peaceful means, and to outreform the Congress party reformers. Their administration of Kerala, the first state of any size in the world where Communists have won by constitutional means, is being closely watched for indications of their future intentions.

The 1956–57 elections showed that the influence of the orthodox communal parties — the Hindu Mahasabha (Great Assembly), which wants India to go back to Vedic times, and one of whose members assassinated Gandhi, and Ram Rajya Parisshad — is declining, and is found mostly in the northern states. However, the more moderate right-wing party, the Jan Sangh, which is particularly active on the Kashmir question, doubled its percentage of the popular vote in the 1957 General Elections, and more than doubled its percentage of the votes polled (from 3 per cent and 3 million votes in 1952 to 5 per cent and 7 million votes in 1957). The Scheduled Castes Federation, which was organized to fight against high caste Hindus on behalf of the outcastes, was not successful in the election, and was weakened by the death in 1957 of its leader, Dr. B. R. Ambedkar, an able and eloquent lawyer trained at the Columbia Law School, who not long before his death led 200,000 outcastes in a mass conversion to Buddhism to demonstrate their resentment at the exclusion of outcastes from Hindu temples and other acts of discrimination.

Some commentators outside India, notably the *New York Times*, believe that the new anti-socialist party formed in June 1959 by Chakravarti Rajagopolachari, for decades a leader of the struggle for independence and after 1947 for two years Governor General of India, will offer influential opposition, but this view is not shared by informed Indians. This party, which assumed the name of Freedom party, after objections had been raised to its initial title of Conservative, opposes the trend toward socialism. Under existing circumstances it is not expected to garner sufficient votes to play a significant role.

The lack of a strong and respected opposition group, which could provide an alternative to the Congress party, is often regarded both in India and abroad as an obstacle to democracy. Yet the question may be asked whether a single strong but democratic-minded and conciliatory party is not better suited for an underdeveloped non-Western country in the early stages of independence than a congeries of conflicting smaller parties. Whether Congress would have succeeded in holding power as long as it has if it had not been for the unrivaled prestige of Mr. Nehru, who is also Prime Minister and Foreign Minister, is open to doubt. In the meantime, the dominant figure of the Prime Minister has served both to keep possible contenders for his office at a safe distance, for even the Communists recognize the impossibility of challenging him, and at the same time has shielded his party against criticisms which might have brought reforms within its ranks long before 1957, when the elections revealed that the party had lost ground in several states, and had been defeated by the Communists in Kerala.

Among the many faults from which, it is now acknowledged, the Congress party is suffering are poor grass-roots organization, especially as compared with the Communists; nepotism; the predilection for the fleshpots of some of its leaders, who had spent long terms in jail under the British; corruption reported from a number of areas, with which Nehru failed to deal; indifference to the interests of the voters; lack of appeal to youth; and in general a condition of sloth engendered by easy and prolonged success for which the party had not had to fight. Mr. Nehru's 1958 threats to withdraw from office, while remaining ready to answer the call of the nation from outside, brought outcries of shock and promises to reform from party leaders. If this shock is not forgotten, and these promises are implemented, responsible observers believe that the Congress party may yet have a decade of useful work ahead of it. If not, then in the next election which is scheduled for 1962, when the second Five-Year Plan is to come to an end, the voters may have surprises in store for the Congressmen.

Thus, while India has the appearance of a one-party state, the reality — as in many other aspects of the Indian scene — does not always correspond to the appearance. The political opposition to Congress is not effectively organized, but its voice, in Parliament and in the press, is often powerful and influential, notably in the case of Hungary, and even more in the case of Tibet, and is not to be discounted by the government. The freedom and vigor of the opposition, which cannot be measured solely by its numerical representation in Parliament, constitute an important force in India's political life.

For the new political pattern in India — unknown in the centuries before the British came as well as under British rule — is the process of free general elections determined by secret ballot. Not only are such elections still unusual in non-Western countries with no tradition of Western-type democracy, but India's experience with universal suffrage has confounded the assumption previously made by political scientists that literacy is a prerequisite for democratic voting. In two general elections the citizens of India, 80 per cent of whom are peasants living in primitive villages, and 85 per cent of whom are still illiterate, voted, according to impartial outside observers, not only with enthusiasm which might have been expected, at least the first time an election was ever held in India but, what is more important for the long run, with understanding of the local issues at stake and with shrewd discrimination between contending candidates. And, although preferences often — too often, from the point of view of liberal-minded Indians — were shown for candidates of the same caste as that of the voter, yet voters again and again voted for the candidate they regarded as most capable of serving their interests, irrespective of whether he might be a former maharajah or, as happened in Bombay, a man who ran errands in a government office.

In terms of sheer numbers, the Indian general elections are the largest free elections in the world. In the first elections of 1951–52, 173,213,635 names out of 180,307,684 listed in the 1951 census were on electoral rolls, and of these 88,612,171, or 51 per cent, cast their votes for elections to Lok Sabha, the lower house of Parliament. Five years later, as a result of population growth, the total of persons eligible to vote was 193,128,924, of whom 115 million, or 60 per cent, cast their ballots for 488 members of the Lok Sabha, for 2,901 members of the lower houses of 13 state assemblies, and for councils in two Union Territories.

The government, recognizing the physical difficulties of

voting in a huge country, with sharp variations in climate and many physical obstacles, such as the high mountain passes of the Himalayas, covered with snow during the winter months, has taken extensive measures to facilitate the task of the voter. Elections have been spread over a period of three months (in 1951-52), or three weeks (1957), making it possible for voters to adjust their ballot to climatic and travel conditions. In order to insure that no citizen will have to travel more than three miles to cast his vote, 200,000 polling stations were set up for the 1956–57 elections, as compared with 196,084 in 1951–52. In accordance with the Indian system of having a separate box for each candidate in the constituency, 2,960,000 steel ballot boxes were used, and 575,000,000 ballot papers, printed under the same security arrangements as those that govern the printing of bank notes, were provided for the voters.

In spite of the fact that the elections were spread over three weeks in 1957, instead of three months, as in 1951–52, one million officers had to be appointed to carry out the elections. To assure an honest secret ballot by a predominantly illiterate population, the ballot boxes are marked with the symbols of each of the principal parties — two bullocks for the Congress party, a thatched house for the Praja Socialist party, a sickle and an ear of corn for the Communist party, and a lighted lamp for Jan Sangh. The voter obtains two ballots in consecutive moves — first his ballot for the State Assembly election, and then for the Lok Sabha, and entering a screened area, drops each into a box bearing the symbol of the party to which his candidate belongs.

In spite of the inexperience of the voters, remarkably few have been challenged, and even fewer have been charged with fraud, and practically no incidents involving violence or intimidation have been reported. What has particularly impressed foreign observers are the voters' enthusiasm for the electoral process, their genuine desire to inform themselves about the qualifications of candidates, and their common sense in making their selections. These qualities of the Indian voters do not seem to be, as some had believed, merely the result of curiosity about a new experience which provided some of the drama and excitement of fairs or public ceremonies, but might soon give way to boredom, for the second general election brought an even higher percentage of voters to the polls than the first. It would be interesting to explore the question whether the millennial custom of participation in the selection of village councils (*panchayats*), as well as councils of the various castes, may have given the Indians the habit of thinking in terms of an electoral process. And the selectivity shown by the voters may cause political scientists to rethink their belief that the operation of democracy requires literacy — although, one must hope, not to the point of wondering whether democracy in the United States would be better served if the process were reversed, and voters were guarded against exposure to literacy. But, looking at Indian elections, we might ask ourselves whether the important thing is to know how to read, or rather to know what to read once the alphabet has been mastered.

Nor can it be assumed that, just because the majority of Indians cannot read, this means that they are ignorant beings who go into a deep sleep of apathy between elections. What a book, or a radio or television program is for Americans, the public speeches of India's political leaders are for the rank and file of the people. It is a common thing for a popular speaker like Jayaprakash Narayan or Asoka Mehta to speak half a dozen times or more a day when traveling around the country, addressing 100,000 or more people at a given meeting. And when it becomes known through the village grapevine that Prime Minister Nehru is to be in the neighborhood, men, women, and children travel, on foot, by bicycle, by oxcart, often for many miles over rough territory and in bad weather, to hear Panditji, as he is affectionately called (ji is a suffix of affection). Then, up to 400,000 may gather in the open, sitting on the ground, chatting with each other, patiently waiting for Mr. Nehru's arrival, listening intently as he speaks — in Hindi, or in English which he uses particularly in the South, where the use of Hindi is opposed — and hoping that perhaps they might come near him, but satisfied just to hear his message, which always has to do with some aspect of the country's problems and carries words of exhortation.

This process of intimate communications between the leaders and the people becomes accelerated during the pre-election campaigns. But at any time it conveys something of the spirit expressed by Emperor Asoka when he said that the ruler must always be accessible to the people. And as one watches Indian public speaking, it becomes clear that political leaders, as some will frankly admit, feel their way along in determining the mood of their audience, establish a rapport with their emotions, their fears and hopes, and often play on them as a musician plays on an instrument.

The most distinctive feature of India's democracy is that it has succeeded, under conditions which are centuries remote from those of the Western democratic nations, in combining free secret elections unknown in Russia and China with a strongly centralized authority represented by the Prime Minister and his cabinet colleagues, on the one hand, and the Central Parliamentary Board of the ruling Congress party on the other. This Board, consisting of six powerful members, including until 1959 U. N. Dhebar, president of the party (who was succeeded by Indira Gandhi), and Prime Minister Nehru, in turn, with the cooperation of five others elected by the All-India Congress Committee, form the Central Election Committee (CEC) which screens party candidates at all levels. The CEC follows the rule that new party slates should give adequate representation to the minorities (Muslims, Christians, Parsis, Anglo-Indians), about 15 per cent of the seats in Parliament to women, and about one-third to persons of "new blood," that is who are not already legislators. The process of selection within the party is not free of tension and dissatisfaction, or even minor rebellions on the part of individuals or local groups who consider that they have been slighted by the top leadership.

In preparation for the 1957 elections, the CEC renominated only 243 out of the 369 Congress members who had seats in the Lok Sabha, and put up 249 new candidates for the 492 seats for which the party entered the lists. Of the new candidates, 27 were Muslims, 9 Christians, 11 Sikhs, and one Parsi. The rest were apparently caste Hindus or members of the Scheduled Castes or tribes. The party nominated 28 women for the Lok Sabha and 268 for the State Assemblies, a figure which showed a marked increase over the previous election but did not yet reach the 15 per cent promised by the party leaders.

The expenses of the elections, which include the use of pamphlets, loudspeakers, jeeps, posters, and so on, are financed largely out of contributions by wealthy individuals and business firms. This feature of India's political life, familiar to Americans, has been criticized by some Indian commentators on the ground that the party's financial supporters thus obtained special privileges and distorted party policies. The suggestion has been made by a former civil servant, A. D. Gorwala, now a commentator, that two million contributors should give six rupees ($1.25) a year, or a total of a billion and a quarter dollars for each period of five years, to a common fund to be used for the election expenses of all of the Congress party's candidates. This, it is argued, would broaden the base of India's democracy, and prevent the use of influence by a small minority of the wealthy for their own, rather than the nation's, advantage.

What has been hitherto missing in India's political structure — both under the British and since independence — is a local political self-governing unit which would express the will of the people at the grass-roots level, and mobilize the energies and enthusiasm of India's millions of villagers for the national task of reconstruction. As the Indian government pointed out in 1958, "For centuries the Indian villager has not only been illiterate and isolated, but not even permitted to practice democracy. For many villagers, in many villages, the sense of independent citizenship in an independent country is wholly new; the responsibilities of citizenship, of local initiative, of public impulse and cooperation are as yet only dimly perceived."

To remedy this lack, the government in 1958 decided to establish elective Block Development Committees in organized village blocks, each of which is composed of 100 villages, totaling 50,000 to 80,000 people. In 1959 there were 2,400 of these blocks, and by the end of the Second Five-Year Plan in 1961 the number is expected to rise to 3,500. Members of the Block Committees will be chosen by indirect elections: groups of five village panchayats (councils of five) will elect one representative, and thus each Committee will have a block membership of 20. Each Committee, following training to be provided by the government and a period of experience, will be made into a statutory body and equipped with both the power and the resources to function effectively.

This far-reaching program of democratic decentralization has exceptional importance, from India's point of view, as a contrast to the communes of Communist China, which cover an area roughly comparable to the Indian block, and are tightly controlled by the central government, itself controlled by the Communist party. The block development committees are regarded as in harmony with the Gandhian traditions of village service and responsibility. According to the Indian government, they will "test and demonstrate the crucial issue of our times — whether the long illiterate villagers, long deprived of the opportunity to practice democracy — can now, with training and guidance, successfully participate in and direct their own advancement." This program, as the Indians see it, constitutes their most significant new pattern of political democracy.

But, towering over the political scene is the figure of Mr. Nehru, a striking example both of the advantages and disadvantages of the "charismatic personality." There is little dispute that in the turbulent decade of India's political, economic, and social reorganization the Prime Minister was the common denominator between conflicting groups, languages, material interests, religions — and thus became a spokesman for his multiracial, multireligious, multifaceted people. His critics speak harshly of his many weaknesses — his lack of experience in the complex problems of a rapidly changing economy and a new technology, his love of power, his incapacity to delegate authority, his predilection for abstract ideas, his double standard about communism — opposing Communists at home yet dealing with them abroad — his lack of conviction on crucial issues such as the Hungarian revolt, his reliance on a few personalities to whom, for one reason or another, he feels indebted or who are sympathetic to his temperament, notably Krishna Menon, and most of all his unwillingness to listen to or accept criticism. The main criticism of Nehru, however, is that he has not tried to discover and bring forward men who could take over the succession, as, in Britain, Churchill did with the Edens and the Macmillans and Attlee with the Gaitskells and the Wilsons. The only person, except for Jayaprakash Narayan whose participation in his cabinet he failed to enlist, who stands out in Nehru's entourage is Krishna Menon, whom many Indians, as well as Western friends of India, regard as the principal threat to India's democracy.

Yet, when all is said and done, and all the dangers of his personal rule over his cabinet, and thus over the country are recognized both for domestic and foreign policy, it is gen-

↑ A fifth-grade class in northern India

A mobile library in India ↓

↑ A worker in the Dhakeswari Cotton Mill

The Tata Iron and Steel Company ↓

erally agreed that no successor of comparable stature is in sight — a problem which arose after Churchill and Franklin D. Roosevelt — although this, too, is attributed to the very fact that Nehru has so long dominated the country's politics, blocking the emergence of a younger successor. And it is agreed that even if he were to carry out his threat of retiring to the Himalayas, he would still, no matter how remote from day-to-day affairs, be the most potent influence in the country as long as he lives.

Moreover, these criticisms, more widespread in 1958 than at any time since independence, are a healthy sign of a new awareness that the nation's business is not just the concern of government leaders in New Delhi, no matter how popular or competent, but of all the people. Nor should criticism of Nehru be interpreted abroad as indicating the decline of his influence and the near-disintegration of his rule. Whatever else may be said about India, it remains what it set out to be in 1947 — a genuine democracy functioning under non-Western conditions, determined to develop its backward economy by voluntary means, and not by force. Nehru, who is often criticized for his autocratic temper, nevertheless continues to be the symbol of his country's democratic faith — in spite of his own impatience with his critics. By being a party leader yet retaining a vision of the nation's interest as a whole, he has succeeded in being the great reconciler of conflicting forces, thus preventing in the first decade of independence a disruption that might have proved fatal for the country, and embodying in his political rule the conciliatory philosophy of Hinduism.

As one watches him day after day in Parliament answering members' questions with unflagging interest and frequent flashes of humor, or standing erect in the drenching rain, in his knee-length, cream-colored jacket with a rosebud in his buttonhole, on the ramparts of the Red Fort on August 15, India's independence day, to address a vast throng, one realizes anew the truth of Franklin D. Roosevelt's 1928 remark: "There is no magic in democracy that does away with the need for leadership."

To thoughtful Indians the question is not, as Americans often put it, "After Nehru, what?" Other leaders will emerge in case of need, these Indians say, just as Gandhi came in his time, and Nehru took over when Gandhi succumbed to the bullet of an assassin. Rather, the real question is which way India will go politically in the next decade, admitted by all to be critical for the future of its democracy.

India's prospects of maintaining its new pattern of democracy — a middle course that avoids extremism, encourages reconciliation, and gives an opportunity for free expression by the people through their elected representatives — depend on the success it can achieve in developing its new economic and social patterns.

Chapter 7

New Economic Patterns: A Mixed Voluntary Economy

Just as independent India had to give new direction to its political life, so it had to give new direction to its economy. At short notice it had to carry out a series of simultaneous telescoped revolutions which, in the Western nations, had been spread over several centuries. Within a decade India tried to modernize its agriculture, which except for a number of large irrigation schemes and agricultural research the British had left practically as they found it three and a half centuries before; to establish new industries that would serve modern agrarian needs as well as produce a modicum of essential manufactured products, such as steel (about two million tons a year were being produced by the Tata and the Indian Iron and Steel works), locomotives, and tools for which the country would otherwise have to depend on imports; and to form capital resources among a population 80 to 85 per cent of whom live under substandard conditions, with an annual per capita income in 1958 of $59.00. In short, India had to modernize an archaic economy of the type usually described as "colonial" — that is an economy which provided raw materials such as cotton and jute for the industries of advanced nations, as well as some consumer items such as tea, and imported the bulk of its manufactured goods.

Today it is pointless to argue, as some of the Indian leaders did before 1947, that the country's poverty was due solely to the erroneous policies of the British, on the assumption that, once the foreign ruler had left, India's economy would come to full bloom. It is equally pointless to assert, as some Western critics tend to do, that if it were not for the Hindu detachment from material possessions and lack of concern for such practical things as thrift and private investment for private profit, India's economy would soon catch up with that of the West.

The tragic truth, as the French anthropologist Germaine Tillion has pointed out in her brilliant book, *Algeria: The Realities*, in discussing the crux of the problem faced by most underdeveloped countries, is that no one is wholly guilty or wholly innocent — neither the colonial power nor the colonial people. For the conditions which India — like Algeria, and many other non-Western areas — is trying to correct, are conditions that arose long before the East India Company started its trading operations or the generation of Indians which began to agitate for independence from Britain had come upon the scene. Had the advanced nations of the West, and the non-Western peoples which for a variety of historical reasons did not share in the process of modernization precipitated by science and technology, remained apart, it is conceivable that the populations of the non-West might have been kept stable by the positive checks Malthus had in mind — disease, civil strife, wars, and famines. Then the ratio of food and other resources to people might have been gradually altered without the shocks caused by injections of Western democracy and Russian and Chinese communism, and the process of adapting primitive societies to modern concepts and practices might have been stretched, if not over the centuries enjoyed by the West, at least over a century or more.

But the sudden, dramatic, encounter of West and non-West through conquest, trade, and cultural infiltration shook the non-Western civilizations to their foundations. As Germaine Tillion points out, the underdeveloped peoples were deprived of the values that had once given them cohesion and, because of the sudden spurt of the birth-rate combined with the decline of the death-rate, were deprived of the modest well-being they had once enjoyed but which now had to be shared among new millions of people increasing in geometric proportion. The British, except for a few experts in the latter years of their rule, when it was already too late, were not aware of the stark conditions which their very efforts at what were indubitably humane reforms had engendered. But, to be fair, neither were the Indians. And, neither the British nor the Indians realized before 1947 the revolutionary changes which would have to be made if India was to escape the disaster predicted by Malthus for Europe that a continuing increase of the population, with little or no increase in agricultural or industrial productivity, would require heroic measures, financial expenditures as yet undreamed of not only by Britain and India, but also by the United States and the United Nations, and a complete revolution not only in the people's way of life but also in its way of thought.

Nor is it any longer believed by Western experts that it will be possible to carry out this urgently necessary, many faceted revolution by laissez-faire methods prevalent in Western Europe and the United States in the nineteenth century. These methods, it is agreed, would merely compound and perpetuate the gradualness that has held back India's economic development over the past three hundred years. If the process of change is to keep pace with the growth of population and with its rising expectations for improved living standards, the government cannot do piecemeal patching of the economy here and there, without regard to its over-all objectives and requirements. It must plan the most effective way of using the country's limited resources of food and raw materials, of foreign currency and human skills, and it must direct these resources to the enterprises whether public or private, which seem most essential for the survival and welfare of the country.

The issue today in underdeveloped countries is not whether they should plan. There is no debate about this in the non-Western world. The London *Times*, in a 1957 article on "Planning in Asia," said: "If there is a tide that is really sweeping across Asia, it is not so much nationalist or Communist, religious or political. It is the tide of enthusiasm for economic planning. It is becoming Asia's religion, the new light of the East. Planning, as the latest annual report of the United Nations Commission for Asia and the Far East remarks, 'has become a watchword in Asia.' Even countries 'dedicated to private enterprise in principle, have met with the reality that their Governments have to assume responsibility for establishing new industries.' " The issue, then, is whether planning is to be blueprinted and applied by totalitarian methods, as in Russia and China, or by democratic methods, as India is trying to do.

India's new economic pattern which it describes as "the Socialist Pattern of Society," represents an attempt to create a mixed economy which combines private enterprise with government planning, over-all direction, and control, as well as government initiative in fields that private entrepreneurs might not find attractive, and to subject both the plans and their implementation to the scrutiny of a parliamentary democracy. This pattern, which as already noted resembles that of semi-socialized Britain and in many respects has drawn for its models on the ideas and practices of the British Laborites, is being applied in a country which is technologically two or more centuries behind Britain, although politically India strives to maintain the level achieved by the British in the twentieth century. This attempt to live, at one and the same time, in several centuries, which is characteristic of most underdeveloped countries, imposes an indescribably heavy psychological strain on both the people and the leaders which no one in the West who has not been exposed to it can thoroughly understand, no matter how sympathetic he might be to the problems of non-Westerners. The Indian leaders, who during the struggle for independence had understandably concentrated primarily on political objectives, had nevertheless even then given some thought to the need for planning. As they turned away from the task of liberation, and came face to face with the harsh realities of the country's economy, for whose future they were henceforth solely responsible, they elaborated their ideas in the Election Manifesto of the Congress party in 1951. This manifesto declared that the party favored a planned approach to economic development in order to make it possible for the people to live a good life. It emphasized the need for an increase in agricultural productivity and improvement in cattle breeding; stated that small and cottage industries would be encouraged; declared that there would be state ownership or control of basic industries; and defined its objective as a mixed economy consisting of a public and a private sector, both of which were to be fitted into an overall national plan. Mr. Nehru has stressed that in India there is no private sector and no public sector, but only one national sector. What India intended to undertake, to quote the former Indian Ambassador to the United States, G. L. Mehta, was "a bold experiment in industrial democracy . . . on an unprecedented scale."

This experiment has been embodied, so far, in two five-year plans, the first of which, inaugurated in 1951, was completed in 1956, and the second, now under way, is to be terminated in 1961. The major goals of the two plans have been to increase productivity throughout the country and to reduce social inequalities through improved living standards. The plans, however, do not envisage complete nationalization of all the country's resources and means of production. In fact, as the government has gained economic experience, it has tended to reduce rather than enlarge the public sector, in this respect, again, following the course set by Britain after completion of the Laborites' economic reforms, 1945–50. India's economic system has often been described, both by its admirers and its detractors, as "socialism." The applicability of this description to present-day India (whatever the future may hold) depends on how "socialism" is defined. If socialism is defined as complete government ownership and operation of economic enterprise, then India is no more "Socialist" than Britain, or Japan which Americans regard as "capitalist"; and Indian observers could point to the United States as a country which has many features of what they regard as "socialism." As of 1958, in "Socialist" India, it was estimated that 90 per cent of the country's enterprises, including agriculture which is entirely in the hands of individual owners, were in private hands, and furnished 92 per cent of the country's total income, with only 8 per cent of total income coming from government-owned enterprises.

But while India's economic system cannot be described as "socialism," still less can it be described as "communism." In contrast to Russia and China, which enforce on the population plans that are not subject to public criticism, India refrains from the use of coercion, maintains a democratically elected representative government, and stresses voluntary participation by the people through various forms of cooperation. In agriculture, instead of imposing collectivization of peasant farms, as has been done by the Russians, or of militarized agrarian communes, as was done by the Chinese in 1958, the Indians encourage agricultural cooperatives, cooperation of the peasants in community development projects that embrace hundreds of villages, and voluntary contributions of labor by the peasants to various projects in their villages or their neighboring areas such as the building of schools, dams, roads, and so on.

When the Indian government surveyed the economic scene,

it had to make cruel but essential choices between priorities, such as have been faced by all underdeveloped countries whose resources and level of technological and entrepreneurial competence were not adequate to fill the multiform needs of a society in full spate of transformation. Should agriculture be developed first, even if this meant a delay in creating industries that might draw people off the land into urban centers, and thereby start the process which in the West had led to a decline in the birth-rate? Or should industry be given precedence, even if this meant that the people would have to reduce still further their already shockingly low intake of calories — but, if so, how would human beings stand the physical strain of building dams and factories, unless they were driven by force, like the Jews who built the pyramids of Egypt, or the Russians who were made to open up new lands, and build new facilities in once virgin territories, by ruthless methods that disregarded human dignity? Or should a modest halfway attempt be made to develop a little more agriculture and start a little more industry?

The Indian leaders, faced by these disheartening choices between several evils, decided to concentrate, under the first Five-Year Plan, on increasing agricultural productivity, and on expanding irrigation and transportation, both necessary for agrarian development. Their difficult decision appeared justified, in fact made inevitable, by statistics. According to the 1951 census, 51 per cent of the gross national produce (GNP) came from agriculture, which constituted the occupation and source of employment of 70 per cent of the people (with dependents, this figure was 83 per cent). According to the All-India Rural Credit Survey, published in 1954, the agricultural population can be divided into three categories: big cultivators, who form 30 per cent and have large tracts of land, some of whom are absentee landowners; medium-size cultivators, totaling 40 per cent, who have five acres or more and are considered the backbone of the agricultural population, with enough land to support themselves and to improve their lot; and small cultivators with five acres of land or less, who make up 30 per cent. In addition, as mentioned earlier, there are 10 million landless peasants who, with their dependents, total 40 million people. It is for them that Vinoba Bhave, seconded by Jayaprakash Narayan, is trying to obtain five acres per family from the big cultivators.

The government has made a four-pronged approach to the vast agricultural problems that confront the country. First, in the 1950 constitution it has provided for land reform, through the breakup of large estates, and the distribution of land thus obtained to the landless, in return for compensation to the landowners. This program has thus far revealed three major difficulties. The amount of land obtainable from the big landowners is modest relatively to the needs of the landless millions. The states, which were charged with the responsibility for land reform, do not have the funds — and neither does the central government — to pay compensation to the landowners. And, as has proved true in other underdeveloped countries, it soon becomes clear that land reform is only a beginning, and that the distribution of land in small parcels to peasants who lack the machinery, seeds, fertilizers, and farm animals to cultivate it properly diminishes, rather than increases, agricultural productivity. The necessity then arises for consolidating these small parcels into cooperative projects, as Vinoba Bhave and his associates are now trying to do.

Bhave, who, in accordance with Gandhi's philosophy, abhors violence and believes that the only way communism can be checked in the countryside is by accelerating land distribution, at the same time refuses to violate the constitution by seizing land without compensation. He therefore tries to circumvent the need for such payment by asking landowners to make a "gift of land" to him, as the representative of the landless. While he has so far collected about 4 million acres of land, critics claim that most of the land given to him is of poor quality, or even unusable because of rocky or arid soil, and that in any case the landless do not have the physical means to cultivate such land as is arable — a need recognized by Bhave, who also asks city-dwellers to make gifts of money for the purchase of bullocks, farm implements, seeds, and fertilizer.

The need for consolidation of redistributed land parcels also raises a far-reaching political problem. Should consolidation take the form of cooperatives, as urged by the Socialists, or of farm collectives, as urged by the Communists? An official answer to this question was given at the annual convention of the Congress Party held in January 1959 at Nagpur. There it was decided, on Mr. Nehru's proposal, to move with all urgency toward the transformation of as many as possible of India's 650,000 villages into genuine working cooperatives. Land titles will be retained by individual owners, although Mr. Nehru hopes that at some time in the future there can be village ownership. Meanwhile, the village will become a unit for pooling resources. Cooperative credit, cooperative marketing, and cooperative seed selection and seed procurement will be important features of the proposed new arrangements.

The second prong of the government's farm program is its attempt to stabilize the rate of population growth through sponsorship of planned parenthood. Neither the Hindus nor the Muslims have religious objections to the limitation of birth, and India is one of the three non-Western countries which officially supports planned parenthood clinics, the others being Egypt and Japan, similarly faced with grave population problems. Mr. Nehru has brought family planning experts such as the late Dr. Abraham Stone of New York to stimulate public interest and to advise Indian specialists, and start planned parenthood clinics, which are encouraged and supported by the Indian Planned Parenthood Association, headed by Lady Rama Rau, whose husband was at one time India's Ambassador to the United States and chairman of the Reserve Bank. It is realized, however, that even the most energetic efforts cannot reduce the present size of the population; the best that can be done is to slow down future population growth. From the point of view of the Indians, "the population explosion" is not a topic of academic discussion but a frightening reality. The need to discover a simple formula, preferably manufactured out of local materials, which would be practicable among a predominantly illiterate population, where women have little or no privacy in village mud huts which house both people and animals, is a top priority. While we in the West talk about crash programs to manufacture missiles, the Indians are forced to think of crash programs to manufacture contraceptives.

As in the case of agricultural production, India, while officially accepting a family planning program, has not yet taken effective action to implement it. As of 1959 only a small fraction of the second Five-Year Plan funds earmarked for family planning had been spent; and training was inadequate, with only ten to twelve planned parenthood experts available per state. At the International Planned Parenthood Conference in New Delhi in February 1959 Prime Minister Nehru admitted that planned parenthood measures had not achieved success, and urged voluntary sterilization after three children as a measure to check population growth.

The third prong of the government's program is to increase agricultural productivity through the use of fertilizer, improved seeds, insecticides, control of animal diseases, and other methods. The resources available for this purpose are still pitifully limited. For example, the country's first fertilizer plant at Sindri has been supplemented by two more, but their output does not begin to meet the needs of the peasants who, having discovered the effectiveness of fertilizer, clamor for more. However, the introduction of improved production methods is being accelerated through the use of the community development projects, India's counterpart of the agricultural extension projects in the United States, whose contribution to the country's development is discussed in Chapter 8.

The fourth prong is the mobilization of the financial resources of the peasants through the rural credit system, introduced in 1954. Previously the peasants, whose annual cash earnings vary between $21 and $59, had had a hard time making both ends meet, and had found it difficult, if not impossible, to finance purchases of such essential items as a new bullock or a plow without resort to the moneylender, who was apt to charge up to 40 per cent interest on small loans. The result was that many peasants were permanently in debt, and had no surplus, however small, for savings, or any nearby place where they could deposit what they saved and borrow at low rates of interest. The moneylender, vividly described by the talented author B. K. Narayan in his novel *The Financial Expert*, in effect dominated the rural scene, and, since more often than not he was also the local big cultivator to whom his poorer neighbors sold their crops, the vicious circle of moneylender-plus-landowner control over the peasants could seldom be broken. Peasant indebtedness seemed to be a permanent fixture in village life.

Now, however, this control has been challenged by the creation of a network of rural credit facilities. These facilities are made available, with the aid of the State Bank (the former Imperial Bank, nationalized by the government in 1954 for this purpose), by cooperative credit societies and cooperative banks reorganized under a program which is being carried out by the cooperators, the State governments, and the Reserve Bank. The State Bank helps by opening additional branches and assisting the cooperatives with finance, especially for marketing and processing. This rural credit system makes it possible for the peasants to deposit their small savings, which then become available to the government for the financing of irrigation projects and other undertakings — and to borrow on the security of their savings at 2 or 3 per cent interest. When it is borne in mind that Japan, which started its industrialization about a hundred years ahead of India, made very effective use of its system of rural credit institutions for the formation of capital needed for industrial investment — Japan's example in this respect was carefully studied by India — it can be seen that this approach holds promise for the future. However, the moneylender remains an important factor in the village. The credit system, whatever its intentions for the future, has not yet reached the "non-credit-worthy" peasants, who have too little land to put up as security — and they are a very large segment of India.

These four approaches — land reform, supplemented by Vinoba Bhave's "land gift" movement whose effectiveness is largely moral; the drive for planned parenthood; efforts to increase agricultural productivity by new techniques; and mobilization of the peasant's financial resources through the rural credit system — are all integrated into a single process through government planning. The urgent need for such planning can be understood when it is realized that under the first Five-Year Plan the country, by strenuous efforts, increased the production of food grains by nearly a fourth, or 11 million tons, and agricultural production as a whole by 19 per cent. Yet, because of the continuing increase in population it was estimated in 1957 that under the second Five-Year Plan it would have to achieve a 28 per cent rise in agricultural production by 1961, with a 25 per cent increase in food grains output alone. As Mr. Nehru has wryly commented, India must run very hard, agriculturally speaking, just to stand still. Nor can the anticipated increase in food production be expected to improve the standard of living, for it will just be barely adequate to keep the people from starving unless the population growth can be checked.

The government's emphasis on agriculture, however, has not yet been translated into an administrative emphasis on increasing agricultural production. So far India has concentrated not on producing more food but on bringing a backward rural population forward through the community development projects. Two significant examples illustrate the situation. After eleven years of independence, only 15 per cent of the Indian farmers have improved seeds. And in 1958–59, following two years of poor harvests, the shortage of food grains was estimated at 6.7 million tons.

The key problem has been an almost total absence of any sense of urgency about increasing food production, and even an actual acceptance of traditional village farming methods which yield very little. The government agencies concerned with agriculture have continued, as before independence, to emphasize regulation rather than the accelerated development required by the urgent, in fact emergency needs of the nation today. In 1959, however, a sense of urgency about food production began to emerge. Important studies by a parliamentary team on the antiquated hierarchical structure of the agricultural departments were expected to lead to reforms. A top-flight team of United States experts on all phases of agriculture, from water and soil conservation to price policy, sponsored by the Ford Foundation, visited India to help the government plan a genuine program to raise agricultural production levels. The Ministries of Food and Agriculture and of Community Development are to plan and organize the national program for increasing food production.

At the end of the first Five-Year Plan, India still had to import wheat, but had reached near self-sufficiency in rice, needing only about two million tons in imports. This seemed like an impressive achievement, since only three years before, in 1953, India had suffered from a dangerous shortage of both wheat and rice. Thoughtful observers, however, pointed out that this success might be dangerously illusory, since the period

1953–1956 had been marked by two to three good monsoon seasons, with the rains neither too heavy nor too scant — a situation which could not be counted on to recur annually. And, unless India manages to accumulate and store surpluses of wheat and rice for future emergencies, it will have to import grains for its expanding population, as proved to be the case in 1957, when near-famine conditions developed in several areas of the country following an arid summer with insufficient monsoon rains, and again in 1958–59. Critics of the government, notably the distinguished economist Professor D. R. Gadgil, director of the Gokhale Institute of Politics and Economics at Poona University, contend that the government must make long-term plans for production and storage of food, and control food prices if necessary.

Even when the food grain crops are good by Indian standards, the diet of the average person is seriously deficient in proteins. While Western critics contend that the Hindus could easily remedy this deficiency by abandoning the custom followed by orthodox believers that they must never touch meat, some experts believe that this custom may have been due, in the first place, to the impossibility of obtaining meat in sufficient quantities, or in the absence of refrigeration, in usable condition, and that the Hindus made a virtue of necessity. However the case may be, today India's cattle are in poor condition. And, while cow-worship inhibits the Hindus from killing cows, which are a drain on the country's scarce resources of fodder, the survival on short rations of ill-fed and poor-quality animals prevents efforts that might otherwise be made to improve the quality of cattle by proper breeding and care.

While Mr. Nehru and other modern-minded leaders recognize the problems created by the persistence of cow-worship, they think it wise to avoid a head-on clash with the religious sensitivities of millions of devout Hindus. The government, however, has established special areas where cows from all over the country which are not claimed by their owners (and are often seen wandering serenely and unconcernedly about the streets of large cities like Calcutta and New Delhi with no regard for traffic) can be removed for "protective custody." This, however, under schemes tried so far, has not proved a success.

Meanwhile, the government is trying to overcome the country's protein deficiency by an increase in the output and consumption of fish. One of the most constructive measures taken in this connection has been made possible through a cash contribution raised by the Norwegian people. This contribution — Norway's own Point Four plan — has been used to provide Norwegian deep-sea fishing experts and boats for the training of Indian fishermen, who had traditionally limited their fishing to coastal waters. The government, for its part, is endeavoring to develop refrigeration facilities, so that fish can be transported inland. It is also hoped in India, as in other underdeveloped countries, that foods produced by photosynthesis may ultimately increase the country's food resources, just as the Japanese, when confronted with similar exigencies, have used various kinds of seaweeds, although few are as yet enthusiastic about the gustatory qualities of these substitutes.

All these measures taken together, however, have not reduced the dangerous unbalance in the ratio between food and population. The seriousness of India's agricultural problem was dramatically emphasized by the team of fourteen agricultural experts from the United States recruited by the Ford Foundation at the request of the Indian government. This team, headed by Dr. Sherman E. Johnson of the United States Department of Agriculture, in a report published on April 20, 1959, declared that India is heading for disaster unless it can increase its food output by 57 per cent during the next seven years. This means that the Indian farmers must learn to grow 110 million tons of food a year by 1965–66, the end of the third Five-Year Plan, as compared with the unusually favorable crop of 70 million tons in 1958, tripling the present 2.3 per cent a year increase in food production.

At the present slow but steady rate of increase, the report forecast, the gap between food supply and demand will be 28 million tons by 1966. The team warned that "no conceivable program of imports or rationing can meet a crisis of this magnitude."

Dr. Johnson's group of experts insists that a food target of 110 million tons a year is both reasonable and attainable. "The best in Indian agriculture is comparable to the best in other countries," the report asserts. "The task is to develop ways of raising the low average to the highest levels which some Indian cultivators have achieved."

This goal, according to the United States team, calls for an emergency program of action to mobilize India's resources of soil, water, and manpower. It also requires that India's economic planners assign top priority to agriculture.

Although the Johnson team tried to avoid political pronouncements, it directed attention to the politics of food in these words: "If elementary wants such as food and clothing are not satisfied, other freedoms may be sacrificed for the promise of food enough." It suggested that "food enough" become "a central objective in the crusade for the new India visualized by its leaders."

The Johnson team saw no reason to blame Indian soil, water, or climate for this condition. It found that, by applying improved methods of cultivation more widely, India's yields of many food grains could be doubled.

The report advocated a program of price stabilization for food grains and a public works program that would apply idle hands in the countryside to the tasks of drainage, irrigation, and terracing against erosion.

In this way India could conceivably turn to advantage its vast surplus population. The inflationary effect of additional government spending on public works would be offset, the report maintained, by a substantial increase in food production. At present, farm prices fluctuate wildly. They are generally lowest at harvest time when the farmer must sell his produce quickly to pay off his debts. The report proposes that the government guarantee the farmer a minimum price for his rice and wheat well in advance of planting time. Such guarantees, along with provision of markets and storage facilities within bullock-cart distance of his own village, are essential if the farmer is to invest in better seed, fertilizer, and draft animals, it was said.

The report also contends that the Indian government must complete its land reform program as soon as possible and end the insecurity of many farmers about the future of their own acres. It cautions against breaking up the relatively few large farms that are efficiently managed.

The Johnson team stressed the importance of providing a rural credit system that would release the villager from the grip of the moneylender. Cooperatives may be one answer, the United States experts said, but only if they have sufficient resources provided by the government to perform economic functions "better than they are now being performed."

The government realizes that it must rebuild not only the strength of its people but also the strength of the soil which must provide their food. The lack of forests, depleted over the centuries, together with the impact of heavy monsoon rains, has caused dangerous soil erosion. New trees must be planted and carefully nurtured for the future protection of the soil. Meanwhile, the lack of wood for fuel has led to the use of cow-dung for this purpose, thereby depriving India of natural fertilizer, with the result that the land has become progressively poorer. At first the government hoped to replenish the vitality of the soil by the importation of nitrates from Chile or phosphates from Morocco, and such products as Krillium, an artificial fertilizer produced by the Monsanto Chemical

Company in the United States. These imports, however, are a drain on the country's limited reserves of foreign currency. Instead, the government has started to produce its own fertilizer. It also hopes to perfect and adapt for popular use a solar stove which, under India's climatic conditions, with a long season of intense heat, could make available a cheap source of fuel for cooking purposes.

Thus, one of India's principal economic targets is to improve the output of its agriculture and, at the same time, to stabilize the growth of its population, so that increased food resources can eventually lead to a rising standard of food consumption. Its second principal target, embodied in the second Five-Year Plan, is to start India on the road of industrialization, which, it is hoped, would have the dual effect of providing the population with at least a modicum of manufactured consumer goods, and of reducing the birth-rate as a result of increased urban living.

Western observers, basing their conclusions on the experience of the Western nations before the Industrial Revolution, are inclined to emphasize industrialization as the most promising answer for India's population problem. But India, as already indicated, faces an acute difficulty which did not exist in the Western nations before 1800. This difficulty is that the presence of a vast and growing population of itself discourages and impedes industrialization, since any government which has humane instincts finds it necessary either to concentrate first on minimum agricultural production just to keep its people from starving, or at best to use its limited resources for the simultaneous development of industry and agriculture — in contrast to the West, where industrialization came only after considerable agricultural modernization.

But, some critics of India ask, are there not other measures that could be taken to relieve population pressure at this critical stage, in addition to planned parenthood which, as Mr. Nehru has said, is not the only key to economic planning?

Another approach often suggested is emigration. Today, however, this possibility is almost nil for the Indians, although in the past thousands did emigrate, and settled in Ceylon and Malaya, in Kenya and South Africa, where they usually became merchants and professional men. Their success, however, provokes hostility, not only on the part of the white settlers with whom they compete for prestige, position, and financial gains, but also on the part of the natives, who hope to achieve the positions won by the Indians, and regard them as interlopers. This is particularly true in those countries — notably Ceylon and Malaya — where the Indian emigrants want to maintain their Indian citizenship and vote in their new country, too, thus raising the delicate problem of dual citizenship. Prime Minister Nehru, in an effort to conciliate neighboring countries, has suggested that the Indians of Ceylon, to take the most important example, should either give up their Indian citizenship or their claim to the right of voting. In many areas Indians are prevented from emigrating by the maintenance of a strict color bar — in Australia, which has a "whites only" policy, although it welcomes individuals of color who go there for purposes of study or training; South Africa, with its stringent policy of *apartheid* which has forced Indians already there to move out of the cities where they had their homes and their work into new locations in the countryside assigned to the "colored"; and some of the Latin American countries. And when India takes up the cudgels in defense of its emigrants, the Afrikaner in South Africa and some of the British in East Africa accuse it of practicing a form of imperialism in the African continent, and of spreading "radical" doctrines.

Nor does internal migration, which at first sight may seem feasible when one looks at areas of India that are either practically empty or only sparsely settled, offer much promise for the future. It is true that today, with the start of industrialization and the gradual erosion of the caste system, the mobility of the population has greatly increased. But even now 85 per cent of the people live on the land, and are strongly tied to their familiar, if impoverished, homes. It is hoped, however, that the construction of new dams and the opening of new industries will encourage young people to leave the land and seek employment in areas of the country which had previously failed to offer opportunities for livelihood. The trend toward job-seeking away from home is beginning to break up the joint family, which had had as strong a hold on the individual in the past as the caste but whose cohesion becomes increasingly difficult to maintain as one young member after another, before or after marriage, moves away and often seeks new occupations. This weakening of family ties has also been accelerated by the migrations of Muslims from India to Pakistan and of Hindus from Pakistan to India following the 1947 riots, which brought about a large-scale resettlement of peoples in both nations, and has not yet ceased, with Hindu refugees still entering West Bengal from East Pakistan every time that the Pakistanis seem to grow more intransigent.

So, India's chief hope for stabilization of its population is to lay a basis, no matter how modest it may be, for industrialization. The marked shift from agriculture to industry which the government made in the second, as compared with the first, Five-Year Plan, is indicated in Table 1 which shows percentages of the country's resources allocated to major categories of production.

It will be seen from this table that India's planning is markedly different from that of Russia and China in its emphasis on the choice of priorities. In India industrialization was deliberately postponed until a modicum of food — now recognized to be still inadequate — had been provided. In contrast, also, to the crash-program character of the Russian and Chinese five-year plans, which stress speed irrespective of the sacrifices, physical and spiritual, inflicted on the people,

India's planning is "gradualistic," in keeping with its political policy of slow peaceful adaptation of the country to the needs and opportunities of a modern society. Russia and China, animated by motives of national prestige and military security, as well as by the determination to improve the lot of their people, are trying to "catch up with and outstrip the capitalist world," to use Stalin's famous slogan. By contrast, India, which is not trying to compete with the West but only hopes not to be outdone by China, has as its first consideration the welfare of its people.

TABLE 1. Percentages of India's outlay on major categories of production.

	First Five-Year Plan (1957 figures)	Second Five-Year Plan (Estimate)
Agriculture and community development	14.0	11.8
Irrigation and power	29.0	19.0
Industry and mining	5.0	18.5
Transportation and communication	26.0	28.9
Social services and miscellaneous	26.0	21.8

India's industry shows the characteristics of socialism far more clearly than its agriculture. For, while land remains in the hands of private owners, a small sector of industry, representing only about 8 per cent of the national income, is controlled, directed, and operated by the government. The pattern for some government-operated enterprises had been set by the British long before independence. Transferring to India their own tradition of government ownership of basic utilities, the British built, owned, and operated the railways, as well as posts, telegraphs and telephones — a practice also customary in other democratic countries of Europe.

When the Indians first came to power, they were inclined —
like the British Laborites with whom some of their leaders
had been well acquainted during their studies in Britain —
to believe that nationalization would be a universal panacea
for industry. They nationalized a number of enterprises,
among them the Indian airlines, eleven internal and two external, and more recently also the life insurance companies.
As time went on, however, they became disillusioned with the
curative powers of nationalization if taken alone, and after a
series of readjustments settled for a relatively limited number
of government-controlled enterprises. This list includes industries working solely for defense, the production of steel
(which was nationalized by the British Laborites after 1945
and then de-nationalized by the Conservatives in 1950), and
enterprises regarded as in the national interest — such as
fertilizer plants — which private owners may not be interested
in initiating.

The government, however, is concerned not only with large
industries, such as steel and locomotives, but also with small
industries, which are expected to play an important role in
the country's development. Small-scale industry is important
not only in terms of production (currently, as much pro-
portionately as large-scale industry), but also in terms of employment, which is desperately needed in a growing population and of the growth of a middle class, which is needed
for the stabilization of a democratic society. Small-scale industries generally use some power machines and make some
effort toward improved techniques. They include all industries employing less than fifty persons when using power, and
having a capital investment of less than $100,000. Some of the
principal small-scale industries are footwear, bicycles, locks,
surgical implements, sewing machines, builders' hardware,
agricultural instruments, hand tools, electrical appliances,
knitted textiles. The small-scale industries are a significant
portion of the private sector. With the aid of the Ford Founda-

tion, which has done an exceptionally imaginative job in India, experts in small-scale industries have been brought from the United States, Italy, Sweden, and Denmark, to help the Indians think through how to establish small factories, and how to market their products most effectively. The small industries, in turn, stimulate greater agricultural productivity, as the villagers try to earn additional cash for future purchases.

The change in the government's definition of what is the public and what the private sector was indicated in the statement on Industrial Development Policy, read in Parliament on April 30, 1956. This statement pointed out that in 1948, one year after independence, the state took exclusive responsibility for establishing new undertakings only in six fields: coal, mineral oils, iron and steel, aircraft manufacture, shipbuilding, and manufacture of telephone, telegraph, and wireless equipment (exclusive of radio sets). Today industry is classified into three categories, and the role of the state in each is clearly defined, as follows:

Category I includes the six industries in the fields mentioned above, whose number has now been expanded to seventeen. Among these are heavy castings and forgings of iron and steel; heavy plant and machinery required for iron and steel production, for mining, for machine tool and such other basic industries as may be specified by the government; heavy electrical plant, including large hydraulic and steam turbines; mining of iron, manganese, chrome, gypsum, sulphur, gold, and diamonds; mining and processing of copper, lead, zinc, tin, molybdenum, and wolfram; and aircraft. In the seventeen fields listed under Category I the government is responsible for all new undertakings.

Category II includes twelve fields in which the state will generally take the initiative in starting new enterprises, but may transfer them eventually to private owners. In this category "private enterprise will also be expected to supplement the effort of the state either on its own or with state participation." Among the enterprises in this category are several which had been registered as private in 1948. The Category II list includes aluminum, machine tools, antibiotics and other essential drugs, fertilizers, certain minerals, basic and intermediate products required by chemical industries, sea transport, road transport, ferro-alloys and tool steels, synthetic rubber, chemical pulp and carbonization of coal.

Category III includes all fields not otherwise specified, which are left to the initiative and enterprise of the private sector. The state, however, may start any industry not included in the first two categories "when the needs of planning so require or there are other important reasons for it." This is an escape clause which may prove narrow or broad according to the government's discretion.

The government not only controls and directs important industrial activities, but also regulates the development of both the public and the private sectors. To this effect, it has passed three basic legislative measures. These are:

The Industrial Development and Regulation Act of 1951, which provides that all private industries, numbering forty-two, must be registered with the government. It gives the government the right to investigate and inspect industry, check prices of goods, and see to it that proper materials are used in the production. A Central Advisory Commission advises the government on matters concerning the development of the industries listed, and a Licensing Commission reports to the Ministry of Commerce and Industry.

This act sounds restrictive to Americans concerned with the maintenance of free enterprise in the United States. It must be borne in mind, however, that India is faced with shortages of all kinds — of available raw materials, managerial talents, skilled workers, and hard foreign currencies (the dollar, the pound sterling, the Swiss franc, the German mark, and so on). The government believes that it must assign priorities to certain industrial fields ahead of others, regarded as less necessary from the point of view of national interest and well-being, and that new industries must come within the frame of reference of the five-year plans. This act, in effect, provides for a mixed regulated economy.

The Government-Owned Industrial Development Corporations Act of 1954, which prescribes the ground rules for the way in which basic enterprises are to be started by the government. After establishing the enterprises, the government can sell them to private owners. Among the enterprises which have been started and operated on this basis are the Sindri fertilizer company, and two other fertilizer plants subsequently built; the antibiotics factory built by the government with the aid of the American Cyanamid Company; and the Chittaranjan locomotive works.

The Industrial Investment Corporation Act, also passed in 1954, which allocated $235 million in capital to start new industries and to expand existing ones. Foreign investors who are interested in exploring the possibilities of investment in Indian enterprises can discuss with this Corporation the country's plans for the future to discover how their projects might fit into its planned economy.

In general, it can be said that since 1954 India has moderated its initial predisposition toward nationalization of now existing industries and the creation of new ones under state auspices. The 1956 Resolution, which has been described as an "economic constitution," based on the political constitution of India, declares that ownership and control of the material resources of the community are so distributed as best to serve the common good; and that the operation of the economic system does not result in the concentration of wealth and means of production to the common detriment.

As compared with the 1948 statement on nationalization, however, the 1956 Resolution is less sweeping and dogmatic. Henceforth, greater emphasis is to be placed on the government's development of an expanded public sector. A steadily increasing proportion of the activities of the private sector are to be developed along cooperative lines. Existing private industry is to develop along with state-owned undertakings in all three industrial categories defined in the 1956 Resolution, provided private industry is properly directed and regulated so that it does not seize advantages which react adversely to the welfare of the people. The door is left open for private enterprise to enter the industrial field reserved for state development if it is found that exclusive government jurisdiction would retard development or otherwise be adverse to the national interests. Thus, it appears that with the possible exception of one or two industries dealing with public utilities and natural resources, India has abandoned the over-all program to nationalize private industry falling within the public sector. The state has assumed monopoly rights with respect to arms and ammunition, atomic energy, and railway and air transportation. Private enterprise may be authorized to operate in all other fields in the public sector if it is considered advantageous to the nation's interests.

As a result of this change of attitude on the part of the government, there is an increased proportion of activity in the private sector, and growing cooperation between the private and public sectors. The government assists and encourages private enterprise in a variety of ways, including financial assistance, tariff protection, tax concessions, and technical research. For example, of the loans amounting to $225 million given by the World Bank to India, over $150 million are for projects of private enterprise.

The steel industry is an example of how public and private enterprise exist side by side. Three new units of a state-owned steel industry which are expected to produce three million tons of steel a year are being completed — at Rourkela by West German engineers; at Durgapur by a British combine;

and at Bhilai by the U.S.S.R. Meanwhile, the privately owned steel plant operated by the Tata family at Jamshedpur since the end of the nineteenth century, received active assistance from the government in obtaining a $75 million loan for its expansion from the World Bank, as well as loans from private banks in the United States. In short, as former Indian Ambassador to the United States, G. L. Mehta, pointed out in an address to the 52nd Annual Conference of the League for Industrial Democracy in New York on April 12, 1957, in the Indian conception, "a welfare state is not a totalitarian state and there need be no insistence on nationalization as a matter of creed." Like the British, whose experience they have closely studied and in many respects followed, the Indians are pragmatic, not dogmatic about their economy.

Nevertheless, the government's policy of control and regulation over the country's economic development has frequently brought criticisms from Indian private investors. They claim that the government has not given private enterprise a fair opportunity to develop new industries, and has not shown sufficient confidence in the judgment and spirit of adventure of the private businessman. They also believe there is an inherent danger that the industrial development of the country will bog down because the government does not have sufficient trained personnel, and that India will ultimately suffer from the overbureaucratic system of government control. There is a general feeling in the business community, however, that private enterprise faces a brighter future since the government's 1956 declaration of industrial policy than it did in 1948.

Meanwhile, critics to the left of the Congress party, which has a strong representation of businessmen and industrialists in its membership, take the opposite view. They contend that the business community is unduly pampered by the government; that government controls over new enterprises are inadequate; that in 1957, to give one example, the Ministry of Commerce and Industry, then headed by T. T. Krishnamachari, who subsequently became Minister of Finance, had given out an excessive number of import licenses to private enterprises, thereby gravely depleting the country's meager reserves of foreign currency. What the Communists would do with private industry if they came to power is not yet clear. While in their manifestoes they proclaim their intention to take over all industries, the decision of Kerala's Communist government to invite the industrial magnate Birla to invest in new industries seems to indicate that at the present stage of the country's development, at least, even they are not prepared to dispense with businessmen.

A detached study of the pros and cons of India's industrial policy, published by the Federation of British Industries in 1956, "India: A Survey for British Industrial Firms," states unequivocally that "the issue of nationalization is very much of a red herring in the study of Indian economic prospects." Although, in the opinion of the Federation, the Indian government has not made its own policy clear abroad, there were "reasons of an eminently understandable kind" for those acts of nationalization which have taken place. "The Indian air-lines were nationalized because they would have required Government support for the replacement of aircraft on such a scale that they would have remained private only in name; the Imperial Bank of India was nationalized after an exhaustive survey of the country's requirements of agricultural credit because it offered the most direct way toward an adequate system; life-insurance business was nationalized not because the Government wanted power over the investment of funds, which it already had in ample measure, but because of cases of malversation of funds, which have occurred in Indian insurance companies which in many cases have been developed simply as convenient adjuncts of large privately-manipulated industrial and commercial combines."

The difficulties in the way of private industrial enterprise, according to this survey, "lie to a very large extent within the field of the Government's income tax policy." If this "foolish" policy could be moderated, foreign investors would have good reason to seek opportunities for investment in India. For, in other respects, "India is prepared to welcome foreign investment on terms which are not unreasonable, have been conscientiously adhered to, and compare well with those enforced by other underdeveloped countries . . . There is no rigid insistence on a majority Indian holding in foreign-initiated enterprises; some one hundred per cent subsidiaries of British firms have been welcomed. The employment of Indian personnel in all possible positions is insisted upon, but not at the expense of managerial experience or technical skill, which it is well understood necessarily accompany foreign capital."

The report adds: "There are people who seem to find the prospect of the industrialization of underdeveloped countries an alarming one, but it is impossible to contemplate the course which Indian industrialization seems likely to take without the broad conviction that it will create for Britain more opportunities than it destroys. In any case the role of an economic Canute is an impossible one. History cannot be stopped at some convenient stage in the life-cycle of a firm or an industry."

In another impartial analysis, the financial editor of *The Manchester Guardian*, after a survey of the Indian economy, wrote as follows on December 18, 1958: "Few people in the West realize what rapid strides have already been made towards the industrialization of the country. A number of splendid modern plants and factories now exist in many parts of the country, and many more are on the way to completion. Over a period of a few weeks I visited some of them in different areas and found almost every one beautifully laid out, lavishly equipped and efficiently run. That is true of both

Government and private enterprise units. The experiment of 'democratic planning' has begun well. There are weaknesses, there are problems; but what has been achieved is far more than an average Western observer like myself could have imagined.

"In a number of cases I was told that 25, 30 or 40 per cent more direct labor hours are required in India to produce one unit of output than in Europe. That is a very good achievement considering the absence of an industrial tradition and the shortage of trained workers and technicians. Everywhere the management was confident that the gap between Indian and European productivity will be narrowed when the great training drive has continued a little longer and more experience has been gained."

In its attitude toward private investment India has traveled far since 1947 when, still fresh from its long experience with economic colonialism, it was cautious about accepting investments by foreign capital in its projected enterprises, for fear that they would prove a new form of Western intervention to prevent its rise from backward agriculture to an economy combining modern agrarian practices with native industry. With time, however, when Britain, the United States and a few other Western countries possessing capital resources indicated their willingness to meet India's principal investment conditions, the government became less suspicious of the motives of private investors. It still insists that private investments should fit into its over-all framework of economic development, and should not be to the detriment of the nation's interest. But, as in the case of Indian private industry, the government since 1956 has made it clear that it is willing to give foreign private investment an opportunity to justify itself in a Socialist state.

And foreign investment could unquestionably be of considerable value to India in the years ahead as it expands its economy. For at present the country must draw, for the bulk of its investment capital, on domestic resources, which constituted 90 per cent of the funds used for the first Five-Year Plan, and probably will reach the same figure under the second. The principal sources of India's capital formation are taxes; savings made through various channels, but particularly through the rural credit system; savings effected by cuts in imports; and the sterling balance in London created by Britain's debts to India for purchases made there for the British Armed forces during World War II.

The sterling balance, estimated at 300 million in 1957, is a diminishing asset, since, when it has been drawn down, India will have no more reserves of English pounds. Savings effected on imports can play a significant part, but they actually constitute a limitation on the country's future development if they are effected by the curtailment of imports of industrial goods needed for industrial growth, rather than of luxuries required by a tiny percentage of the population who can afford foreign wines, cosmetics, clothes, foods, and other amenities.

Thus, the principal sources of internal capital are taxes and savings. However, in a country where the majority of the population live at substandard conditions, taxes, no matter how steep, can necessarily be collected only from a small minority; and that minority — professional men, businessmen, industrialists — are apt to protest that the government is killing the goose that might lay the golden egg by discouraging further investment. The government, nevertheless, has persisted in maintaining high corporation and personal income taxes, and in 1957 added wealth and expenditure taxes. Although increases in some levies, especially excises, have been made, the Central government has felt that indirect forms of taxation — notably a sales tax — would impose an unduly heavy burden on the poor, who in India are a vast majority. Every state, however, has a sales tax on all kinds of articles.

At the present time, only about 10 per cent of the national income is obtained from taxes and other current revenue. Foreign observers, for example Professor William W. Lockwood of Princeton University, point out that out of 110,-000,000 income earners, only 500,000 pay any personal income tax at all to the Center, as compared to 11,000,000 in Japan. India, he said in the October 1958 *Foreign Affairs*, "grants total exemption up to a higher level of income. She then applies lower rates — even with allowances for the new wealth tax — on incomes as high as $12,000 or more." One of the principal problems of taxation in India, as Professor Lockwood emphasizes, is that agriculture, which produces just over half of the nation's income, is entirely exempt from direct taxation by the Union government, and land taxes paid to the states have declined "to the point where they take little more than 1 per cent of farm income. Indirect taxes on the farmer, too, are lighter than city people pay. The more prosperous landowners are grossly undertaxed, even though they reap much of the benefit from the development outlays and better farm prices. As a result the states as a group are failing to provide even the modest revenue increases asked from them under the Plan." Since the States, under the Constitution, have major revenue rights and major development responsibilities for agriculture and small industry, the main problem of increasing taxes from the agricultural sector of India's economy is political: for the large landowners, who are well represented in the Congress party, have been opposed not only to land reform but also to rises in their taxes. This problem could conceivably be gradually adjusted, either if the government succeeds in persuading the representatives of landowners in Parliament to accept changes in the tax structure, or if opposition political groups less sensitive to the influence of landowners should come to power.

Meanwhile, the prospect for an increase in the other principal source of internal capital — savings — is not bright for the immediate future, again because of the prevailing poverty. Over the long run, however, the country would greatly benefit if the habit of saving were to be inculcated, even though the actual returns remained modest. For, as in many other countries at the same stage of development, there is a marked predilection among Indians for conspicuous consumption. The rich spend money for their own comfort, adornment, and pleasure, as well as for travel abroad when foreign currency is available (as the Russian aristocracy did before the Bolshevik revolution): and even the poorest family is apt to throw caution to the winds when it has a wedding or other festivity to celebrate, and will spend all its savings on a great feast, and on jewelry for the bride. Until recently, the peasants were not only bowed down with economic woes, but had no facilities readily at hand for regular saving of such small sums as they accumulate after taking care of current expenses. Here the network of rural credit banks will, it is hoped, prove of value in encouraging small savings.

Of the resources which India obtained from abroad for the financing of its first Five-Year Plan, the bulk was supplied by the United States, through grants and loans, and by the World Bank, to which the United States is an important contributor, as can be seen from Table 2.

TABLE 2. Expenditures of the first Five-Year Plan coming from abroad, 1951–1956.

Country or agency	Amount (millions of dollars)
United States	285
United Nations	3
Colombo Plan	47
World Bank	100*
Private U. S. organizations (Ford Foundation, missionary groups, etc.)	40

* Mostly for railroads and irrigation.

During the first Five-Year Plan, as can be seen from this table, American assistance to India amounted to approximately $300 million. This sum was supplemented by the wheat loan of $190 million and by the American share of loans to India by the World Bank (about $40 million). Early in 1957 the United States entered into an agreement with India by which it was to deliver about $300 million of wheat and other agricultural products under the surplus food program within the next three years. Including freight charges, this represented a commitment of nearly $300 million. Of this amount $234 million was to be covered by a long-term loan, $54 million was to be in the form of grants, and the remaining $72 million was to be spent by the United States in India.

If the United States continues its present levels of aid, it will provide India with about $350 million of economic development and technical assistance during the second Five-Year Plan. Even so, however, India was expected to have a gap of about one and a half billion dollars between the goal it had fixed for itself under the second Five-Year Plan and the amount of foreign currency it had hoped to obtain abroad through loans, grants, and exports. In 1958 Britain, after considerable delay and uncertainty, gave India a loan of approximately $150 million; and the United States made loans totaling $225 million, one for $110 million through the Export-Import Bank, and the other, for $75 million, through the new Development Loan Fund of the International Cooperation Administration. The first of these is for fifteen years at 5¼ per cent interest. The terms of the second will vary according to specific projects. The Indian government, however, had hoped that it might obtain from the United States a total of $500 to $600 million in new funds to maintain the pace of the second Five-Year Plan. As of January 1, 1959 United States assistance to India under the second Five-Year Plan stood at about $1,030 million, more than half of which was surplus food given under Public Law 480. On July 20, 1958 India informed the United States and international institutions that it was in urgent need of about $300 million before the end of the year in dollars or other hard currencies — not loans for big development projects. Frankly admitting that "we simply ordered more than we could pay for," the Indian leaders said that if the aid they needed was not forthcoming, their only alternative was to stop paying the country's bills or to "starve the economy."

For in spite of its strenuous efforts, India found that no sooner had it completed its first Five-Year Plan than it was confronted in the spring of 1957 with the prospect that lack of funds — and particularly of foreign exchange — might force curtailment or "rephasing" of its second Five-Year Plan.

Since this second plan was designed to carry the country forward along the road toward industrialization on foundations laid by the first plan through the development of agriculture, irrigation, and transportation, the government had to ponder a grave question. Would the substantial and impressive economic efforts it has made in the decade since independence reach a dead end? Or would this nation, which is trying to modernize its backward economy by democratic, voluntary methods, in contrast to Russia and China, stage a break-through to success by 1961?

The first reaction of some critics, both in India and abroad, on hearing about the difficulties of the second Five-Year Plan, was that the Indian leaders must have been overambitious when they formulated it. The truth, however — and it is a sad truth for the Indians — is that the plan, far from being overambitious, is modest in scope. A Swedish expert has estimated that the general scale of financing in India is approximately that of highly industrialized Sweden with a population of 7 million. Given the country's continuing population growth (which may bring the number up to 408 million by 1961 and to nearly 500 million by 1975–76), the people's unfilled basic needs, and the extent to which the primarily agricultural economy must be modernized before industry can function effectively, this is indeed a modest estimate. Even if the plan is fulfilled, it is estimated that by 1961 India will have increased the average per capita income from $59 to only $69 — which is hardly a luxurious figure when compared to $300 in the U.S.S.R. and $2,000 in the United States — and will have raised the rate of investment from 7 to 11 per cent of the total national income as compared with an average of 16 to 20 per cent in Japan between 1913 and 1939 and of 15 to 20 per cent in the U.S.S.R. today. To give another example, by 1961 India expects to be producing 6 million tons of steel for its vast population, as compared with the over 100-million-ton capacity of the United States, and the 60-million-ton projected capacity of the U.S.S.R.

Why, then, has India run into difficulties in carrying out the second plan? Basically, as then Finance Minister T. T. Krishnamachari, a businessman by background, put it in Parliament on August 23, 1957, "the present 'crisis' — if that term is to be used — is a crisis of development; it is not a crisis of stagnation or of confidence." If India is to build up its economy for future expansion, it must spend money, and some of the money required must be foreign currency for the purchase abroad of capital goods India cannot produce itself. Once these purchases have been made and utilized by the economy, then India will have achieved sufficient momentum to continue developing with less stress and strain. The next five or ten years are therefore crucial, and call for maximum effort at home and maximum aid that can be given India from abroad.

As to whether or not the government has followed the right course, there are a variety of views, depending on those with whom one talks. Critics say that the government, unduly heartened by improvement of the food output plan due to weather conditions that cannot be counted on to recur continuously, allowed itself to become complacent and approached the much tougher tasks of the second plan, with its emphasis on industrialization, in a state of dangerous euphoria.

Most important, the critics continue, the government failed to do the essential thing about planning — that is, to plan adequately. In particular, it failed to take into account the difficulties of calculating agricultural output, which is entirely in the hands of the private sector. Nor did it keep a sufficiently firm watch on the issuance of import licenses, with the result, it is argued, that a portion of foreign exchange was frittered away on the import of consumer goods instead of being husbanded for the payment of capital goods purchases. In fact, say the critics (some of whom regard planning as anathema), the government did not plan enough.

In reply, government spokesmen as well as some private observers contend that India is faced, not with insuperable problems, but with the natural growing pains of an underdeveloped land which is trying, in a short period of time, to change over from a feudal agrarian society to a modern industrial economy — a process which in Western Europe was spread over several centuries. India, moreover, must accomplish this at a time in history when foreign capital resources are scarce, and such resources as do exist — in the United States, and to a much lesser degree in Britain — are being sought by a long line of countries which share India's dilemma.

Nor has India's economy developed to the point where it can count on its exports, which for the most part consist of raw materials and light industry products, to provide sufficient foreign exchange to close the gap between its domestic sources of capital and the expenditures on machinery, steel, and so on required by the second plan. To make matters worse, the prevailing inflation has affected a number of India's suppliers in Europe, raising the cost of essential commodities, and efforts to obtain deferred-payment arrangements, notably in Britain and West Germany, even when successful, only add to the over-all expense of the plan. Meanwhile, India, alarmed by United States military aid to Pakistan since 1950, has felt forced to spend, on mounting defense measures, money it can ill afford.

All this does not mean that the Indian rupee is in danger of devaluation, as some of the more panicky commentators had predicted. In fact, the rupee has so far been rated internationally as one of the stablest currencies of the postwar period. But it does mean that India continues to be faced with a crucial decision: whether it should keep cutting back its plan and tailor its projected development to the resources it can obtain by measures of austerity at home, by stepped-up exports, by drawing on its sterling balances in London, and by obtaining such loans as it can from the United States and from international agencies — or, if these prove inadequate, whether to abandon the hope of carrying out the plan.

Confronted with this painful dilemma, some Indians have shown signs of defeatism. They point to the tremendous effort required by the plan, doubt that the results anticipated will be sufficient to justify the effort, and talk about fulfilling just "the core" of the plan. As defined on March 3, 1958, the core of the plan included, in the public sector, the following items: Steel (the three new steel plants at Rourkela, Bhilai, and Durgapur, and the ferro-sillicon expansion at the Mysore Iron and Steel Works); seven National Coal Development Corporation schemes; coal washeries; a lignite project; the railway development program; the ports development program at Bombay, Calcutta, Madras, and Vizagapatnam; and power projects, including the Bhakra-Nangal project in the Punjab and Rajasthan. In the private sector the core includes expansion of the Tata Iron and Steel

Works and of the Indian Iron and Steel Works, and of coal output.

Others, refusing to yield to pessimism, contend that it will be impossible to pull a "core" out of an integrated plan without jeopardizing the plan as a whole — to build steel plants or set up power and transportation projects without, at the same time, modernizing agriculture, clearing slums, constructing houses, and educating India's millions for the jobs they must perform in a technological age. They urge the country to face squarely the reality that it may have to rely primarily on itself and to regard this need for self-reliance as an asset rather than a liability. For then, they say, India would not be subject to the fluctuations of international politics and the vagaries of the cold war.

Those who take this austere but undismayed view of India's future believe that before doing anything else, the country must assure itself a stable supply of basic foods — wheat and rice — out of domestic production. Supporters of the second Five-Year Plan contend that it can succeed only if the government, while leaving food production in the hands of individual farmers, intervenes in the marketing of wheat and rice to assure fair distribution and stable prices. And the Nehru cabinet is sharply aware that the labor unrest among government workers in the summer of 1957, with threats of a narrowly averted postal and telegraph strike, was due primarily to rising prices of food. The soundest approach, agrarian experts believe, is to do everything possible to double productivity by using some of the rice-growing techniques long employed in China and Japan, which respectively produce twice and four times as much rice per unit of land as does India. But how to give the peasants new incentives to produce more is still a matter of debate.

It could be argued, and is by some, that if India were resigned to being an essentially agricultural country, producing only light industry goods, it would not face the dilemmas and hardships that beset it today. But, would stabilization at the existing low level be feasible in a country where, even under the best of circumstances, current planned parenthood programs will not begin to show results for about a century or more and where people, awakened from age-old lethargy in isolated villages, are beginning to insist on a better life in terms of schools, medical facilities, roads, fertilizer? In the United States we often talk about "the revolution of rising expectations" in an abstract way. In India one can physically sense this "rise" in village hovels and city slums. Any government which would try to check it might buy short-term survival, but only at the cost of creating an ultimately explosive situation which would rebound to the benefit of the Communists, as it already has in Kerala. For the Indian people, sparked by the government, are creating new social patterns of voluntary community action which the authorities, whatever their political ideology, could now stop only at their own risk.

Chapter 8

New Social Patterns: Voluntary Community Action

Independent India has as its objectives not only the creation of a political democracy, based on a synthesis of Indian and English ideas and practices, and of a mixed socialist economy. It is also determined to create at the same time a "good society," not by government fiat and coercion, but through voluntary community action. This third objective, like the first two, is an integral part of the 1950 constitution, which spells it out in detail in what might be called a Bill of Social Rights.

The character and scope of the social revolution which was to be carried out after independence had been clearly stated by Gandhi. In the Mahatma's opinion, political independence (*swaraj*, or self-rule) was part and parcel of the struggle for social and economic equality. "The two things," he said, "social re-ordering and the fight for political *swaraj*, must go hand in hand; there can be no question of precedence." Swaraj was not to be merely the substitution of an Indian government for a British administration, but "the poor man's swaraj," with full economic freedom for the "starving toiling millions."

"Economic equality," Gandhi said, "is the master key to non-violent independence . . . A non-violent system of government is clearly an impossibility so long as the wide gulf between the rich and the hungry millions persists. The contrast between the palaces of New Delhi and the miserable hovels of the poor laboring classes cannot last one day in a free India in which the poor will enjoy the same [political] power as the richest in the land. A violent and bloody revolution is a certainty one day unless there is a voluntary abdication of riches and the power that riches give and sharing them for the common good."

Gandhi urged the city people to go to the villages and there come in "living touch" with the poor by "working for them in their midst, sharing their sorrows, understanding their difficulties, anticipating their wants." He contended that "whether the British remain or not, it is our duty always to wipe out unemployment, to bridge the gulf between rich and poor, to banish communal strife, to exorcise the demon of untouchability. . . . If crores [millions] of people do not take a living interest in this nation-building work, freedom must remain a dream and unattainable either by violence or non-violence." He enjoined the ancient Hindu principle of trusteeship on the big landlords, the princes, and other rich people, reminding them that wealth is held in trust to share with and serve the interests of the poor.

At the same time, in contrast to the Marxists, who argue that the end justifies the means, Gandhi declared that the new social order he envisaged should be achieved by non-violent means. For Gandhi "means are everything; as the means, so the end." Force to accomplish a purpose, no matter how worthy it might be, was repugnant to him. "The spirit of democracy cannot be imposed. It has to come from within."

"A new social order cannot be forced; that would be a remedy worse than the disease. I am an impatient reformer. I am all for thorough-going, radical social re-ordering, but it must be an organic growth, not a violent superimposition. . . . What is needed is not extinction of landlords and capitalists but a transformation of the existing relationship between them and the masses into something healthier and purer. . . . In India a class war is not only not inevitable but it is avoidable if we have understood the message of non-violence. . . .

"Let us not be obsessed with catchwords and seductive slogans imported from the West. Have we not our own distinct Eastern tradition? Are we not capable of finding our own solution to the question of capital and labor . . . ? It is surely wrong to presume that Western socialism or communism is the last word on the question of mass poverty."

The pattern of an egalitarian society where justice is assured to all — a "socialist pattern of society" — includes, according to the Indian constitution, a wide range of rights of a kind not explicitly stated in the American constitution, but found in two such diverse documents as the 1936 constitution of the U.S.S.R. and the 1946 constitution of the Fourth Republic in France. The Indian constitution, in the section on fundamental rights, provides for equality before the law and for equality of opportunity in public employment. It prohibits discrimination on grounds of religion, race, caste, sex, or place of birth, and abolishes untouchability, forbidding its practice in any form — thus striking a double blow at the caste system.

In Part IV of the constitution, on directive principles for the policies of the state, it is provided (Article 38) that "the State shall strive to promote the welfare of the people by securing and protecting as effectively as it may a social order in which justice, social, economic and political, shall inform all the institutions of the national life." Equal pay for equal work is to be assured for both men and women (Article 39). The state is to "make effective provision for securing the right to work, to education, old age, sickness and disablement, etc.," foreshadowing some form of social security. The state is also to "make provision for securing just and humane conditions of work and for maternity relief" (Article 42), foreshadowing labor legislation. The State "shall endeavor to provide, within a period of ten years from the commencement of this Constitution, for free and compulsory education for all children until they complete the age of fourteen years" (Article 45). And Article 47 emphasizes that it is the duty of the state to raise the level of nutrition and the standard of living and to improve public health.

This article also provides for the introduction of prohibition, which was close to the heart of Gandhi who believed that excessive drinking was demoralizing, particularly for the poor, who would be tempted to fritter away their meager earnings on drink. So far, complete prohibition has been introduced in a few states — Andhra, Bombay, and Madras, with a progressive system of prohibition in New Delhi which is slowly strangling the social life of the capital. Other states, although paying lip service to Gandhi's principles, have hitherto preferred to maintain a business which brings substantial revenue, but agitation for the extension of prohibition is growing. Moreover, it has been found that, where prohibition is in force, the rich circumvent it, as Americans did under similar circumstances, by obtaining liquor for "medicinal" purposes, or through smugglers, while the poor continue to suffer from inebriation by manufacturing their own potations, the best-known of which is toddy, made out of fermented cocoanut juice.

It would be easy to say, as come critics do, that the constitution's Bill of Social Rights is but a list of pious hopes, which the government can hardly expect to fulfill in the lifetime of this, or even a subsequent, generation. Leaving aside the only partial, and mostly ineffectual, realization of Gandhi's ideal about prohibition, it is admitted that the harsh realities of an underdeveloped country make it extremely difficult to implement the admirable social principles enunciated in the constitution. The official abolition of untouchability has not yet closed the economic and social gap between the four castes on the one hand, and between the castes and the outcastes on the other, nor has the prohibition of discrimination on grounds of religion, race, caste, sex, or place of birth, brought about equality. Provisions about equality of opportunity in matters of public employment and equal pay for equal work for men and women are challenged every day in a country where a population which increases by five million a year is faced with underemployment, as well as unemployment, and two million new workers come into the labor market annually, with little hope of obtaining stable work.

In a country where capital resources for minimal economic development are in short supply, provisions about free and compulsory education for all children until the age of fourteen, and for protection against old age, sickness, and disablement, are blocked by lack of funds. And recurring shortages of basic goods, while food consumers continue to multiply, make the task of raising the level of nutrition and the improvement of public health a Herculean undertaking.

For India is trying to do something that has never before been attempted in history. It is trying to provide, on however modest a scale, measures of social welfare regarded as essential by Western nations in the twentieth century, but within the framework of an economy which, except for a few industries, is approximately at the level at which the West was in the fifteenth century — and to do this without resort to force and violence.

Critics might say that, given this vast gap between ideals and realities, the Indian government would be well-advised not to arouse the hope, which may prove illusory, that improvement can be expected by people now living, for fear that when the illusion becomes apparent, the masses may rise up in revolt and seek alleviation of their ills in some form of political extremism — whether reactionary communalism or communism. But, the leaders of India are confronted with two ineluctable facts. First, the people, exposed to information about the economic and social improvements that have taken place not only in the West, but also in Russia, will not be put off by pleas that nothing can be accomplished for them at this stage of the country's development. And, second, Gandhi and Nehru and their associates could not have failed to try to implement their promises, without betraying the very cause for which they had fought during the struggle for independence. True, available facts and figures inevitably raise the question whether the government has not "oversold" social advancement in a backward country. But, there is one element in the picture which, while it can neither be weighed nor measured scientifically, may prove to be the unpredictable yet decisive factor in the forging of a new society in India.

This element, which in tables of statistics appears only in terms of depressingly rising population figures, or discouraging numbers of more mouths to feed, more children to be educated, more men and women to be given some sort of work, is the Indian people itself. As is so often the case in countries with vast population figures, the numerically staggering millions, seen in impoverished villages and crowded city slums, appeared to the British, and still appear to Western visitors and to their own fellow-citizens who dwell comfortably in cities, as "masses," a term which conveys an impression of hordes of human beings, faceless and voiceless, who press relentlessly on the resources of the land but have no ideas or initiatives of their own. For decades, the British, and many Indians as well, thought of India's millions of peasants as human beings who had humbly accepted the station in life to which God, and the caste system, had called them, who bowed their heads to natural disasters such as drought or flood, who produced innumerable children with no heed for their health, nutrition, or education, and who could never be expected to stir out of their fatalism and apathy.

The signal achievement of Gandhi and other leaders of the independence movement is that they recognized the human being in the face of the peasant, that they sensed his potential capacity for enterprise, for self-discipline, and for sacrifice on behalf of his children, and of the community in which he lives. These qualities, they believed, were like veins of ore that had never been mined, but that would produce great riches once they had been probed. Fatalism and apathy, as they saw it, were not ineradicable features of the Indian's outlook on life, nor were they an inevitable product of his Hindu faith which, as we saw, dictates a life of action where action is the result of careful meditation about the deeds that are to be performed. Nor did they believe, as some Westerners had assumed, that the Indian lacks the gifts of business acumen, thrift, and acquisitiveness which Western experts often attribute to the Protestant ethic, yet which are frequently displayed by Indian merchants not only in their own country, but in the countries to which they have emigrated — Ceylon and Malaya, Kenya and South Africa. What was necessary, in their opinion, was to find the key to unlock the storehouse of initiative which, they believed, was latent in the Indian peasants. This key has been provided by voluntary community action.

The government encourages active self-help and participation by villagers in a wide range of projects through the community development program, which was launched on October 2, 1952, the anniversary of Gandhi's birthday. "The community projects," Mr. Nehru has said, "are of vital importance not only for the material achievements they will bring about, but much more so because they seek to build up the community and the individual, and to make the latter a builder not only of his own village center but in a larger sense of India."

This program, which started in 1952 in 25,000 villages, by the end of the first Five-Year Plan in April 1956 was reaching 123,000 villages containing 80 million people, or about a fourth of all the country's villages. It is hoped that, by the end of the second Five-Year Plan in 1963 (the date originally set was 1961), the program will cover all of India. The two extra years were asked by the Committee on Plan Projects, appointed by Parliament, which in November 1957 urged better training of rural workers at all levels to man the projects. Community development is carried out through the national rural extension service which was founded in 1953. This service is based both on the experiences of India's own rural workers, stimulated by Gandhi and the poet Rabindranath Tagore before independence, and on the agricultural extension systems used in the United States and Japan. As the Indian Planning Commission has stated in its book, *The New India*, the essential method of the community development program is "education and persuasion; never coercion and dictation. Its incentive is the advancement both of the individual and the community."

The government, in effect, proposes reforms in the village areas, but it is the village community that disposes. The representative of the government is the multipurpose village extension worker — a young man, or, less frequently, a young woman (the ratio of men to women village level workers is ten men and two women per block of one hundred villages) — with high-school education or better who has been specially trained in rural extension work. He, or she, goes from village to village, from farmer to farmer, introducing techniques with which we are familiar in American extension work — field demonstrations, individual talks, and group discussions, audio-visual teaching, and other ways of arousing the interest of the villagers. The multipurpose worker gives help and information on improved methods of cultivation, on health care and sanitation, on cattle diseases and their prevention, and so on. He encourages not only the individual farmer, but the village as a whole, to start new enterprises — a dam, a latrine, a school, a hospital. The government provides technical advice and advances part of the funds, but the decision to build a school, for example, must be made by the village, and the villagers must pay a share of the cost in cash, labor, or materials.

As a result of this democratic process of voluntary participation in a community undertaking, the villagers acquire the habit of working with their neighbors, as well as with other villages in the area covered by the multipurpose village worker. The rapid expansion of the community development program has roused the Indian peasants to see what can be accomplished by pooled efforts to improve living conditions. It is a heartening experience to visit villages where community development projects are under way, and to see the interest of men and women in taking steps, modest as they may seem to a Westerner, toward a better life for their children for whom the Indians have a deep affection.

They listen avidly, with respect and even reverence, to those who bring expert knowledge to the village — the multipurpose worker, the school teacher, the veterinary, the midwife — and show endless ingenuity, with the limited resources of tools and knowledge at their disposal, in carrying out suggestions they regard as practicable. If animals have been sharing the one-room mud house with the family, and the villagers are told this is not a hygienic way to live, they will take the animals out and arrange to tether them in the village square. After watching the teacher intently as he or she instructs their children under a tree, for lack of a schoolhouse, in the mysteries of the alphabet and the operations of addition and division, they want eventually to build a school, providing the land, the building materials (usually local stone, or bricks they make themselves), and the labor. Almost always the plot of land set aside for the school is well situated, open to the sun, and great care and pride go into the construction work. The adults, when they know that their children are beginning to become literate, want to follow suit, and welcome help from the teacher in training themselves, after the men return from the fields at night, or after the women are through with their morning chores, so that they in turn can form classes to teach others. They will put together their few annas to buy a newspaper, so that there will be something to read — and later perhaps try to get a few books. They adorn their homes, not only with the beautiful traditional copper vessels and the designs women paint on the floor and on walls, but with added amenities purchased from local craftsmen or in the bazaar of the neighboring town on an infrequent visit there.

The moment hospital facilities, to use Asoka's phrase, "for man and beast," become available, they flock to see the doctor — often a "lady doctor" — and the women, with time, when they find out about planned parenthood clinics, go in for consultations, while the men bring in their sick animals to be looked at by the veterinarian. New ideas for improvement of agricultural production are eagerly seized upon, as the government discovered after it had established just one fertilizer plant, thinking the peasants would be slow to make use of the new product, only to be swamped with orders. They are eager to have electricity brought into their villages. These peasants, who had once been considered as unwilling or unable to change, who often know hunger and thirst, are hungry and thirsty for knowledge, and look forward to a better life for their children.

It is easy, in the glow of a deep longing for improvement, however modest, of the Indian peasant's miserable lot, to be carried away by overoptimistic expectations about the impact of the community development projects on India's long-stagnant villages. An outside observer, who would like nothing better than to share this glow, must admit that some of India's administrators as well as Western visitors have allowed themselves to be carried away by overoptimism, and to confuse the goal with the actual performance. There is a constant danger that the sparks started by government initiative will die out after a brief period of activity, and that the villages stirred by new ideas will relapse into lethargy for lack of sustained effort.

Many peasants are afraid of change of any kind. This is more true of men than of women, and of the very poor than of those who have some resources of their own. Many, too, are suspicious of all government, and look askance at any undertaking in which they have to deal with officials. The multipurpose village workers, for their part, must not only be skilled in the tasks they are called upon to perform, but must have a sympathetic concern with the villagers without falling into a "lady-bountiful" bathos; must be willing to start with small improvements which are within the peasant's reach rather than with large schemes that may frighten him off; and must have a sense of the equality of human beings, irrespective of wealth or poverty, of caste or religion. This is a strenuous assignment for any young man or woman — yet it is perhaps the most important assignment an Indian citizen can undertake today in a land of villages.

The poignant mixture of hope and apprehension one feels during visits to the villages has been vividly described by Margaret Parton, the most perceptive American journalist to write about India, in her book *The Leaf and the Flame*, when she says: "And as we drove away over the rutted earth, I found myself with hands clasped in lap, praying in a sort of way that they would keep up the zeal even when the illustrious leaders had left, that they would build their road to the future, that they would not relapse into a 'pathetic contentment,' which in India is another phrase for stagnation and sometimes for death. But they must do it themselves; they must understand that they must do it themselves, for the government is too harassed, too financially burdened, too lacking in trained personnel to do it — to build the roads to the outside world which are a key to so many village problems."

The same point has been made by a distinguished American

rural sociologist, Dr. Carl Taylor, in his article, "Two Major Evils," published in the January 26, 1959 issue of *Kurukshetra*, the monthly journal of the Community Development Ministry. Dr. Taylor, who had seen the start of the Community Development Program, which he regards as "excellently designed and soundly launched," believes, after studying it in operation, that corrections are needed both at the village level and in the "administrative assembly line." He contends that administrators doubted the villagers were clearly and keenly aware of their needs, and assumed they would have "to be baited to work at the improvement of their own life." As a result, "an undue and unwise amount of material and financial assistance was given "to motivate the people." This, in turn, caused the program to become more and more an administrators' program and less and less a "community development–extension" program. The remedy he recommends is as follows: "The development of the people, the development of unpaid local leaders, the maximum possible contributions of village level workers, who work with the people and the people's chosen leaders and self-created groups, are the very essence and genius of community development." It is hoped in India that the newly adopted "democratic decentralization" of the villages, through the creation of the Block Committees described in Chapter 6, will help to make community development, as Dr. Taylor suggests, a "people's program instead of what it has been so far, a government program."

But if the overoptimists are to be deprecated so are the overpessimists — and no Westerner can be as critical of India's conditions as are some of its most thoughtful critics — who contend that the community development program has proved a complete failure. For in spite of mistakes, disappointments, and setbacks, thought and action are stimulated by two important factors. First, independence, although it has brought many new difficulties, has given the peasants a sense they had not had for centuries — the sense of working for themselves in their own country, not under foreign rule. The electrifying effect of independence cannot be overestimated in the non-Western countries which have known colonial rule. First, even if the native rulers prove unsatisfactory, the Indian peasants know that they have the right "to throw the rascals out" — a right they did not enjoy while the British were there. And, second, the government has tried to make clear that it is not directing the peasants' decisions. What the government workers do is to ask the peasants: "What do you want? We are here to help you in every way we can, but it is you who must choose." This attitude of respect for the individual and for the community of which he is a member gives the peasants a feeling of dignity they had not enjoyed before. And as the individual becomes involved in improving his village, then his community, then the surrounding area, he also starts to think in terms of building the nation as a whole. In this respect, the community development program acts as a cement to hold the disparate elements of a vast subcontinent together.

But the program does more than that. It also creates new needs, which must be filled if the program is to succeed. There must be more and more trained personnel capable of handling community development projects — more multi-purpose workers, teachers, doctors, midwives, home economists, veterinarians, public health experts, engineers. It is estimated that under the second Five-Year Plan 200,000 new workers will be needed at all levels, whose training will require 61 training centers and 95 agricultural schools.

But as plans are made for obtaining these trained people, new ideas arise about the kind of education India should have. It becomes evident that, by modeling its schools and colleges and universities on the British experience, India has produced vast numbers of white-collar workers and intellectuals who, literally, have no place to go at the present stage of economic development, when most of the available jobs are in government, and industry, as it becomes more specialized, needs men and women trained in science and technology, not in the humanities — as do the community development projects.

And yet, encouraged by the promise made in the constitution of free and compulsory education for all, more and more young people every year hammer at the doors of educational institutions, which are short of funds, of buildings, of library facilities and, most important, of trained teachers in practically all fields of knowledge. The thirst for knowledge, released by independence and by the start India has made on modernizing its social and economic system, cannot be readily slaked. Desperate educators, confronted with a tidal wave of students, are busy trying to rethink the purpose and methods of education for vast masses of people, still 85 per cent illiterate, who must be prepared as soon as possible to man, not only government offices and newspapers and law offices and hospitals, as was done in the past, but also primary and secondary schools, and the multifarious activities of community development projects.

New methods are being studied, on the basis of information about general education in the United States, of American agricultural extension schools, of the training the Russians give in science and technology to a people who only forty years ago were at approximately the same educational level as the Indians. New textbooks must be written and published. But the Indians are so poor that hard-cover books would be accessible only to a few — so paperbacks are being published not only in English, spoken by but 10 to 15 per cent of the population, or in the official language, Hindi, which is not yet familiar to many of the people who speak other languages, but also in the various major tongues of India — Marathi, Gujerati, Telugu, Bengali, and so on.

And still another question arises — should instruction be

given in English, as it was under British rule, or should the government bow to nationalist sentiment, exclude English, and insist on having all instruction given in Hindi, the newly proclaimed official language, along with the local or regional language? The argument made in favor of the adoption of Hindi as the language to be spoken by all officials was that, first, it would provide a common tongue for the nation as a whole, replacing English, the language of the ousted foreign ruler; and, second, that it was the language of the largest language group in India.

While the first argument carried great weight during the years of the nationalist struggle against Britain, the second argument, once independence had been achieved, aroused fear in the non-Hindi areas of the country that the Hindi-speaking regions of the north would attempt to dominate the rest of the new nation in more than linguistic terms — particularly since Hindi was being pushed by the extremist Hindu religious groups. At the All-India Languages Conference held in Calcutta in 1958, Master Tara Singh expressed this fear vigorously when he said: "The conquering Muslims imposed Persian and Arabic on us and the conquering British imposed English. Now, the Hindi-speaking people are trying to impose their language because they are more numerous than any other language-group in the country." And, Chakravarti Rajagopalachari, former Chief Minister of Madras state in the South, where Tamil is the prevailing language and the opposition of the predominantly Dravidian population had taken dramatic forms, such as the use of passive resistance and the destruction of Hindi railway signs, declared: "God alone knows what will happen if Hindi was pushed like that!" Bearing in mind the agitation for Hindi, backed by violent demonstrations, which had occurred in the state of Punjab in the north, Rajiji, as this elder statesman is affectionately called, also said that a secular state should have a secular language as its official language. These mutual denunciations by supporters and opponents of Hindi seemed to justify Mr. Nehru's earlier warning that, "Language is both a binding force and a separating one and we have to be very careful in the matter of languages in India lest in our enthusiasm we might encourage disruption."

This issue, which threatened to assume dangerous proportions in 1957, has gradually been eased as responsible leaders have pointed out that English is not merely the tongue of a former colonial power, but a medium of expression essential for work in scientific and technical fields, not to speak of diplomacy, the press, and other media of contact with the outside world. C. D. Deshmukh, former Finance Minister and now president of the University Grants Commission, strongly pressed the case for retention of English at a conference on the problems of teaching English held in New Delhi in 1958. He described English as "the main gateway of learning," and contended that development of the mind would be impossible without extensive and reinforced resort to the English language which opened "the doors to us of at least two-thirds of the current scientific and technological literature and 'belles-lettres.' "

The mere thought of having to find substitutes, in Hindi and other languages, for the terms used in nuclear physics, which is of such importance to India, conscious of the possibilities of atomic energy for peacetime use, has caused even nationalists to reconsider their opposition to the use of English. The compromise that will probably prove workable is to teach students Hindi, the official language for all of India, and the local language through the primary school, and to introduce English, the language used by the literate minority for 300 years, for study during the seven or eight years at the secondary level, continuing with it in colleges and universities. To those who have protested that the process of learning more than one language would be too arduous for the young, Mr. Nehru pointed out in 1958 that, in the

Low Countries and the Scandinavian countries he had just
visited, children thought nothing of speaking two or three
languages; and he particularly singled out the example of
Finland where, he reported, children speak five languages —
Finnish, German, English, Swedish, and that of their neighbor Russia. Thus, the needs of modern education seem to
assure that India will remain a multilingual country from
which English, even if it is not taught as well as when the
British were there, will at least not be excluded, as at one
time seemed possible. This seems to be assured by the government's decision to establish an English-language Training
Institute.

As the villagers begin to improve their living conditions,
they become eager to start saving through the rural credit
system, and begin to have new wants which before they had
either not experienced or had had no hope of satisfying.
Where once they could walk on foot in their villages, now
they need bicycles to get around the community development
area. The men want an extra shirt, the women an extra sari.
They begin to look for leather sandals. Perhaps new pots and
pans are coveted by the housewife. Radios and sewing machines may be seen, and dreamed about for the future. Slates
and chalk and pencils and paper have to be obtained for the
schools. If the house is enlarged by the addition of another
room, new furniture may be required. Slowly, imperceptibly,
but in a way that eventually makes itself felt, the peasants
turn to nearby sources of modest industrial goods.

The government, following Gandhi's injunction to try to
take industries to the villages, instead of villagers to the industrial towns, has encouraged the growth and modernization
of the traditional and "cottage industries," which still form
an intimate part of Indian village life and economy, and of
the towns as well. These industries include hand-loom
(cloth hand woven from mill-made yarn), *khadi* (hand-spun
yarn, and cloth hand woven from homespun yarn); silk; hand-

icrafts, such as art metalwork, toys, ivory carving, ceramics; and the manufacturing of raw sugar, matches, and leather footwear.

Thus, slowly — much too slowly not only from the point of view of Western critics but also of the more impatient Indians — ancient ways of life are being changed, old customs are being replaced by new, and the individual gets a glimpse of the wider horizons of the modern world without having to tear up his, and his nation's, past by the roots. The gains achieved by these gradual methods seem modest, even pitifully so, compared with the spectacular victories reported by the Russians and the Chinese from industrial and agricultural battlefronts. But the Indian leaders believe that by building without haste they are laying solid foundations for the country's future, and that the preservation of human values — of life, and liberty, and a sense of personal dignity in a mass society — is in the long run more important than sudden transformations of an existing order, no matter how dramatic or, in the short run, desirable from a practical point of view. India accepts mechanization, and collective effort, and the latest contributions of science and technology, including atomic energy for peacetime purposes — but it regards them not as ends, but as means to achieve the end it has set for its people: and that is the welfare of society as a whole, with as close an approximation to equality of rights, opportunities, and well-being as its resources and level of economic development permit.

A similar approach has been made to the task of reorganizing the social order since independence. This, too, — except for the initial Muslim-Hindu riots — has been accomplished with little or no violence, and with a striking degree of mutual respect between social groups which in other countries at a comparable stage of economic growth have clashed in bloody political strife or brutal class warfare. Instead of eliminating some groups by force, on the "we or they" principle, the Indians, without fanfare, have readjusted themselves to new circumstances, have averted potential clashes, have sought accommodation and reconciliation rather than clear-cut victories for one section of the population over another. Within a decade, the princely heads of 561 states, instead of trying to overthrow the central government by revolution, or nursing grievances in exile, have for the most part accepted their new status with good grace, and have not been above seeking lucrative employment in business or political responsibilities as members of parliament. Some, like the Maharajah of Jaipur, have transformed their palaces into attractive hostelries for tourists. Others, for example, the Maharajah of Patiala, who heads Coca Cola in India, have gone into business enterprises. Still others, entering electoral contests alongside commoners, have garnered the votes of their former subjects who, far from being hostile to dethroned rulers, are ready to choose them as their representatives in a democracy, provided they display the necessary qualifications. A readjustment which, in a country like France required the 1789 revolution, followed by Napoleon's seizure of power and by several restorations of the monarchy before the country settled down to being a republic, has been carried out smoothly, leaving no significant residue of ill-feeling on either side.

Similarly, while the Indians are still suspicious of the private entrepreneur, fearing that he may be ready to sacrifice public weal for private gain, the government, as already pointed out, far from making martyrs of businessmen, has encouraged private enterprise, has welcomed wealthy leaders of commerce and industry to the ranks of the ruling Congress party, and has operated on the theory that partnership between government and business is far more beneficial for the country than the suppression of merchant, banker, and investor. The business community, for its part, although often critical of specific governmental policies, has not been alienated, realizes that it would be unable to win enough votes in the country to form a viable opposition party, acknowledges the need for state initiatives in some basic sectors of the economy, and does not hesitate to turn to the state in obtaining financial assistance at home and abroad. And, while labor conditions in India leave much to be desired, particularly in some of the textile mills of Bombay and Allahabad, industry does not question the freedom to form unions, and the government, often acting as mediator, tries to maintain a balance between the interests of capital, labor, and consumer.

Nor has India's predisposition toward egalitarianism spared even the group which, in another society, might have assumed the role played elsewhere by monarchy or aristocracy — the civil servants. These men, usually educated in England, and nurtured in the traditions of British administration and justice, might have aspired to the role once played by British rulers; or, alternatively, their past association with the foreign ruler might have made them unacceptable to the new political leaders, who had suffered imprisonment and repression at the hands of the British.

Yet, neither of these alternatives occurred. The government of independent India made effective use of the civil servants it inherited from Britain, integrating them into the new system, but did not set them up on a pedestal. On the contrary, the civil servants soon discovered that they were responsible not only to the executive, as in the past, but also to the representatives of the people, as chosen by the voters for service in Parliament. This was not always an easy adjustment to make for men who had had no experience with parliamentary democracy, and who still often look with distaste, even contempt, on legislators who may not be their equals in education, *savoir-faire*, and knowledge of the world — even though they are much closer to the hopes and fears of the average citizens. But, here again, although there have been some important instances in which civil servants have received what they understandably regard as unfair treatment at the hands of politicians appointed to the top cabinet posts, and even at the hands of Mr. Nehru, the balance of power and interests between political leaders and administrative technicians who today must master the intricacies not only of government operations but also of state industrial enterprises, is being gradually adjusted without revolt on either side.

There is one problem, however, which will require greater clarification than it has so far received. The ruling Congress Party has indicated on a number of occasions — and Mr. Nehru himself has publicly made this point — that members of the civil service should not be "neutral" and should come out of their "ivory tower." The implication of these remarks is that the civil servants are too aloof from the political ideas of the Congress party — particularly from its socialist plans — and fail to achieve an emotional integration with the government's policies. It has even been suggested that the concept of the British civil service as a group of trained administrators uncommitted to any given political course but ready to serve every government, whatever its policy, is not a good example for India to follow. Critics of the government — notably *The Eastern Economist* — have pointed out that if civil servants are today to associate themselves with a given political party simply because it happens to be in power, they will be obliged to become equally associated tomorrow with a different party which may subsequently take the helm. Thus the civil service would become a weathervane, turning with every political wind. On the contrary, critics say, if the civil service is not to be recruited solely from the ranks of "yes" men careful to avoid taking the initiative, they should be encouraged to exercise detachment and independence and, through fearless criticism of the proposals made by politician-Ministers, produce a creative "cross-fertilization" of ideas which would enrich the country's administrative development. This issue — whether, as claimed by some government and Congress party spokesmen, the civil service is becoming an ossified bureaucracy, incapable of adapting itself to the country's new economic and social needs, or, as critics of Nehru contend, is being forced to bow to the will of politicians — will have to be resolved if the growing requirements of an expanding economy and an increasingly complex administrative system are to be adequately met with both imagination and integrity.

The armed forces, which in some underdeveloped countries have either assumed, or been forced by lack of other strong leadership to assume responsibility for government — as in Egypt and Iraq, Pakistan, and some of the Latin American countries — have so far remained completely aloof from politics. They have displayed a discipline, loyalty, sense of public service, and intellectual qualities which are not only respected by their own people, but have impressed observers abroad wherever Indian troops have performed military assignments, as in the repatriation of prisoners at the end of the Korean war, or in the United Nations Emergency Force in Sinai after the Suez crisis.

Thus, without mobilizing the entire population for national tasks, without subordinating the individual to the state, without trying to brainwash citizens into excluding all private thought and feeling, the Indian government, in spite of the appalling problems with which it has been confronted since independence, has succeeded in maintaining an orderly society, based on voluntary cooperation by a wide variety of religious, linguistic, economic, and social groups, and guided, through their own decisions, by objectives common to a majority. Purists might argue that the Indian system is not a true democracy in the Western sense, since it is ruled by a single-party government, under the leadership of an individual who exercises vast personal authority. Yet, under the conditions of an underdeveloped economy only now emerging from the Middle Ages, and of a social order faced by the strains of adaptation to technology at home and of cold-war tensions abroad, India's multiracial, multireligious, multilingual society, animated by a drive toward egalitarianism and dedicated to voluntary cooperation, cannot but be regarded as evolving new patterns of democracy. These patterns may not be properly comparable with those of the West, but they hold rich promise as an example to other non-Western countries — provided, of course, they can be maintained in the future. Whether or not India succeeds in pursuing a democratic way of life, or is forced to follow the road taken by Russia or China, will depend not only on its own resourcefulness and sense of dedication but also on the understanding and support it may receive from the advanced Western democracies.

Chapter 9

New Patterns of Diplomacy: Neutralism or Non-Alignment?

Vast and complex as were the problems India faced after 1947 in reorganizing its political life, its economy, and its social order, its leaders at least could draw for inspiration on the country's ancient traditions as well as on its more recent experience with British rule. There was need for reorientation of thought, for renovation of institutions, for new construction — but these tasks, urgent as they were, could be carried out in a familiar environment, and an environment, too, over which the Indians themselves had control. The materials they had at their disposal — climate, resources, population growth, grinding poverty, the restrictions of the caste system, illiteracy, lack of technical skills, shortage of capital — were hard to work with, often seemingly unyielding. Yet, the Indians had won their long struggle to become molders of their own destiny. However inadequate the end result of their efforts might be, they would have the satisfaction of knowing that, at last, after three centuries of foreign rule, it was of their own making.

The problems they faced in world affairs were far less malleable. At the peak of their power and glory, Hindu emperors and Mogul rulers had welcomed trade and what we would call today cultural exchanges with lands outside their borders. Greeks and Syrians, Persians and Chinese, English and French and Portuguese successively left their imprint on India — some through influence on the arts, some on languages, others on religious beliefs, still others on political ideas and administrative practices. Visitors from the Middle East and from China, impressed by the high level of civilization they found in India, bequeathed to us the best available descriptions of achievements in administration, education, religious tolerance, and the arts of living as reflected in day-to-day occurrences among rich and poor. The most enlightened of India's rulers — Asoka and Akbar — were eager to learn the lore of their neighbors and to benefit by their experience.

But in a vast subcontinent which, until the development of naval power in the sixteenth century was difficult to reach except by long journeys overland — and in the case of China by perilous travel over the passes of the Himalayas — there was relatively little need to seek the military support of neighboring countries through alliances, as France and England and other European nations had done in a comparable period of national growth. It was not with other countries that the Indian princes fought or made pacts before the coming of the British. It was among themselves that they waged bloody wars such as shocked Asoka and drove him to reject the use of force and to accept the "middle path" preached by Buddha. And once the British came, they soon took over the direction of India's contacts on the world scene and the protection of its frontiers, which after 1858 had become the frontiers of the British Empire. India had no foreign policy of its own. The British made its foreign policy. And even when the lines of India's struggle for independence had been clearly laid down, and it was increasingly apparent that the final parting of India and Britain was not far off, the British did not consult leaders like Gandhi and Nehru about taking their country into World War II on Britain's side. In world affairs India was an object, not a subject.

Thus, when independence came, India had no choice but to start with a clean slate in foreign policy. And it started at a time when the international landscape was undergoing

seismic changes which even the more experienced powers —
Japan and the Western nations — found it difficult to assess
and to fit into existing patterns of policy. India, a newcomer
to the world scene, was confronted with not only the need
to initiate relations with dozens of countries of which it had
no recent direct knowledge but the necessity of doing this at
a time when its attention, perforce, had to be concentrated
on domestic problems of staggering difficulty which brooked
no delay.

World War II, like a tornado, had overturned empires,
cast national idols from their pedestals, shattered age-old
alignments, destroyed untold wealth of manpower and resources. Communist Russia, despite the losses it had suffered
at the hands of Nazi Germany, had emerged as one of the two
great powers to survive the holocaust. Britain and France had
been gravely weakened at home and had lost colonial domains
overseas. Germany, Italy, and Japan, the defeated nations,
had experienced grave psychological as well as economic disasters. The nationalist aspirations of peoples liberated from
colonial rule or struggling to be liberated — as in the case
of India — were remaking the map of the globe with dizzying
speed. China, racked by Japanese depredations and torn by
civil strife, came under Communist rule within three years
after India had won independence. The Arab lands were
striving to complete the process of self-determination that had
started with the breakup of the Ottoman Empire after World
War I, but had been temporarily checked by British and
French administration in the area under League of Nations
mandates. The United Nations had been in existence for two
years, and had barely begun to function. Everywhere one
looked around the world, change seemed to be the only common denominator. The cold war was emerging before the
debris of the hot war had yet been swept up. The United
States, alone untouched by foreign invasion, had enhanced
its power, and had reluctantly but resolutely assumed respon-

sibilities in world affairs it had hitherto sought to avoid. As the curtain rose on this bleak scene, worthy of the brush of a Brueghel or a Goya, the Indian leaders, overwhelmed by anxieties at home, had to make far-reaching decisions abroad. What was to be the fulcrum of the new nation's policy? Was it to align itself unquestioningly with its former ruler, Britain — or become its opponent? Was it to assert its faith in democracy, and reject relations with all nondemocratic countries, but particularly with the totalitarian Communist regimes of Russia and, later, China? Was it to support the aspirations of peoples who, just as the Indians had done before 1947, were still struggling to achieve independence, or counsel them to move cautiously, for fear that they might merely aggravate postwar confusion and disorder? Was it to accept unreservedly the leadership the United States had assumed in the cold war, or plead its domestic problems as a legitimate excuse for isolationism? Was it to make clear that the independence it had won after so many years and at such great sacrifice would mean just what the word said — freedom to choose its own course in world affairs, as seemed best for its national interests?

Varied and bitter as have been the many criticisms made of India's foreign policy, particularly in the United States, it would be difficult to argue that India, confronted with this list of harsh ineluctable choices, adopted a dogmatic and rigid position. Far from it. The new nation, instead of irrevocably choosing "this or that" developed a policy based on a continuous acceptance, adjustment, and interweaving of "this and that."

This policy, for lack of a more precise term, has been defined as "neutralism." It has also often been described as noncommitment and nonalignment. The most accurate description for these shorthand terms would have to be phrased something like this: "Don't any of you great powers push us into a corner. We find something good in each of you, but by no means everything, and we feel we have the right, as an independent people, to choose those things which we find good and reject those we find bad. Having just succeeded in obtaining our freedom, we naturally object to any form of colonialism, but this does not make us any less friendly toward Britain, many of whose qualities we greatly admire — although, understandably, we sympathize with all those who are still trying to emulate our example and become free. The totalitarian pattern of Russia and China is unsuited to our national temperament and is alien to our traditions — but we want to be free to learn what we can from the Communist experience with industrialization. We admire the many achievements of the United States, but we do not see why our admiration should make it inevitable for us to join the American-led bloc in world affairs when we do not share some of the American estimates about the future of Russia, China and, above all, of the uncommitted nations of Asia, the Middle East, and Africa. We increasingly believe in the value of the United Nations, which offers the best hope of avoiding a polarization of the world into two contending blocs — led by the United States and the U.S.S.R. — whose clashes could sooner or later unleash a nuclear war which would jeopardize, if not destroy, all the efforts we, who are underdeveloped and abjectly poor, have been painfully making to improve the lot of our people. Let us make more and more use of the United Nations, and other international agencies, to stabilize a world wrenched out of balance by two world wars, and to help the underdeveloped nations achieve the modicum of well-being which modern science and technology make possible for mankind."

This definition, although obviously unsuitable for crisp and vivid newspaper headlines, may make it possible to understand the inner coherence of what seem like contradictory decisions by India in world affairs. The newly independent nation, a republic which owes no allegiance to the British

Crown, far from becoming an opponent of Britain, voluntarily joined the Commonwealth, and has proved loyal to this loose yet closely knit alignment, in spite of the strains imposed by the Suez crisis of 1956, and the controversy over the Greek Cypriotes' demand for self-determination to be followed by self-government. In this case, India's decision not to challenge Britain about Cyprus in the UN was facilitated not only by concern for British interests, but more so by the belief in India that the Greco-Turkish struggle was not between a white nation and a people of color, but between two white and comparably advanced peoples — and therefore, according to the Indian yardstick, did not constitute a case of colonialism. At the 1958 United Nations General Assembly, however, Krishna Menon, on behalf of India, reversed this position, and attacked Britain's policy toward Cyprus.

India, however, was shocked by Britain's military intervention, along with France and Israel, against Egypt in the Suez zone in 1956, and made no secret of its dismay that its partner in the Commonwealth, which had shown its willingness to relinquish colonial possessions in Asia, should be reverting to colonial practices in the Middle East. Although Mr. Nehru firmly resisted demands in Parliament for termination of India's association with Britain through membership in the Commonwealth, the Suez crisis left in its wake a feeling of uneasiness on both sides — with the Indians becoming more cautious in their belief that Britain had turned its back on colonialism, and the British feeling resentful about the attitude taken at that time by India, as compared with the more friendly attitude of Pakistan which, as a Muslim country, might have been expected to back Egypt without qualifications. In this case, as contrasted with that of Cyprus, India saw a conflict between an overseas white colonial nation with a people of color striving to achieve independence from past colonial rule.

India's anticolonialism, a product of its own experience

which is still fresh in the minds of the generation now ruling the country, has also caused it to demand the withdrawal of remnants of Western colonial possessions on its own territory. France, under the premiership of Pierre Mendes-France, voluntarily relinquished in 1954 its two small territories — Chandernagore and Pondicherry — under friendly circumstances, and India took that occasion to assure France that its cultural influence in these areas would be respected. In keeping with its sympathy for peoples who are struggling to free themselves from Western domination, India has been sympathetic to the cause of the Algerian nationalists. Yet, when, in 1956, France walked out of the United Nations General Assembly, refusing to be present during discussion of the Algerian problem which it regards as an issue of domestic affairs, it was India's delegate, Krishna Menon, usually known for his intransigence toward the United States, who initiated moves in the UN to make possible France's return to the Assembly. Similarly, Mr. Menon not only forbore from attacking Britain's administration of nonselfgoverning territories in Africa, notably British Togoland, in the UN Trusteeship Council, but actually praised Britain for its policies.

India, however, has vigorously denounced Portugal for its determination to retain its colony of Goa, which Portugal describes as an integral part of its territory, but which Mr. Nehru has described as "a pimple on the face of India." In spite of repressive measures taken by the Portuguese authorities against Indians in Goa who oppose their rule — including the jailing and deportation of critics to Portuguese Africa — and rising demands in India for measures of retaliation, Mr. Nehru has determinedly resisted the use of violence, even though it is generally recognized that a small Indian force could easily occupy Goa and oust the Portuguese. But the Indian government has been shocked and disturbed by what it regards as Washington's unqualified support of Portugal's claim to Goa, which the Indians find it difficult to recon-

cile with the traditional American opposition to colonialism.
India's resentment on this score came to a climax in 1956,
when, at the close of a conference between Secretary of State
John Foster Dulles and the Foreign Minister of Portugal in
Washington, a joint communique was issued in which the
United States declared its concern for the preservation of
Portugal's rule over its colonies in the Far East. Although it
was eventually explained by the Department of State that
the communique was intended to refer to the Portuguese
colony of Macao, bordering on Communist China (this seems
to have been indicated by the use of the term Far East, instead of Southeast Asia where India is located), the damage
had been done; and the United States made no subsequent
official gesture to dispel the impression that it was taking the
side of Portugal against India. This American stand, which
seemed incomprehensible to the Indians, was assumed to
have been determined by the fact that Portugal is a member
of the North Atlantic Treaty Organization (NATO), and
that the United States wanted to retain the goodwill of the
Portuguese in order to assure maintenance of its bases in
the Azores.

The issues of Cyprus, Algeria, and Goa are examples of
the difficulties India has faced in steering its newly established
foreign policy among the shoals of the cold war. Mr. Nehru
has often been accused, particularly in the United States, of
using neutralism in such a way as to embarrass and damage
the cause of democracy, and to enhance the prestige and influence of communism. American commentators have frequently asked India: "Are you with us or against us? Why
don't you stand up and be counted on the side of democracy?"

If the issue is narrowed to the question, "Is India against
democracy?" then it can be answered in the negative. For
there is no doubt that no sooner had India achieved independence than it joined the Commonwealth of its own free
will — when, presumably, had it desired to strike a blow

against the Western democracies, it could have chosen to co-operate closely with the Union of Soviet Socialist Republics. Nor has India, in spite of tremendous domestic problems and frequent lack of understanding of its views on the part of the United States, departed from its initial determination to maintain a democratic society.

But, if the question is, "Does India intend to deal exclusively with the democracies, and to support the Western-led bloc against the Communist bloc?" then the answer is again in the negative. Responsible Indians do not believe it is in the interest of their country to join one military alliance against another. This view is due not only to the Indians' traditional predilection for nonviolence, or to fear that a nuclear war would destroy all they are trying to achieve. It is due, at a far deeper level, to a prevailing conviction that neither side in the cold war has a monopoly of virtue and wisdom, and that each has legitimate interests and aspirations which, amidst the rigors of the cold war, either are not seen, or if seen are rejected, by the other. India's response to the cold war is, first, negative — an overwhelming desire to be left out of a struggle which, Indian leaders are convinced, can only lead, if unchecked, to the greatest catastrophe in human history; and, second, positive — a profound conviction that if the potential combatants can be kept apart, India, together with other like-minded countries (high on the list are Tito's Yugoslavia and Nasser's Egypt) could eventually bring about a reconciliation between seemingly irreconcilable ideologies and national ambitions.

Undeterred by foreign, most frequently American, criticism, Mr. Nehru, as principal spokesman for India, has endeavored to maintain a balance — not between East and West, a common Western phrase which makes no sense to India, since it is an integral part of the East, and sees Russia as a Eurasian nation — but between democracy and communism on the ideological plane, and between the two power blocs on the plane of politics and military force. Here still another question arises: "If, as India claims, it is neutralist, has it kept the balance even? Or, in spite of its best intentions, has it shown greater partiality toward the Communist nations — if not by choice, then because of fear for its own safety?"

The answer to this question is complex, and must be given in three parts. First, there is no doubt of India's special regard for Britain and the Commonwealth — and this in spite of the fact that one of the members of the Commonwealth, the Union of South Africa, pursues a policy of rigid discrimination against all people of color among its population, including Indians and Pakistanis. If India is partial, it is partial to Britain — and that means to democracy, assuming that we regard Britain as a democracy. Yet this point is not always clearly understood in the United States where adherence to democracy is usually equated with unquestioning support of this country and its policies — although it could be equally and, in this case, more easily equated with support of Britain. It sometimes seems as though Americans did not realize the democratic quality of Britain and of other members of the Commonwealth, and did not give them due credit for the role they play in world affairs.

The second part of the answer is that India, although it has grown increasingly friendly toward the United States in the past two or three years, is not as much at ease with this country as it is with Britain, or Canada, and is much more ready to question the motives of the Americans than of the British. This is understandably puzzling to Americans. For we know — and the Indian leaders know — that no country in the world so outspokenly and unremittingly supported the cause of India's independence, and so openly denounced British "imperialism" as the United States, to such an extent that it could be convincingly argued it was the Americans, rather than the Russian Communists, who did most, before 1947, in bringing about the disintegration of the British

Empire, sealed during World War II by Japan's victories in Asia. What, then, caused what can only be described as the estrangement between the United States and India after independence? How could the Indians, instead of showing eternal gratitude for the backing their cause had received in the United States, display aloofness, at times downright suspicion, toward this country's foreign policy?

For this seemingly mysterious transformation there are several explanations. First, Britain, shorn of its imperial power, was no longer a threat to India's national interests, and the Indians, once free, found that they could benefit by a new-found friendship with their former ruler, whose political ideals and administrative methods they had admired in the past. No such ties existed between India and the United States and, to make the situation more difficult, it was now the United States which, replacing Britain as the premier Western nation, had assumed, albeit with great reluctance, the role of a great world power and, many Indians feared, might proceed to become a new empire-builder. While suspicions about the intentions of the United States might not prove true, caution seemed to be indicated until the policies of the new great power had been clarified. And this attitude of caution was confirmed when, as the cold war succeeded the hot, the United States, particularly at the time of the Korean war, began to press Asian nations to align themselves with the West in the struggle against not only Russia, but also Communist China.

Second, the Indians were disappointed to find that the United States, which they had regarded as the champion of anticolonialism, yielding to the pressures of the cold war, appeared to be tempering its former support of self-determination of nations, proclaimed by Woodrow Wilson in World War I, so as not to disturb the remaining overseas possessions of its NATO allies. From the point of view of the Indians, NATO, although designed for the defense of Western Europe against aggression by Russia, had the aspect of a coalition in which the United States would be enlisted by its allies for the defense of their interests in the Middle East, Asia, and Africa. This fear was strengthened by the Suez crisis, in which Britain and France were reported to have used American weapons; by the seeming indifference of the United States toward the long-drawn-out war in Algeria, which reportedly took a toll of several hundred thousand lives; the diversion to Algeria of four French divisions which had been placed under the command of NATO, and were said to be using American equipment and planes provided to NATO forces; and in 1958 by the use of NATO airfields in West Germany for the transport of American troops and equipment to Lebanon. To Indian critics of the West, it seemed as if NATO was a new instrument of Western intervention in non-Western areas.

But the most serious, because most direct, threat to the development of Indo-American friendship was the decision of the United States, at the end of the Korean war, to create a series of bases along the periphery of Russia and Communist China which would serve to implement the policy of "containment" first initiated at the suggestion of George F. Kennan. Washington had hoped to enlist all of China's neighbors in this containment task, and had offered military as well as economic aid to a number of Asian countries, including India and Pakistan. India, adhering to its policy of noninvolvement, declined military aid, although it welcomed, and has since increasingly made use of, American economic aid. Pakistan accepted both, and subsequently became a member of two military alliances sponsored by the United States — the Southeast Asia Treaty Organization (Pakistan, Thailand, the Philippines, as well as Britain and the United States), and the Baghdad pact (Pakistan, Iran, Turkey, and Britain, with Iraq a member until the July 14, 1958 coup which toppled the Hashemite dynasty of King Feisal).

Pakistan's acceptance of American military aid struck a severe blow at India's relations with the United States. Even thoughtful and well-informed Indians found it difficult to believe, in spite of American efforts to explain the sequence of events which had led to this decision, that the United States was concerned solely with its over-all policy of containing Russian and Chinese communism. They deprecated the possibility of attack by Russia and/or China, or the capacity and willingness of Pakistan to fight off such an attack if it occurred. They contended that the United States, fully aware of the hostility between India and Pakistan since partition, was deliberately arming India's potential enemy and, since the principal controversy between the two nations was the problem of Kashmir, was in effect intervening in the Kashmir issue on the side of Pakistan. Even those Indians who took the time to hear the American side of the case pointed out that, whatever the motives of the United States, the mere fact that modern weapons were being supplied to Pakistan made it imperative for patriotic Indians, who had hitherto opposed the creation of a large military force, to demand an increase in India's defenses and, consequently, an increase in defense expenditures which the country, faced with mounting difficulties in fulfilling its second Five-Year Plan, could ill afford to spare.

The anxiety created in India by publicity about the arrival of American tanks and other equipment in Pakistan which, it was argued, could hardly be used in the visible future against Russia or China, redounded, according to our friends in India, to the benefit of Krishna Menon, close associate of Mr. Nehru and regarded by some of his critics as sympathetic to the Communists, who, as his representative in the United Nations, had antagonized American public opinion by his unconcealed attacks on the United States. Mr. Menon, who on his return to India in 1957 had been appointed Defense Minister, responded to demands in Parliament for modernization of the country's armed forces, and thereby not only appeared in the role of champion of national security, but won the sympathy of the armed forces, whose requests for re-equipment he readily met. Thus, Indian friends of the United States contended, by giving military aid to Pakistan, Washington, in effect, was enhancing the importance and influence of the principal political leader who had unmistakably indicated his hostility to American policy.

But, Americans might ask, if it is true that India had some reasons to be concerned about the role played by the United States in world affairs, and particularly about the course it was following in Asia, is it not true that India, far from acting impartially between this country and the Communist bloc, actually bent its neutralism in favor of Russia and China?

This is the third aspect of the question raised above about the impartiality of India's neutralism. It is true — and thoughtful Indians, although few in number but on occasion influential would be the first to admit this — that the Indian leaders have seemed more ready to give the benefit of the doubt to the two great Communist powers than to the United States. For this, too, there are several explanations.

First, and this is something that is difficult for Americans to understand, the Indians have a fellow-feeling for the Chinese — far more than for the Russians, only a minority of whom are Asians — not because of admiration for totalitarianism, but because they see in China a struggle comparable to their own to achieve independence from Western intervention and to create a new economic and social order. Unlike most Americans, the Indians cannot bring themselves to regard Communist China as an outlaw from international society. They are aware of the danger that China might try to infiltrate or dominate neighboring areas — they have already seen this happen in Tibet, and hope to prevent it in Nepal, the Himalayan kingdom whose foreign policy and defense are controlled by India. But, in contrast to Americans, they believe that the wisest way of dealing with Communist China is to recognize Peiping and admit it to represent China in the United Nations, where the power of world public opinion could then be brought to bear on the Chinese, no longer isolated from the West by the American economic boycott and Washington's refusal to grant recognition. Consequently, the Indians are not prepared to adopt the policy of intransigence and nonintercourse followed by the United States with respect to Communist China. Nor do they agree with the United States in regarding Taiwan as the spokesman of mainland China.

Second, India, although committed to the democratic way of life, and convinced that the totalitarianism of Russia and China is unsuited to its economic and social needs, nevertheless believes that it can learn many useful lessons from the experience of Russia, and even more of China, in its efforts to achieve rapid industrialization. The Indians see no advantage in isolating themselves from their two great neighbors to the north. And, while it has become increasingly apparent that in order to fulfill its series of economic plans it will have to depend more and more on aid from the West, it wants to be free to accept aid also from the Communist bloc.

Third, India, fearful of war, has no desire to antagonize Russia and China by actions which might bring about military reprisals. With an army of 400,000 as yet inadequately equipped with modern weapons, India would in any case be no match for its neighbors. Nor does India see any advantage in joining the United States-led bloc, which might conceivably give it the military protection it does not command itself, but would at the same time, it believes, greatly increase the danger of a clash with Russia and China.

Fourth, the Indians are not, as sometimes appears, insensitive to ruthless deeds committed by Russia and China. The

Hungarian revolution of 1956 brought protests from many leading Indians, among them the Socialist Jayaprakash Narayan, and although Mr. Nehru was slow to express his own views until an inquiry on the spot had been made by his Ambassador to Moscow, who was also Ambassador to Budapest, he did indicate his concern when the results of this inquiry became available. Even sharper was the reaction of Indian opinion to the execution of former premier Imre Nagy and other Hungarian leaders in 1958, which was widely condemned by the press, by spokesmen of various points of view, and by Mr. Nehru. Condemnation of Russia and China, however, would be far more prompt and vigorous if it were not for the fact that many Indians are apt to compare what the Russians and Chinese do with what they know of past and present actions by Westerners in colonial areas. And, while the West points out that the days of colonialism are over, the Indians insist on discussing current or recent happenings in Algeria or Kenya which, in their opinion, are no better than the actions of the Russians. As they see it, both the Western nations and the Communist powers do not hesitate to use force and violence when they believe it necessary for defense of what they consider their national interests. And here again, the Indians are apt to be more sympathetic to the sufferings of people of color than to those of the white peoples of Eastern Europe.

A sharp reassessment of India's foreign policy, however, was precipitated by the March 1959 events in Tibet. The Tibetan revolt against the rule of Communist China, news of which began to seep out through Indian sources in mid-March, promised to mark a historic turning point in the triangular relationship of non-Western countries with the West, on the one hand, and the Communist bloc on the other. Experts on Chinese affairs did not expect that, over the long run, this revolt would affect the power of the Peiping government in mainland China. But Peiping's treatment of the Tibetans deeply affected the attitude of India, as well as other Asian countries, toward Communist China as a world power.

It is important for the West to understand the reason for this change. Hitherto, many Asians had regarded "imperialism" as synonymous with "colonialism." This, in turn, was associated with the Western nations — Britain, France, the Netherlands, Belgium, Spain, Portugal — which in the Age of Exploration, and Expansion had acquired territories in Asia and Africa, and, after the breakup of the Ottoman Empire in 1918, in the Middle East as well. Thus, in non-Western eyes imperialism became a symbol of the unequal treatment accorded by the white man to his non-white colonial subjects. What Westerners referred to as "the white man's burden" was regarded by non-Westerners as the white man's yoke.

Japan's conquest of Southeast Asia in the 1930's did not dispel this conviction; for the Japanese, being Asians who challenged and, for a time, seemed on the point of defeating the West, were regarded by many Asians as harbingers of their own long-hoped-for liberation from Western rule. Had the Japanese consolidated their victories and retained power they would doubtless have suffered the onus of being regarded as new imperialists — as was the case with Japan's domination of Formosa and Korea, and its aggression against China in the 1930's. Their defeat and withdrawal left the Asian colonial peoples once more face to face with white rulers, some of whom made an orderly peaceful withdrawal (the British in India, Pakistan, Burma, Ceylon, Malaya), while others relinquished their possessions with marked reluctance (the Dutch in Indonesia) or after bloody struggle (the French in Indo-China as late as 1955).

Meanwhile, China had long been regarded by Asians not as a colony of the West — even in years of most far-reaching internal disintegration China preserved its own government

— but as a victim of the kind of intervention and unequal treatment by Western powers which colonialism had come to represent.

Given these circumstances, the assumption of power by the Chinese Communists in 1949 was viewed by many Asians not merely as an internal revolution but as a legitimate national liberation from Western encroachments. Nor was Peiping's military occupation of Tibet in 1950 regarded as an imperialist move, because this remote land high in the Himalayas had been dominated in the eighteenth century by the Manchus of China who, after a brief invasion of Tibet by the British in 1904, restored their hegemony in 1910, and suppressed a revolt at that time, quartering troops in Lhasa. Thus, historically, Tibet, which in the nineteenth century had been a bone of contention between Britain and the Tsarist Empire, was regarded as having been under the suzerainty of China.

The Tibetans, however, in their mountain retreat difficult of access, had developed a society of their own, dominated by Lamaism, a form of Buddhism, whose high priest, the Dalai Lama, with his seat in the Tibetan capital, Lhasa, is believed to be a living god, the incarnation of Lord Buddha himself. Thus, the present Dalai Lama, aged 23, is a national as well as a religious symbol. The rival Panchen Lama, aged 21, who heads a smaller sect of Shigatse, is regarded as an incarnation of a lesser Buddha, Amitabha.

When the Chinese Communists, in their drive to assert their rule over all areas historically claimed by China, occupied Tibet, they imposed a treaty in 1951 in which they pledged autonomy to Tibet, with no change in the political position, status, or power of the Dalai Lama. Under the treaty a Chinese military and administrative committee was to be established in Tibet, the Tibetan army was to be absorbed into that of China, and Peiping was to control Tibet's external relations.

Peiping, however, found it difficult to establish its authority over the Dalai Lama and the Buddhist monks who comprise a considerable portion of the population of about 1,300,000. The Chinese Communists tried to strengthen the influence of the Dalai Lama's rival, the Panchen Lama, who is believed to be more amenable to Peiping's influence. The Khambas, a warlike tribe located in the southeast area of the country, had revolted against Peiping in the summer of 1956, and had established their own local authority. When the population of Lhasa joined the Khambas, Peiping tried to arrest the Dalai Lama in March 1959. At that time some 13,000 Buddhist monks — whom the Chinese Communists, intent on secularizing Tibet, had described as "unproductive" elements — joined the revolt, which subsequently spread to the neighboring Chinese province of Sinkiang, where many Tibetans are settled. Fierce fighting broke out in Lhasa, and the Dalai Lama, accompanied by members of his family and four members of his cabinet, fled southward. The Tibetan cabinet, on March 25, denounced the treaty with China and proclaimed the country's independence. On March 28, Peiping, in turn, proclaimed the end of the Dalai Lama's rule and his replacement by the Panchen Lama. The Chinese then charged that the revolt had been sparked by Western "imperialists" abetting the Chinese Nationalists on Formosa (who had meanwhile stated they had made air-drops in Tibet and had pledged aid, and ultimate independence, to the area); and that Tibetans settled at Kalimpong, on India's territory, had played a part in the uprising. They also declared that discussion of Tibet in the Indian Parliament constituted intervention in China's internal affairs.

The Asian country most immediately concerned with events in Tibet is India, which borders on that area. Prime Minister Jawaharlal Nehru had questioned China in 1951 about the status of Tibet, and had urged Peiping to give it autonomy. While Peiping had not directly answered Mr.

Nehru's suggestion, the pledge of autonomy contained in the 1951 treaty had been accepted by India as satisfactory. Subsequently, India had endeavored to maintain friendly relations with its powerful neighbor, China, and had encouraged other Asian countries — notably at the conference of Asian-African countries at Bandung in 1955 — to accept the Five Principles of peaceful coexistence (*Panchsheela*) which India and China had agreed on in New Delhi in 1954. The Five Principles are mutual respect for territorial integrity and sovereignty, nonaggression, noninterference in one another's internal affairs, equality and mutual benefit, and peaceful coexistence.

Peiping's ruthless suppression of the Tibetan revolt came as a shock to India. Speaking in Parliament on March 30, Mr. Nehru, who had previously rejected Peiping's complaint about parliamentary discussion of Tibet, said that the Chinese Communists had violated their pledge of autonomy. Mr. Nehru also expressed India's sympathy for the Tibetans, and subsequently declared that he was seeking to bring about a peaceful settlement through diplomacy. On April 2, it became known that the Dalai Lama had taken refuge on India's territory, and was to reside at a hill-station, Mussoorie. On April 18, in his first public statement, the Dalai Lama accused Peiping of having broken all its promises to respect Tibet's autonomy. Again, the Socialist leader Jayaprakash Narayan, was more outspoken than Mr. Nehru, and in July 1959 urged that the case of Tibet should be discussed in the United Nations.

Whatever may be the outcome of the Tibetan revolt, it has had the effect of causing Asians, even those who follow a neutralist policy, to assert that the non-white rulers of Communist China are practicing "imperialism," which was once associated solely with Western whites. For example, *The Daily Times* of Jakarta in Indonesia said: "The picture of Asians kicking Asians is not a pleasant one." Another Indonesian newspaper said that this event "may cause Communist China to lose all her friends." *The Hindustan Times*, in an editorial entitled "The Rape of Tibet," declared: "Much else could die with Tibet if we do not even now heed the warning," and urged reassessment of "the basis of our foreign policy."

What happened in Tibet stirred Asians far more than events in Hungary, because the Hungarian revolt was regarded as a struggle between two white peoples. This does not mean that the Asian countries will intervene militarily on behalf of Tibet. India, the most powerful of them, with an army of 400,000, is not in a position to attack Communist China, with an army of 2,500,000. It should be borne in mind that the United States, the strongest military power in the world, did not issue a military challenge to Russia in the case of Hungary, in spite of its promises of "liberation." Nor will China's actions in Tibet make Asians less sensitive to Western methods in Algeria or South Africa, where whites continue to treat non-whites in a colonial manner.

The significance of Tibet is that it has aroused Asians to put moral pressure on Peiping, as they had previously done on the West, for independence or autonomy of peoples under foreign rule. Paradoxical as it may seem to Americans, many Asians believe that this pressure could be more effectively applied if Communist China was in the United Nations.

Meanwhile, India does not contemplate a change in its policy of nonalignment, as demonstrated by Mr. Nehru's rejection of a bid by Pakistan for a military alliance. Some observers, in fact, believe that the events in Tibet may have reinforced India's belief in nonalignment, on the ground that, as the threat of China grows, India should more than ever shun foreign entanglements and concentrate on its own economic and political progress. At the same time, it is expected that India will view Communist China with increased suspicion and distrust; will take precautions against possible

Chinese encroachments, both political and military, along India's Himalayan frontier, where Peiping has long been conducting a "cartographic war" by including some of the border areas of India within the boundaries of China as represented on Chinese maps; and will increasingly identify the Indian Communist party with international communism.

Indian critics of Mr. Nehru's foreign policy, although agreeing with him on the desirability of keeping the country free of what George Washington called "entangling alliances," contend that the government is not genuinely "neutralist," because of its marked tendency to be more lenient about the mistakes and misdeeds of the Communist dictatorships than about those of the Western democracies. To this contention government supporters reply that the Indian leaders expect far more from the advanced industrial democracies of the West, with their long tradition of freedom, than from Russia or China, which have grappled with the problems of industrialization only in recent years, and, having lived for centuries under autocratic regimes, had little or no opportunity to acquire the habits of thought and action that are prerequisites for democracy. This argument may sound specious to Westerners, particularly in moments when India seems more shocked by Suez than by Hungary. Yet, whatever we in the West may think of its merits, it, too, reflects a deep-seated belief that India may be in a position to act as a mediator between the West and the Communist dictatorships just because its own experience is a unique synthesis of Asia's past and the West's present which, it hopes may prove to be the world's future. It is only after several years of American condemnation of India's neutralism that the *New York Times* (one of the principal critics) said editorially on July 29, 1958, speaking of the Arab states: "Nationalism and even neutralism do not automatically mean victory for communism and Soviet imperialism."

The role of mediator between democracy and communism

and of activator if not acknowledged leader of the new nations of Asia, the Middle East, and Africa to which Nehru has aspired since he came to office, might have been more readily attainable had India itself escaped the dilemmas of power politics for which it has been quick to criticize other great nations. These dilemmas are a direct result of its as yet unadjusted relations with Pakistan which, through the accidents of geography, borders on it in West and East, with the two wings of the Muslim nation — West and East Pakistan — separated by one thousand miles of Indian territory.

The failure of the two religious groups, Hindus and Muslims, who had found accommodation between their faiths and their ways of life under Mogul rulers such as Akbar, to restore their coexistence on the eve of Britain's withdrawal was not only a tragedy for the subcontinent, but also cast a dark shadow on Asia and, to the extent that Asia is now inextricably part of the international community, also on the world. Unlike India, a secular state which promptly reorganized its political life and adopted a democratic constitution three years after independence, Pakistan, a religious state, has found it difficult to reconcile the interests of its two wings: the western sector, with a predominantly conservative leadership drawn from big landowners, and with militant tribes along the border of Afghanistan, and the eastern sector, with a socially and economically more advanced population which has pressed for increasing autonomy from the central government in Karachi.

As in India, the political group which led the fight for independence and, in this case for partition — the Muslim League founded by Jinnah, a brilliant Bombay lawyer — has found it necessary to adapt itself to the tasks of developing a new nation. In Pakistan, however, the influence of the religious leaders, the *ulema* or priests, slowed down the process of reorientation. But, in the course of forging the constitution political scientists, economists, and other leaders of secular thought who believed that a narrow interpretation of the Koran was not suited for the needs of a modern state, sought to achieve a synthesis of modern ideas with Islamic principles. The constitution, adopted on March 23, 1956, nine years after partition, had a preamble which began with the words: "In the name of Allah, the Beneficent, the Merciful. . . ," and declares "That Pakistan would be a democratic state based on Islamic principles of social justice."

According to the constitution, democracy, freedom, equality, tolerance, and social justice were to be observed, but as enunciated by Islam. There was a provision, however, assuring freedom to minority groups — the most important of which are the ten million Hindus — in the practice of their religion and guaranteeing their fundamental rights. But a Hindu could not be elected to the presidency of the Islamic state — although it is also unlikely that in India a Muslim could hope to become president of predominantly secular India. The extent to which the constitution could have operated as an instrument for the modernizing of Pakistan depended on its future interpretation by experts who favor the country's secular development. Meanwhile, however, the ruling Muslim League, headed after Jinnah's death by Premier Liquat Ali Khan and, after his assassination, by Premier Mohammed Ali, later Ambassador to the United States, gradually began to disintegrate, and was succeeded by the more liberal-minded Awami League, with its principal strength in East Pakistan, headed by the former Premier, Hussein S. Suhrawardy, who before partition had been governor of Bengal. The Awami League and other political groups were disbanded on October 7, 1958, when President Iskander Mirza abrogated the constitution and established a military government, only to be subsequently ousted from office by his aide General Mohammed Ayub Khan on October 27, 1958. With the abrogation of the constitution, the secular-religious issue may once more be reopened.

The travail of partition, which wreaked human misery on both sides of the new frontiers, and left each country economically crippled — with Indian factories deprived of Pakistan's jute, and Pakistan's jute producers deprived of India's manufacturing facilities — was further compounded by the as yet unresolved controversy about division of the subcontinent's canal waters.

Next to Kashmir, the problem of the canal waters is the most difficult issue between India and Pakistan. The background of the problem is that, in the undivided Punjab under British rule, 26 million arid acres had been brought under irrigation by thirteen complex canal systems. Ten of these systems, using 88 per cent of the irrigation water, were on the Pakistan side of the frontier at partition, and nearly all of them depend on rivers flowing from India or from India-held Kashmir. Pakistan has charged that India could, at will, divert these canal waters from its territory, and leave it to face a disastrous drought — a charge which India has vehemently denied. The fact that the sources of some of the waters needed for the irrigation of Kashmir are involved in the controversy has added to the bitterness on both sides.

The controversy was submitted to the World Bank which, after a careful study, made four proposals in its report published in February 1954:

1. Ultimately, Pakistan should have the exclusive use of the waters of the three western rivers (Indus, Jhelum, and Chenab), and India those of the three eastern rivers (Ravi, Beas, and Sutlej).

2. This division should take effect after a transitional period, estimated at about five years, during which link canals would be built to bring surplus-flow water from the western rivers across to the Pakistani area that now depends on the eastern rivers.

3. India could progressively reduce deliveries to Pakistan as replacement water from these link canals became available.

4. India would pay for the building of the link canals.

India accepted the 1954 proposals in principle, but Pakistan expressed doubts about the adequacy of the link canals and the time required to build them. After further discussion, the Bank adjusted its proposals by an *aide-mémoire* in May 1956. Its experts reported that link canals alone could not free Pakistan from severe water shortages, and advised that more reservoirs on the western rivers would therefore have to be built too. This time Pakistan agreed, but India objected, largely on the ground that the bill for link canals and reservoirs, which it would have to pay and which was then estimated at over a billion dollars, was too high.

Eventually, at the advice of the Bank, Pakistan trimmed its program down to $700 million, but India offered only $150 million, and complained that Pakistan was delaying a payment of normal water charges and was slow in building the link canals. India contends that it must put into operation without further delay its Bhakra dam and its Rajasthan Canal, slated to start functioning full-scale in 1962, when deliveries of water to Pakistan would have to be discontinued. Pakistan, for its part, fears the shortage of water which, it insists, would result from the operation of India's new dam and canals, and expresses suspicions about India's ultimate motives in withholding water deliveries to which, India retorts, Pakistan has no right in any case.

In spite of these controversies, on April 18, 1959 the governments of India and Pakistan announced that they had signed in Washington a one-year agreement regulating the use of the Indus River and its main tributaries for irrigation. This agreement, reached through the good offices of the World Bank, was to cover "transitional arrangements" for the period between April 1, 1959 and March 31, 1960. The bank was to send a mission to India and Pakistan to discuss new proposals.

Important as settlement of all these problems is, if both

countries are to cohabit peacefully in the subcontinent and to heal the wounds left by partition, none of them has threatened to create the threat of war — although there has been a good deal of sabre-rattling by Pakistan, particularly since General Ayub's rise to power and, occasionally, on India's side by Krishna Menon in his capacity as Defense Minister. Mr. Nehru, however, has firmly opposed a policy of hostility toward Pakistan. According to an urban opinion poll taken in 1958 by the Indian Institute of Public Opinion, nearly 48.7 per cent of the urban population in all age, education, income, and occupation groups is inclined to believe that India's expenditure on defense — which in 1958–59 constituted 35 per cent of the national budget, is not excessive — apparently because of concern about the uncertain state of Indo-Pakistan relations. Of those who regarded defense expenditure as excessive, 11.5 per cent did so on the ground that it is not appropriate to a country which is supposed to be following the Gandhian policy of nonviolence; and 15.4 per cent on the ground that India cannot afford it because of the Five-Year Plan. Of the total polled, 23.1 answered, "Don't know."

In the case of military defense, as in the case of foreign policy, the Tibet revolt marked a sharp turning-point. As late as February 28, India's Finance Minister, Morarji Desai, in presenting his budget to Parliament for the next fiscal year, which begins on April 1, announced a $50 million cut in defense spending — the only significant reduction in expenditures. Spending on the army and navy was to remain unchanged. The saving was to be effected by cutbacks in the purchase of planes and spare parts for the Indian air force.

Yet, when the Parliament debated this cut on April 9, following the Tibet revolt, many members both of the Congress party and of the opposition demanded assurances that the government was not taking a "calculated risk" by cutting expenditures this year in view of Chinese Communist military operations in Tibet, and asked whether the government was taking adequate steps to protect the frontier with Tibet. One Congress party member raised the possibility that Peiping might not be satisfied with the conquest of Tibet, and might have ambitions to extend its influence in other neighboring countries, including Nepal, Sikkim, and Bhutan, India's neighbors to the north, whose foreign policy and defense are controlled by New Delhi. The Defense Minister, Krishna Menon, replied that defense spending for 1959–60, estimated at $510,300,000 compared with $560,700,000 for 1958–59, meant no sacrifice of combat effectiveness and had been made possible by improved planning and the greater availability of trained manpower.

In practice, one of the most striking aspects of relations between India and Pakistan are the good spirit and the mutual respect displayed by the representatives of the two countries whenever they have met on the level of experts concerned with specific technical problems. Not only are the civil servants of India and Pakistan former colleagues in the civil service of India under the British, with the same tradition and intellectual formation, but several of the political leaders on both sides have tried to overcome mutual resentments and fears, aware that if this task is not accomplished now, while those who remember undivided India are still living, it may prove much more difficult for the next generation, accustomed to an atmosphere of hostility. This was the view of Ghulam Mohammed, the late Governor-General of Pakistan, who, even when he was on the point of succumbing to a mortal illness, strained his ebbing strength to find a basis for agreement with India. This has also been true of Mr. Nehru and of several of his associates, in spite of their profound opposition to partition.

All these efforts at accommodation, however, have so far foundered on the issue of Kashmir, the one princely state which bordered on both Pakistan and India and was not originally incorporated into India at the time of partition. In the case of Kashmir, all the emotions which in the past have hampered the settlement of territorial problems in other areas of the world, are present on both sides: the nationalist sentiments of both Pakistan and India; the fundamental split between the secular and the religious state which in the first place brought about partition; the attempt, in which both Muslims and Hindus among the Kashmiris have played a part, to transform a backward agrarian community into a welfare state; the struggle of the great powers over the control of a strategic area which lies at the crossroads of Pakistan, India, Russia, and China, and could be an important jumping-off place for military operations; and the desire of the Kashmiris to determine their own destiny. Unfortunately for Kashmir, as well as for Pakistan and India, it is one of those territories which, because of their desirability, seem destined to be bones of contention between neighboring nations. The list of these territories is long and repeatedly marked by bloodshed: Alsace-Lorraine, the Saar, Trieste, Danzig, the Polish Corridor, Korea, Vietnam.

Both Pakistan and India claim Kashmir, a beautiful state, with its jewel-like lakes set among Himalayan peaks and its sturdy population, which in its long history has known the passage of many conquerors. Neither has shown signs of yielding its claim in the past decade, which is strewn with abortive bilateral negotiations and the failures of successive efforts of United Nations mediators, from Sir Owen Dixon of Australia to Dr. Frank P. Graham of the United States.

As India sees it, Kashmir was one of the 562 princely states of undivided India which were advised by Britain to choose between India and Pakistan. After considerable initial hesitation, its Hindu Maharajah, Sir Hari Singh opted for India at the last minute. The Muslim leader, Sheikh Abdullah, a member of the National Conference, the political party of Kashmir associated with the Indian National Congress, and a close friend of India's prime minister, Jawaharlal Nehru, who was at that time in jail because of his efforts to democratize the Maharajah's absolutist government, favored accession. According to India, Hari Singh acceded after Pakistan had committed aggression by furnishing arms and military direction to "tribesmen" who invaded the western portion of the state, coming within five miles of its summer capital, Srinagar. India, therefore, say its spokesmen, had no choice but to send armed forces to Kashmir, at its ruler's request, to protect a state which had signified its desire to become part of the Indian Union.

True, at that time Mr. Nehru, at the suggestion of India's last viceroy, Lord Mountbatten, agreed that the people of Kashmir should have an opportunity to express their views about the accession, but only after the Pakistanis had withdrawn from the territory they had occupied — a condition Pakistan has so far not fulfilled. Lord Mountbatten's proposal was due to two factors: Kashmir's continguity to both India and Pakistan, and the presence of a population of 4 million, 77.11 per cent of whom are Muslims concentrated in the Vale, 20.12 per cent are Hindus, and the rest are Buddhists (concentrated in Ladakh in the north) and Sikhs. In retrospect, Mr. Nehru's agreement to a plebiscite is regarded as a political mistake, not only in India but also by some outside observers. For no arrangements were made about plebiscites in any of the other 561 states, and none were held, even though after 1947 India experienced difficulties with Hyderabad, where a Muslim prince ruled a population with a Hindu majority, and with Junagadh. Neither of these states, however, is contiguous with Pakistan, and it is difficult to imagine how, had they signified their desire to accede to Pakistan, they would have established a link with that country.

Mr. Nehru now takes the view that a decade later, when conditions in the subcontinent and in the world have changed, a plebiscite in Kashmir would become a new test of the two-nation theory he vigorously opposed in 1947; and that, if it should favor Pakistan, would lead to renewed turmoil and bloodshed among Muslims and Hindus in both Pakistan and India, and might jeopardize India's very existence. However, this view, strongly held by the Prime Minister, whose family are of Kashmiri origin and who has an emotional attachment to Kashmir, is disputed by some leading Hindu experts, who say that the assumption they would maltreat Muslims in India because of Kashmir is a libel on Hinduism.

Many Indians feel puzzled and aggrieved that the Western powers, quick to denounce aggressors elsewhere, have refused to recognize Pakistan's aggression in Kashmir. Others urge the government to have a plebiscite in the Vale of Kashmir for the sake of improving relations with Pakistan while retaining predominantly Hindu Jammu and Buddhist Ladakh. The Vale, they claim, whatever its economic, strategic, and sentimental value to India, is not worth perpetuating a dangerous quarrel with a neighbor whose support in Asia would be valuable for the Indians.

As the debate over Kashmir waxed and waned, the Indian government in August 1953 summarily deposed and jailed Sheikh Abdullah, once its trusted friend, who by that time was the actual ruler of Kashmir, since the Maharajah, son of Hari Singh meanwhile deposed by the Sheikh, had been reduced to the role of a constitutional monarch, appointed for a five-year period. This highhanded action, taken in the dead of night, was justified on the ground that the Sheikh had shown he favored an independent Kashmir which, New Delhi feared, might have gone over to Pakistan. In 1956, Kashmir's Constituent Assembly, under the leadership of the Sheikh's successor, Muslim prime minister Bakshi Ghulam Mohammed, voted to make Kashmir a state of the Indian Union, thereby officially confirming the existing situation. This vote is regarded by many Indians as a consultation of the will of the people, tantamount to the plebiscite which had been promised but never held — although, in fact, this is not the case.

Pakistan, as India knows well, disagrees with all these arguments. It takes the view that the predominantly Muslim population of Kashmir was not consulted about its wishes; that the Pakistanis did not commit aggression, as claimed by India, since the armed action which frightened the Maharajah into opting for India was carried out by "tribesmen" over whom Karachi had no control; that India highhandedly took over Kashmir, and failed to abide by its own promise to hold a plebiscite; that it added insult to injury by disregarding the decisions of the United Nations Security Council before which it had itself brought the Kashmir case; that it rules the Muslims by force; and that it is obligated to hold the plebiscite, which, Karachi contends, would result in an overwhelming vote for accession to Pakistan.

Impartial observers believe that of Kashmir's component parts Jammu — with its predominantly Hindu population — Buddhist Ladakh, and Gilgit would go to India, and that the crucial decision would have to be made only in the Vale of Kashmir. But the Vale, often called India's Switzerland, with its scenic beauties and its attractions for tourists, is an important prize for both countries, quite aside from religious and political considerations.

Gunnar Jarring, former president of the United Nations Security Council, as Sweden's permanent delegate to the UN, undertook a study of the Kashmir problem at the Council's request. In his report of April 30, 1957 he expressed his awareness of "the grave problems that might arise in connection with and as a result of a plebiscite." He called to the Council's attention that "the implementation of international agreements of an *ad hoc* character, which has not been achieved fairly speedily, may become progressively more difficult because the situation with which they were to cope has tended to change." He added: "I could not fail to take note of the concern expressed in connection with the changing political, economic and strategic factors surrounding the whole of the Kashmir question, together with the changing pattern of power relations in West and South Asia."

This statement was interpreted in New Delhi as suggesting that, given the state of the world in general and the unabated tensions between India and Pakistan in particular, the best that can be done is to maintain the *status quo*. Although these tensions emerged in the course of the partition of the subcontinent, in which the United States was not involved, they have been seriously aggravated by American military aid to Pakistan since 1950.

But, even if it were possible, and advisable, to maintain the *status quo* internationally, will it be possible to do it within Kashmir itself? So far as can be ascertained, the Kashmiris are uneasy about their present situation. Recurring attempts to review the case in the UN and threats broadcast by the Pakistani radio create a sense of insecurity which has an unfavorable effect on business and particularly on its most important component — tourism. People in Kashmir say, "Let's get this settled once and for all."

Sheikh Abdullah remains a highly popular leader in spite, or perhaps because, of his four-year imprisonment — from which he was temporarily released in 1958 only to be put in jail again, and then, in October of that year, brought to trial on charges of treason. If he is released once more, he might rally around him those Kashmiris who — although they welcome its economic aid and benefit by it — are discontented with India. The future is further clouded by the struggle for power which developed in the summer of 1957 between Bakshi Ghulam Mohammed, Prime Minister and president of the National Conference (Kashmir's counterpart of India's Congress party), and G. M. Sadiq, believed by his critics to be a fellow traveler, if not a Communist, who after an open break on August 9 left the conference and formed a party of his own. New Delhi has backed Bakshi, but Sadiq also has some support in India — although he was weakened by the outright stand of the Indian Communist party in his favor. In contrast to the Sheikh, who is believed to remain favorable to independence, Bakshi, a forceful personality, contends that Kashmir could not long survive without India. It is economically weak, he argues, and depends on India for both economic aid and military security, with 100,000 Indian troops, one quarter of the army, stationed in Kashmir. According to Bakshi, if Kashmir won independence, it would promptly become a pawn in the cold war. And India continues to fear that independence would ultimately mean that Kashmir would go over to Pakistan.

Supporters of Mr. Nehru point to the achievements of Kashmir, under the Sheikh and under Bakshi, both of whom could be described as Socialist-minded reformers. The state has carried out a land reform more far-reaching than that of India (in fact, Mr. Nehru regards it as a model for Indian study — although, in contrast to the situation in India, no provision was made for compensation), and has made a good start with its Six-Year Plan for economic development, which has included the construction of an all-weather road between India and Kashmir, and of a hydroelectric project. The Indian Planning Commission assisted Kashmir with the drafting of its plan, and India provided three-quarters of the necessary funds in the form of grants and/or loans. With its considerable known mineral resources, Kashmir, it is contended, will be able to achieve a diversified economy and raise the now low living standard of its people. These achievements, say the pro-Indian Kashmiris, would be lost if Kashmir were integrated into Pakistan. Meanwhile, the Pakistanis rule the section of Kashmir conquered by the "tribesmen" in 1947, which is now called Azad (Free) Kashmir.

In India itself there is a feeling of guilt about Abdullah. It was expressed most clearly by the Socialist leader Jayaprakash

Narayan on August 27, 1957 when he said that "the policy followed with regard to Kashmir has led to the deterioration of relations with Pakistan." He favored the release of Abdullah who, he thought, would then be able to persuade the Kashmiris to accept an independent and sovereign Kashmir which could be guaranteed by both India and Pakistan. The Sheikh, however, when he briefly regained his liberty, did not succeed in solving the problem.

For an outside observer the Kashmir problem is fraught with poignant contradictions. If one believes in democracy, then, one asks, is it not wrong, and even hypocritical for Mr. Nehru, who upholds the democratic character of India, to block a plebiscite in the Vale of Kashmir and thwart the inhabitants' right to self-determination? If the Kashmiri Muslims want to join Pakistan, then what right has India to prevent them from doing so? Yet, immediately, the question arises in one's mind: But would the Kashmiris, including the Muslims, be better off with Pakistan — politically, economically, and socially — than they are now with India? Is it possible, in this case, that self-determination might aggravate, rather than remedy, the problems of the Kashmiris?

No solution so far proposed for Kashmir is ideal from the point of view of either of the two nations that emerged from partition. But one thing is clear: responsible persons on both sides, as well as in the UN, believe it is essential to find as soon as possible a basis for restoring good relations between India and Pakistan, which are crucial for the peaceful development of both. Otherwise, both will tend to dissipate their limited financial resources on piling up of more and more armaments, instead of concentrating on their urgent economic and social needs.

India's failure to find a *modus vivendi* with Pakistan has weakened its influence in international councils, where otherwise its voice has become increasingly heard and listened to since 1947. On a wide range of issues, from a settlement in

Korea to the war in Indo-China, from the suspension of nuclear tests to reconstruction of the Middle East, Mr. Nehru intervened again and again with efforts to bring about a reconciliation of conflicting interests or, as in the case of the American prisoners held by Communist China, to speed the settlement of tense situations.

While many Americans have resented the "holier than thou" moral tone of Mr. Nehru (not unlike our own) on a number of critical occasions in which the United States was involved, there has been a growing respect for his broad view of world affairs, his philosophical outlook, and his willingness to work on preventing head-on clashes, as in the cases of the Suez crisis, and of France's decision to leave the UN General Assembly over the issue of Algeria. In this respect India's neutralism has served the interests of clashing nations, since India is one of the few countries of the world which is regarded as an impartial arbiter.

That India cannot consider itself immune to the frailties of other nations has been clearly shown by the Kashmir case. Painful as this is for India and Pakistan, and for friends of both in other countries, it may have the negative merit of convincing the Indians that in the long run they, too, may benefit by the kind of impartial advice which they are always ready to give in world affairs. Humility is a quality seldom possessed by great powers. India, a power great in size, in numbers of population, in the imagination and vision of its leaders, but weak in resources and military strength, has discovered early in the history of its independent foreign policy that it, too, is not without fault. In the years ahead this discovery may prove an asset rather than a liability.

Nor should the prospect for improvement of Indo-Pakistani relations be regarded as entirely bleak. In the past Mr. Nehru has urged a "no-war" pact between the two countries, which could allay the fear, real or imagined, of attack by one on the other — a fear, it should be added, which is discounted by the military leaders of both, who do not believe that either has the capacity to occupy the other's territory.

Hitherto Pakistan had firmly opposed such a pact. But, in July 1958 Pakistan's then Prime Minister, Firoz Khan Noon, who had previously served as its Foreign Minister, declared at a press conference at Lahore that his country would not go to war with India to settle its disputes. He described the talk of war between the two nations "as nothing short of lunacy," and asserted that he would try to seek a solution of Indo-Pakistani problems through peaceful means only, indicating willingness to consider India's no-war pact offer if Mr. Nehru should make it again. When it is recalled that Mr. Noon had previously spoken in menacing tones about the "unfriendly and unhelpful" attitude of the Western powers about Kashmir, threatening to "shake hands with the Communist countries" if necessary to win the controverted state, and that cries of *jihad* (holy war) had been uttered in Karachi by no less a person than Jinnah's sister, Fatima Jinnah, Mr. Noon's statement appeared to open a new approach toward settlement of Indo-Pakistani controversies. *The Eastern Economist*, recalling that, "only until the other day we were a single family," said: "If we cannot reunite politically, there is no reason why we cannot effect unity of the hearts. The next best thing to unity is friendship as between two grown-up brothers." The Noon-Nehru negotiations, however, ended in October 1958 when Premier Noon was thrown out of office by the military government of Iskander Mirza.

If leaders on both sides of the frontiers reach the conclusion that the urgent needs of their peoples for economic and social development are more important, over the long run, than preparation for a war which, in their hearts, they do not believe will occur, and decide to divert the funds they now spend on defense — 70 per cent of Pakistan's budget and 35 per cent of that of India — then both would be able to proceed far more rapidly with their development. And, instead of calling on the United States for armaments which serve to inflame the wounds between the two nations of the subcontinent, Pakistan might ask for an increase of American aid commensurate with the armaments funds it was relinquishing. For, while India has vigorously opposed American arming of Pakistan, it has strongly favored economic assistance to its neighbor. And, in both countries thoughtful men and women realize that, in the race between democracy and communism, those countries have the best chance of success which show most concern for the welfare, rather than the military preparedness, of their people.

Chapter 10

The Eventual Choice:
Democracy or Communism?

If the power of divination were given to man, no contemporary international question probably calls more urgently for prediction than the question whether the eventual choice in India will be democracy or communism. Yet, as of today a responsible answer would have to be given in Delphic terms — in terms sufficiently contingent to permit of diverse interpretations.

In a situation which remains not only fluid but fraught with a multitude of risks, two factors whose significance cannot yet be accurately measured may be expected to have a decisive role. One of these factors is the uninterrupted growth of India's population, which can play havoc with the best-laid economic plans and make a mockery of the most earnest hopes for even a modest improvement of abysmally low living standards. The other is the effect, over the long run, of economic and social developments in Communist China on the minds and hearts of the Indian people.

The obstacles to acceptance of communism in India, as already pointed out, are formidable. The millennial philosophy of Hinduism, reinvigorated by Gandhi for practical application in the twentieth century, is fundamentally incompatible with the ideology of communism. Its emphasis on the individual's contemplativeness, his choice between actions for which he must assume responsibility, and his self-improvement if he is to achieve eventual liberation from his mortal lot, would be difficult to reconcile with the acceptance of a totalitarianism that minutely dictates the acts of every human being, as done by Chinese communism, which in this respect far exceeds the controls imposed in the U.S.S.R. India's deeply felt tradition of nonviolence makes the use of force, both preached and practiced by communism, profoundly repugnant to the Hindus, even those who on occasion have transgressed against this tradition. Its respect for legal processes, reenforced by experience with British law, has assured the existence of an independent judiciary.

At the same time, the concern for human welfare contributed to Hinduism by Buddhism, the belief in reconciliation of conflicting faiths and ideas which proved a common denominator between the Hindu Asoka, the Muslim Akbar, and India's British rulers, and the political and economic liberalism which the Indians derived from Britain but found congenial to the best of their own administrative experience have so far combined to create a protective shield against the penetration in depth of Communist influence. The result is that, in the midst of economic and social conditions in many respects similar to those of Russia before 1917 and China before 1950, India has so far resisted the temptation to seek a solution of its heartbreaking problems through totalitarian means. This resistance was greatly strengthened in 1959 when the Communists refused to join other parties in denouncing Communist China's policy in Tibet, and were attacked by Mr. Nehru and other Indian leaders as opponents of the national interests.

But, will India continue to resist communism, or will it, confronted with the danger of stagnation, either consciously decide to gamble on the possibility that communism may be the best workable system for a country at its stage of development, or indecisively drift toward a Communist regime through failure to adopt and implement effective alternatives? Within the parliamentary democratic system of independent India there are features which directly or indirectly could serve the purposes of leaders determined to establish an authoritarian system. The 1950 Constitution, liberal as it is in wording and intent, leaves considerable leeway between centralization and decentralization of power, between the protection of the rights of the individual and arbitrary use of government power — a leeway of which extremists, whether Communists or Rightists, could conceivably take advantage in a moment of national crisis.

Under the constitution the government, although commanding significant powers at the center, notably for purposes of economic planning, must rely heavily on the states to implement its decisions in important fields, particularly agricultural reform and education. In these fields of decisive influence for the over-all development of the nation the central government has repeatedly been thwarted by states which have defeated or blocked its purposes either by their actions or their failures to act. It is possible that authoritarian-minded groups which succeed in taking control of state governments — as the Communists have done in Kerala — could eventually disrupt the central government. Conversely, if the powers of the states are unduly curtailed, the central government, if taken over by a totalitarian group, could be used, through its control of the nation's well-disciplined and well-trained armed forces, to impose its will upon the states which, whatever their capacity for noncooperation, would not have force at their disposal. Here, then, in relations between the central government and the states, India will need to keep a very delicate balance between the two, to prevent, on the one hand, the danger of disunity leading to disintegration which proved so ruinous in the country's past history and, on the other, the usurpation of overweening power by authoritarian leaders or groups.

Some students of India's government believe that this balancing feat will be all the more difficult, or easy, as the case may be, because of the extraordinary authority assigned by the constitution to the office of the president. It is argued that while the present incumbent of the office, President Rajendra Prasad, has made only moderate use of his prerogatives, this does not mean that under different circumstances — among them the lack of a strong and popular prime minister like Mr. Nehru — another man might not take full advantage of the powers assigned to his office. Among these powers the most important is that of taking over by presidential rule the government of any state or states if he should find that the security of India is threatened, "whether by war or external aggression or internal disturbances," or that "a situation has arisen in which the government" of a state "cannot be carried on in accordance with the provisions of the constitution," or that "a situation has arisen whereby the financial stability or credit of India or any part of the territory thereof is threatened." The language of these definitions is broad enough to permit a president bent on imposing his will on part or all of the country to assert his rule under a variety of circumstances. So far, the president has taken only four states under his rule, and this only for brief periods, but his power to do so could become a deterrent to the exercise of authoritarianism in the states, as has proved true of the Communist-ruled state of Kerala.* But, should an individual hostile to democracy assume the presidency, it is conceivable that he could assert the need for presidential rule in order to install authoritarian regimes in some or all of the states.

Indian constitutional experts, however, contend that the president, except in one instance, can exercise his special powers only on the advice and with the consent of the cabinet. His powers, in practice, are not much greater than those of

* See note on page 78.

the British Crown — to advise, to warn, to encourage, and to assist in anything his prime minister does or contemplates doing. In the opinion of these experts an authoritarian as president would far less be a danger to democracy than an authoritarian as prime minister. The best safeguard against usurpation by the executive, at the Center or in the states, they contend, is the existence of a strong and alert public opinion, whose spokesmen would be undeterred by fear or favor.

Another feature of the constitution which could be used to undermine democracy (although hitherto it has been used to block the activities of the Communists and the Hindu religious extremists) is the amendment of Article 22, which defines the rights of the individual, including *habeas corpus*. This amendment, through the Preventive Detention Act, authorizes the arrest and detention for weeks without trial of persons who are merely suspected of contemplating acts inimical to public safety and order.

This amendment has been used primarily against the Communists — as many as 1,500 have been held in prison at one time — although the courts have insisted that proof of acts, not merely of intent, should be produced against accused persons to justify the continuance of detention. It could, however, under different circumstances, be invoked by the Communists to eliminate their opponents.

Another amendment — of Article 31, which defines the terms of agricultural reform providing that land cannot be taken for redistribution without compensation — removes from the judicial sphere the question of what is reasonable compensation for expropriated property. This amendment destroys the protection given to landowners by Article 31, which provided that "no person shall be deprived of his property save by authority of law," and could be easily used by an authoritarian government to take over all private property in India.

Thus, it is not outside the realm of possibility that India's democratic constitution, as amended since 1950, could be applied to alter drastically the present political and economic system without resort to force and violence.

This would be particularly true if the ruling Congress party fails to revitalize its ranks and to implement its promises, and if its non-Communist opponents, the Praja Socialists, follow the example set by their most popular leaders, Jayaprakash Narayan and Asoka Mehta, and forego partisan political activity either in favor of promoting their objectives through nonpolitical means or of cooperating with the government. Assuming that the Freedom party remains a minor group, the field might thus be left to the only significant opposition party — the Communists — who unless they are disrupted by factional disputes, as has happened in the past, would eventually emerge as the alternative to Congress. If, then, the Indian people became disaffected with the Congress party's shortcomings or outright failures, totalitarianism might come for lack of a viable alternative — even though communism might be sufficiently modified by Indian ideas and practices to be different from that of either Russia or China.

But, assuming that Congress, with or without the support of the Praja Socialists, succeeds in overcoming its post-independence weaknesses, and forcefully tackles India's myriad problems, thereby rekindling popular enthusiasm, the democracy that would emerge could not be expected by the West to be an offprint of Western democracy. We are now beginning to realize that, with the best will in the world, even the most politically experienced non-Western peoples, no matter how generously aided by advanced industrial nations, cannot traverse in a few decades the complex stages of development which have taken the Atlantic nations several centuries. Political democracy in the Western sense, with its array of two or more parties, with its safeguards for the rights of the individual, with its checks on incipient trends toward authoritarianism, is the result of far-reaching economic and social changes which modern science and technology can help to accelerate, but for which they cannot be substitutes — any more than modern preventive medicine and public health measures can replace the process of growth of the human being from babyhood to maturity.

As the experience of the U.S.S.R. and Communist China has shown, economic and social conditions can be profoundly altered through industrialization by totalitarian governments. Whether or not these changes will ultimately create a climate propitious for the development of political democracy, as they did in the Atlantic community, is as yet an unanswered question. In India the question must be put in another form: Can a nation which adopted democratic institutions successfully carry through the economic and social transformations necessary not only for its material modernization but also for the survival of democratic ideas and practices? Or will it have to accept the dictatorial rule of an elite, benevolent and enlightened though it may be, and forego individual liberties, to avoid Communist totalitarianism until it has bridged the gap between medieval conditions and the twentieth century?

The omens for the future are on the whole favorable. The Congress party, which despite many weaknesses and shortcomings has proved that it is dedicated to democratic procedures, increased its share of the national vote in the 1957 elections from 45 to 47 per cent. While it lost seats and votes in some states, it did much better than previously in others, notably Madras and Rajasthan. Even in Kerala, where Congress had not previously had a majority and suffered from accusations of inaction and corruption, the Communist party failed to win an outright victory, polling 35 per cent of the popular vote as against 38 per cent for Congress, and could form a government only with the aid of independents it had aided in the election.

The leaders of the Congress party, moreover, have taken

heed of some of the major criticisms made both by its political opponents and by critics within its own ranks. Reforms in the party structure and in its grass-roots operations may be expected in the future. Meanwhile, the party is becoming more and more representative of the country as a whole, as the lower groups of the population move upward into the seats of power, particularly at the state level. Congress is becoming more democratic in its leadership. At the same time, it is becoming more oriented toward business in its outlook and methods. The party's leadership is not concentrated in one or a few groups. It is widely dispersed, and makes itself felt in the social and cultural, as well as political spheres.

The important thing is that, whatever form the Congress party may take in the future, it remains devoted to democracy as developed in India. In many non-Western countries economic underdevelopment has been more an excuse for dictatorship than a cause of it. India has demonstrated that democracy can thrive in spite of an as yet low standard of living — as long as the leadership shows that it is aware of the need for improvement and makes a reasonable effort to foster it. If the Congress party can rid itself of corruption, and make a major attempt to see that no one in India starves because of lack of food, or its price, or inability to earn enough to buy it, then it can expect to remain in power for a decade or more, and see current development projects to their fruition.

This is no easy task. It will be an accomplishment of outstanding magnitude if India succeeds in maintaining the substance of democratic institutions during its transition from primitive agriculture to a modern agro-industrial economy. The West can greatly further this accomplishment in two ways. It can offer to give long-term aid to assure "the fulfilment of India's second five-year plan and the effective design of its third plan," as proposed in the February 1959 resolution introduced in Congress by Senators John Kennedy,

Democrat of Massachusetts, and John Sherman Cooper, Republican of Kentucky. And, the West can sustain India's morale during the years of the plans' travail through public recognition that in a newly developing country even a modest measure of growing democracy represents a resounding victory over the temptations of totalitarianism.

India after Nehru: Disintegration or Consolidation?

In the perspective of the turbulent decade which has elapsed in India since the publication of this book in 1959, it is impossible to resist the temptation of asking oneself whether the analysis of then current events and the prognosis offered at that time — always a perilous venture amidst fast-moving changes — have proved unrealistic, or have been justified by subsequent developments.

Politics: Survival of Unity and Democracy

The first and most basic question, the answer to which will determine the future course of India, is twofold. Will the political democracy established in 1947 when India achieved independence after three hundred years of British rule prove enduring, and will a nation formed from British India and 562 princely states be able to maintain its integrity? Or has India shown signs of gradual disintegration since the death of Prime Minister Jawaharlal Nehru, an aristocrat by birth, temper, and training, who firmly presided over India's emergence as an independent and dynamic nation? As of 1968, in spite of dire early predictions by many Western and Indian observers that the independent new nation would sooner or later disintegrate into separate, more or less self-ruling and self-sufficient states, and in the process abandon democratic political institutions in favor of various forms of autocracy, India has achieved two major political feats.

First, India thus far has remained a united nation, in spite of wrenching political, economic, and social problems which might have disheartened another people and plunged them into either passive despair or violent revolution, and as of 1968 it showed as yet no serious signs of disintegration. And, second, despite the temptation and the many compulsions familiar to all developing nations, to substitute autocratic rule for nascent democratic institutions in a period of far-reaching and often painful political, economic, and social changes, India has retained its faith in liberal constitutional and secular ideals, continues to maintain democratic institutions based on universal adult franchise, and has the unique distinction of having held four general elections in which the most mammoth electorate in history voted with complete freedom. But, in spite of all these achievements, foreign observers ask, true though this may be of India's first two decades of independence, will the vast new nation find it possible to persevere on this course in the years ahead, in terms both of national unity and of democratic institutions?

As pointed out above, somber prognostications made by both Indian and foreign observers in 1947 have been belied by events. Whereas it had been predicted that, with the passing of Mr. Nehru from the political scene, India would rapidly disintegrate into a congeries of separate states, each with its own language or languages, and that the much-sought unity seemingly achieved under the first Prime Minister's leadership would disappear, leaving behind a confusion of warring political units which would not even maintain the essential link of a common language (the English language used during the erstwhile rule of Britain over British India, and adopted by the 562 princely states), India has outlived Mr. Nehru, and in fact has handled the issue of succession after his death with remarkable maturity and calmness.

As of 1968, not only were dire predictions not fulfilled but, in spite of frequent outbreaks of violence about language problems and economic hardships, political clashes and social struggles, India displayed a remarkable sense of national unity and national purpose. So far as could be determined in so vast and varied a land, the less than twenty-five years of independence had forged within the framework of the independent Indian state many new links — political, economic and social — between the country's multifarious, multilingual and multireligious peoples. Notably, in the autumn of 1965, when India and Pakistan clashed over Kashmir, India gave proof of its fundamental national unity and stability. The entire nation rose as one man to the defense of the motherland, and for the time being all the squabbles over religions, languages, politics, and economic and social problems were completely forgotten. The evidence, in fact, is strong that national consolidation, economic development, and social adjustment of Hindus and Sikhs, Muslims and Christians, have, it often seems miraculously, preserved and, even more striking, further developed a spirit of national concern and national purpose, thereby foreshadowing an increasingly stronger national consciousness.

True, on the political scene by 1968, the ruling Congress party of Gandhi and Nehru, which in itself symbolized the spirit of accommodation among widely varying elements, composed as it was and continued to be of groups of the right, left, and center, had lost ground in terms both of numbers and of power in several of the Indian Union's component states, and, as a result, had been weakened at the center. Yet, in spite of the decline of the Congress party once its chief architects had passed from the scene, and despite the considerable political uncertainty the country then experienced because of the less dynamic leadership wielded by Prime Minister Indira Gandhi, who had succeeded the late Prime Minister Lal Bahadur Shastri, the Congress party continued to retain its greatest asset — its embodiment of the most important aspects of Indian political thought and practice — which had insured its initial success at the time when India achieved independence.

The Congress party, although shorn of the charisma and influence it commanded in the days and the persons of Nehru and Gandhi, remains the keystone of India's political order. It has maintained democracy, secularism, social justice, and a constant search for a middle course at the center of the political spectrum, in contrast to the extremism of both right and left — extremism which, except for recurring but brief periods of political explosion, appears to be basically alien to the Indian character, which is deeply marked by a spirit of give and take. Because of this fundamental asset, the Congress party, in spite of its losses in the 1967 elections, remains in power (see Table 3). It is still the only political group capable of acting as a national party and, what is most important in terms of the Indian ethos, it is the only party still capable of reconciling the major elements of the country's goals and aspirations.

Although the Jan Sangh party on the extreme right has been strengthened and could become still stronger in the future as a result of rising nationalist aspirations and communal fanaticism (and, if so, could pose a serious threat to India's secularism), non-modern concepts and methods have until now held little appeal for the educated youth in general, which is bound to play a significant political role in the years ahead. It is possible that the other important rightist group, the Swatantra party, which remains conservative in its economic and social views, could gain increasing support in the years ahead as the middle class, which had hardly existed before, slowly but steadily grows with the expanding economy. This new middle class clamors for more and more economic freedom and political power, and is becoming a significant force of opposition to the Congress party's socialist

TABLE 3. Allocation of Seats in the
Third and Fourth Indian Parliaments.

Party	Third Parliament (as of April 1962)	Fourth Parliament (as of April 15, 1967)
Congress	375	282
Swatantra	22	44
Jan Sangh	12	35
Communist	17	23
Marxist Communist	15	19
Socialist	8	23
Praja Socialist	9	13
Independent	26	41
Others	19	39
Total	503	519

Note: The difference between the total figures for the 1962 and 1967 elections is due to the fact that the number of seats in Parliament are allocated on the basis of population.

policies. Moreover, its strength within the Congress party is also expanding.

Meanwhile, on the left, the Socialists remain unable to challenge the left wing of the Congress party (which in effect has itself helped to advance many aspects of socialism more effectively than the Socialists), and give the impression of having played out the role they briefly held on the political stage at the time of independence, under the leadership of men such as Asoka Mehta, who himself eventually left the Socialists to head the Planning Commission as a member of a Congress cabinet. In fact, Ashoka Mehta's career symbolizes the tendency of non-Congress social-minded leaders to by-pass the Socialist party, and to find opportunities for achieving their aspirations in the ranks or under the aegis of the Congress party.

Meanwhile, given India's gigantic economic and social problems, the possibility exists that the Communists will gain more power and influence in the years ahead than they have wielded since independence. But, as of 1968, there was little indication that this would be the case, for two reasons. On the one hand, the ideological extremism of Communist theoreticians does not appeal to the Indian temper, which favors accommodation between conflicting ideas and practices; and, on the other hand, the Communists themselves do not appear capable of winning the support of the deeply religious masses on a national scale. Moreover, even some of the prominent Communists who have succeeded in achieving high governmental posts in certain geographic areas of the country, notably E. M. S. Namboodiripad, Chief Minister of the state of Kerala, manage to stay in office only by forming coalition governments with other anti-Congress opposition parties. And, true to the tradition of India's wide variety of political views, even the Communist party is divided into segments which represent the Indian, Russian, and Chinese Communist brands of communism.

It is generally agreed in India that new leadership is urgently needed in the years ahead, as the country seeks to become thoroughly modernized, and that this leadership will come increasingly from the new middle class, which expands as members of the lower classes move upward in the social scale. In spite of losses registered at the polls in the fourth General Elections of 1967, both on the national and the state levels, the Congress party remains the principal source of leadership because of its democratic ideology and its secularism, which continue to hold out the promise of political stability, economic development, and social justice.

It appears that India will withstand attempts from any source to bring about national disintegration. Nor will it succumb to Hindu fanaticism. As of 1968, no responsible leader was ready to contemplate, or accept, the breakup of the Indian Union. Even the DMK (Dravida Munnetra Kazhagam) party, which as late as the early 1960's was threatening to have the state of Madras secede from the

Union, appears to have dropped the cry of secession. And, meanwhile, the spread of education, the emergence of a new generation of Indians determined to see their country strong at home and respected abroad, and India's growing economic and political strength are all contributing to a new sense of national purpose and unity.

Economy: Strengths and Weaknesses

During the decade 1958–1968, notable advances were made in the key sectors of economic development — from food production in agriculture to a wide range of new enterprises in the industrial field. True, during this decade India faced, in some years, critical shortages of basic foods, notably wheat and rice, as its expanding population, which in 1968 had reached over five hundred million (compared with seven hundred million in Communist China), outraced agricultural development. The resulting gap between the rising number of human beings to be fed and the relatively slow expansion of agricultural production widened dramatically. When, in 1966–67, India was hit by the worst drought of the century, this crisis would have brought about a disastrous famine had it not been for massive imports of wheat from the United States, which in 1967 — a year of critical shortage — rose to eleven million tons.

This precarious dependence on wheat imports from the United States has been a major weakness of India, whose basic economy, sophisticated in certain respects — notably in some sectors of industrial production and in atomic energy — remains backward in agriculture, in spite of considerable investment in that sector by the government, which has raised food production from fifty-five million tons in 1947 to ninety-six million tons in 1968. When the rainfall is adequate, and there is enough food to go around, the majority of the Indian people, who are amazingly patient in adversity, feel a profound sense of relief. But whenever the dreaded drought comes, hunger and misery threaten India's millions and create the danger of resulting political unrest.

In contrast to its as yet precarious agricultural situation, India has been making significant advances toward industrialization. In 1968 it was producing over six million tons of steel at three new and very modern plants — built, respectively, by the British (Durgapur), the Germans (Rourkela), and the Russians (Bhilai), who are building a second mill at Bokaro — as well as at two existing Indian-constructed plants in Jamshedpur (owned by the Tatas) and Bhadravathi (built by Mysore State). India has also developed the capacity to manufacture a considerable range of industrial products — from IBM machines and ships to airplanes, from cars and trucks (notably the Tata-manufactured Mercedes trucks) and railway rolling stock to various kinds of precision machinery — which it not only uses at home but also exports, mostly to various countries of Eastern Europe, Africa, and Southeast Asia, although some of the exports have gone also to Britain, Western Europe, and the United States. Moreover, in 1966 India joined the ranks of countries exporting technology. It has exported entire plants for the manufacture of textiles, sugar, cement, paper, and so on, and has installed them in the purchasing countries with its own technical personnel. In addition to its technological progress, India's close political relations with the Arab nations, Southeast Asia, and Africa have also proved a great asset in creating and expanding new markets around the globe. And the visit Prime Minister Indira Gandhi paid to Latin America in the autumn of 1968 had as one of its principal goals the establishment of closer trade ties with the nations of that developing area. Now that India forges technologically ahead of many of the other developing nations, it can look to the prospect of ready-made markets for its manufactured products in less developed countries, while it sells luxury goods, such as its silks, carpets, and jewelry, in developed nations.

A glimpse of India's future plans for economic development was given by Deputy Prime Minister Morarji Desai in a speech at the National Press Club in Washington on October 2, 1968. Mr. Desai expressed confidence that India will become self-sufficient in food grains in the next three years — that is, by 1971 — saying: "Our people all over the country are better fed, better clothed, and are provided with better health facilities"; and he pointed out that a record agricultural crop had been garnered in 1967. Agricultural production, according to Mr. Desai, had gone up by 20 per cent, and the overall national income by more than 9 per cent.

A very considerable part of the increase in food production, according to Mr. Desai, was due to the efforts of the farmer: the adoption of new high-yielding varieties of seeds, the use of chemical fertilizers and pesticides on a large scale, better irrigation practices, and greater overall investment in the land. The area covered by the new seed varieties increased from less than five million acres in 1966–67 to fifteen million acres in 1967–68. During the same two-year period the consumption of nitrogenous fertilizers increased by 50 per cent, and the area covered by plant protection methods doubled. Singling out one of the states of India for special commendation, Mr. Desai said that the Punjab promises to become the granary of wheat in India.

The role that the government seeks to play in agriculture, according to Mr. Desai, is solely to help the farmer in every way to help himself. In this important task of arranging for the inputs and of providing credit, research, and extension facilities, "Indian scientists, administrators, economists and bankers have stood by the Indian farmer loyally and effectively." And, Mr. Desai pointed out, "We have also had valuable help from our friends abroad, both from governments and private foundations in the import of know-how and of material inputs such as fertilizer, agricultural equipment and pesticides. We are particularly grateful to your country [the United States] for help in this area." It is assumed by this author that Mr. Desai's reference to private foundations refers particularly to the admirable work done by the Ford Foundation in India with respect to agriculture, notably the introduction of Mexican wheat.

Mr. Desai stated that it is the declared objective of his government to have India achieve self-reliance in food production in as short a period as possible. As a result of increased productivity, India's imports of food from abroad, according to the Deputy Minister, will be substantially less than in the two previous years, 1966 and 1967. Moreover, a number of projects, many of them organized with the help of foreign private capital, are designed to result in a total production capacity for nitrogenous fertilizers of nearly three million tons, as compared to a domestic production level of less than 500,000 tons in 1968.

In the industrial sector of the economy, Mr. Desai declared that industrial production during the first few months of 1968 rose by nearly 6 per cent, and a similar increase occurred in exports.

Mr. Desai pointed out also that the government was engaged in preparing a new Five-Year Plan, the fourth, which, after some delay, was due to start in April 1969. "Any target of growth that may be adopted," he said, "whether it is 5, 6 or 7 per cent, is to me not the most material consideration, for all these figures are modest in comparison to what needs to be done in India . . . As in the past, the bulk of the resources required for development will be found internally in India. Considerable redistribution of the pattern of incomes is taking place in India, and sectors such as agriculture, which have benefited most in the recent past, will naturally contribute a higher share for development in the future. In taxing the farmer, however, we have to be imaginative as well as somewhat indirect. It makes better sense to tax the consumption of the farmer than his less direct income. It is also possible to tap considerable domestic savings which exist in the rural sector if these savings could be demonstrably channeled into investments such as fertilizer plants and irrigation works resulting in tangible benefits to the rural taxpayer. We are experimenting with these techniques, in India, and I am confident that this problem can be adequately met in the context of the Fourth Plan."

While thus expressing optimism about the economic outlook in India, Mr. Desai also indicated that he was not disturbed by the political outlook — particularly by the proliferation of political parties in the states, which he described as "healthy plurality." The process of "collective decision-making within a federation, giving due respect to the point of view of members of different regions, has indeed proceeded well," he said. "This experience has also, once again, demonstrated to us that ideals and aspirations, from whichever party platform they are derived, have a great deal in common in means as well as in ends. All parties in India are committed to our basic democratic structure and to the achievement of change through persuasion rather than through force. I would submit that the establishment and continuation of this form of secular democracy which, unfortunately, has by no means been a uniform experience throughout the world, is in itself an achievement of no mean order."

Turning to the world stage, Mr. Desai said: "In today's climate in the area of international economic cooperation, the essential question is whether or not the more affluent countries of the world recognize that they have any responsibility for the two-thirds of their fellow-men who are at an average level of income which is about a twentieth of what is considered as the poverty level in the most affluent area of the globe. This is the central problem; and if we are interested in a rational ordering of the world, all of us, to whichever country we belong, have to work toward finding a durable and truly liberal solution to it."

With respect to foreign aid, Mr. Desai declared: "I for one do not feel that we have any natural right to seek assistance from others or to complain that such assistance is not forthcoming in the amount or in a manner which our needs might justify. We have borne our burdens mostly on our own shoulders and shall continue to do so in the future as in the past. We also at the same time have had considerable understanding and help from friendly foreign countries, and what we value most are the goodwill and fellowship built up thereby between us and our friends abroad, not only on a national but often on a person-to-person basis.

"It is also perfectly clear that the primary responsibility of every government is to its own people, and the first charge on its resources is the satisfaction of their domestic needs. While there can be no doubt or disputation about these matters, as members of the same shrinking planet, we cannot forget that while resources may be capable of being shifted from one sector of responsibility to another, there is no escape from the fact that all our responsibilities, domestic and foreign, need to be faced together and as a whole."

As India's economy becomes modernized, two important developments are taking place. First, the once prevalent Brahmin attitude, which expressed contempt for trade and moneymaking as well as for modernization, is being rapidly offset, if not altogether eliminated, by the emergence of a new generation which is keenly interested in modern activities, in technological and scientific development, in business and industry, and basically in a higher standard of living. And, second, if, as seemed possible in 1968, all these new trends coalesce into an intensive drive for technological and economic modernization, then the young generation may begin to find at home the opportunities for research and work they heretofore mainly sought abroad, thereby depriving their country of talents and energy India urgently requires for future development.

Meanwhile, India has assured itself of a large supply, actual and potential, of talented young men and women interested in science by enormously expanding technical and scientific education in the last two decades. With their efforts, India could succeed in creating before the end of this century a firm base for a technological breakthrough — and thus achieve what United States economists call the "take-off" stage for self-sustaining economic growth, for continued future agricultural and industrial expansion, and for still more diversified exports abroad.

It is important to bear in mind that, as in all developing nations (even in Western Europe at a comparable stage of development), consumption at home must be held down to permit exports abroad, perhaps only for one or two decades more, but conceivably longer. However, when and if India reaches the "take-off" stage, industry could be allowed, indeed actively encouraged, to expand enormously the output of consumer goods — and then employment opportunities would become increasingly available, more diversified economic development could be undertaken, and the standard of living could be substantially raised. Already India's leading industrialists are mass-producing electric fans, sewing machines and bicycles, and manufacturing refrigerators, air conditioners, and other domestic appliances in considerable quantities. Indian factories now manufacture radios, and it is expected that before long television will be produced on a mass scale, and will increasingly aid in the gigantic task of mass education. For example, recently, through arrangements with UNESCO, India obtained the use of a sophisticated satellite system to beam nationwide television all over the country.

In the field of atomic science, India has forged ahead with the work which the late distinguished scientist Homi Babha had launched in Trombay with the encouragement and assistance of Prime Minister Nehru. Within the span of two decades, four thousand atomic engineers have been trained and put to work in the Trombay atomic establishment, which now has three reactors, the last of which was built completely by Indian engineers. Atomic power stations which will supply electricity to Bombay and Madras are now under construction, also by Indian engineers. As of 1968, India was one of the top eight countries in the world producing atomic energy, ahead of Italy and Japan, and ranking with Canada and Sweden. In this rapid development of atomic energy, the availability in India of the ingredients essential for atomic development — thorium and monazite sands — has proved a great natural advantage.

As a result of this rapid expansion of scientific and manufacturing capacities, India in the visible future — conceivably by the year 2000 — can reach the point of taking a great leap into the modern age, even though some aspects of its economy, notably agriculture, lag far behind, and remind one of Europe's medieval period. India's many-pronged scientific and technological development may be described as moving within the span of a century from the era of the bullock cart into the era of the bicycle, which is fast becoming the accepted mode of transport both in villages and urban centers; from near-universal illiteracy to the use of television for teaching in villages as well as urban centers; and from the age of coal and iron (both of which India has in large supply), to the age of atomic energy.

Population and Health: Promise or Menace?

This keenly anticipated scientific and industrial success will prove of little avail in solving India's multifarious problems unless the country succeeds in winning two essential victories in terms of social development. It must check population growth; and it must improve the health of its citizens.

Since 1947 India has succeeded, through a determined campaign in which it has been skillfully aided by the World Health Organization (WHO), in wiping out malaria, which in the past greatly reduced the work capability of its population, and in reducing the incidence of tuberculosis, which was its single greatest killer. Through expanded medical facilities, life expectancy, which in 1945 was estimated at twenty-seven years, has been raised to over fifty years in 1968; and under improved health conditions the death rate has declined and the infant mortality rate has been reduced from 13 to 9.2 per thousand. This improved health has made possible increased productivity, and will eventually enhance prospects for an improved standard of living.

This welcome advance in both health and longevity has, however, exacerbated the increasingly serious problem of a rapidly growing population which strains India's relatively limited resources of food, manufactured goods, housing, education, and other resources. India's total population, estimated in 1951 at over 360 million, had risen by 21.5 per cent within a decade, to 440 million in 1961, and in 1968 was estimated at well over the figure of 500 million. If this steady rise in population growth is maintained, India will be confronted with grave problems of feeding, housing and educating increasingly large masses of people. Fortunately for India, its leaders of the late 1960's are keenly aware of the difficulties created by population growth, and have shown themselves ready to adopt a wide range of birth control measures.

During the first decade of independence, India had two Ministers of Health, both women — Princess Amrit Kaur and Sushila Nayar, both supporters of Gandhi and his philosophy of family control through abstinence. This philosophy, however, was not practical among illiterate villagers, who regarded a large number of children as useful for work in the fields, and, fearing that some of them might die young as a

result of epidemics, sought to assure an adequate labor supply by having large families. Indians, however, are basically
not opposed to family planning on religious grounds, and
have shown an increasing interest in its potential success,
provided the necessary facilities and techniques are available.

In the 1960's, the government, with aid and advice from
foreign sources, notably United States specialists on population control, has made use of various devices to limit population — mostly, until 1964, the condom and sterilization,
chiefly of males. In 1964, the government introduced an intra-
uterine contraceptive (IUD) in the form of a loop, hoping
to distribute forty million loops within a decade; but by
January 1968 only two million loops had been distributed
and inserted, because of concern about possible injurious
side effects. Other types of contraceptives, however, continued to be used, and increasing emphasis was placed on
sterilization of males, who are paid bonuses or allowances
for work days they lose; between June 1964 and January
1968, the government had performed three million sterilization operations.

Meanwhile, a new Minister of Health and Family Planning, Dr. S. Chandrasehekhar, not only pressed forward with
the programs of loop insertion and sterilization, but also
suggested that all males who had three or more children
should be sterilized. Although this proposal raised many
questions, both political and personal, many Indian leaders,
as well as foreign observers, believed that a crash program
which would include this measure was essential to check
India's population growth, and relieve the strain it imposed
on the economy. The possibility of a more liberal abortion
policy has also been discussed, as well as raising the legal age
of marriage, from sixteen years to twenty-one for girls, and
from eighteen to twenty-five years for boys.

These various efforts to cut population growth in half, it
is hoped, by 1975, have been aided by the introduction in

1967 of 5,400 primary family-planning centers and about 14,000 subcenters in rural districts; plans have been made to open about 50,000 more subcenters before 1971.

Problem of Languages

These hopeful prospects for rapid development of India's human as well as natural resources may be slowed down by one important factor — and that is the thorny problem of the country's many languages. Of the total population of India, 40 to 45 per cent speak Hindi, and the balance speak Tamil, Telugu, Kannada, and Malaylam (in the South); Bengali (in West Bengal); Marathi, Gujerati, and Punjabi (in Eastern India); and a wide variety of other languages.

It seemed possible that Hindi might, by 1968, have replaced English as the national instrument of communication — even though it has as yet only limited literature — had the Hindi-speaking areas not pressed so hard for its adoption as the national language by 1965, as provided for in the Constitution. This pressure, however, aroused the increasingly stubborn opposition of Indians who speak other languages — particularly those which have a rich literature, notably Tamil in the South and Bengali in West Bengal — and who had already feared that the adoption of Hindi as the national language would place them at a disadvantage with respect to their Hindi-speaking fellow citizens. This difficult linguistic problem was further complicated by the question whether English — used during the three hundred years of British rule in administration, business, and education but spoken by only a small percentage of the Indians — should be abandoned or retained as an associate official language because of its value for communications with the outside world.

It is understandable that in a country as vast as India, with its large population of half a billion, and its bitter experience of colonial rule, many would resist the use of English as a nation-wide official language, regarding English as a colonial symbol. Yet, in practical terms, it would seem that the multifarious, multireligious, and multilingual peoples of India might find the already widespread use of English a boon, not a hardship, at a time in world history when many other peoples who have never experienced the Indians' close contact with Britain find it desirable to teach their students English because of its universal use in such fields as science and technology. This is notably done in the U.S.S.R. and might, sooner or later, be done also in Communist China. Moreover, the use of English in India could serve another important purpose: it could link the various linguistic communities of India, which otherwise might either have to insist on all-national knowledge of the dozen or more languages commonly used in India — and this would impose a great burden on all citizens — or else find it necessary to accept the prospect that only those who speak the local language can be employed in a given state.

If that should happen, India would find it necessary to accept de facto a division of states which, in the long run, could produce the very breakup of the Indian Union into separate, non-communicating linguistic states which was regarded in 1947 as a policy inimical to the creation of a single nation. For the future stability and success of India, it is essential that all its citizens should be free to circulate throughout the country, and to study and work wherever they wish. But continued freedom of circulation will be possible only if communication between multilingual peoples can be assured, and for this either Hindi or English or both would have to be accorded the place of official and link languages.

Need for New Leadership

With all these far-reaching changes — political, economic and social — looming ahead, India urgently needs new, and younger, leaders to lead the nation into modern times. Until the 1960's — when the great architects of India's liberation from colonialism began to pass from the scene — the country had continued to rely on its former leaders, primarily Brahmins and Kshatriyas, who, unlike the aristocracy of France, did not perish in a political revolution like that of 1789.

Now and in the future, however, with the increasing growth of technology and industrialization, the ranks of the educated must be rapidly expanded, and new leadership must be sought not only among men, but also among women. This latter task is not unduly difficult, because Indian women are ready and eager to participate in the transformation of their country; and thanks to the inspiring lead given by Mahatma Gandhi in this respect, women are accepted as leaders to a far greater extent than in most other nations in the past — and in some of the advanced Western nations, including the United States, today. Indian women with the capacity and desire to work in all fields of endeavor, from physics to medicine, from politics to economic development, are welcomed by intelligent men on a basis of equality, and are encouraged to play an increasingly important role in all fields of endeavor. As of 1968, India had a woman — Indira Gandhi — as prime minister. Higher education is increasingly sought by women, as well as by men, and has become an important new status symbol in India — more important, in the long run, than mere social rank or wealth.

Foreign Policy: Non-Alignment and
International Cooperation

Since the achievement of its independence, India has steadfastly maintained the policy of non-alignment initiated by its founders — Jawaharlal Nehru and Mahatma Gandhi. This policy, as the Indians continually point out, is not a policy of non-participation in world affairs, such as the United States followed during its period of neutrality before World War I, and resumed after that war until it entered World War II in 1941, two years after its outbreak.

True, India has not joined any alliances since it attained independence, on the ground that non-alignment is embedded both in its geography and in its culture. But it has been a faithful member of the United Nations, and has made significant contributions to that organization, providing personnel for peace-keeping operations from Korea and the Gaza Strip to the Congo, and supporting all the policies of the UN which it has regarded as beneficial to world peace and stability. The Indians view non-alignment not as a negative concept, but as a natural expression of their historical development and of the ethos of their multiracial and multireligious population.

With this philosophy of non-alignment deeply ingrained in its history and in its ethos, India naturally found it difficult to understand statements such as that made by the late Secretary of State John Foster Dulles who, referring to Indian policy, asserted that "neutralism is immoral." Fortunately, neither the United States nor the world holds this position today. And, as a matter of fact, as of 1968, 75 per cent of the members of the United Nations were professing — and, in various degrees, also practicing — a policy of non-alignment with the great powers as being best suited to their interests.

In her address to the United Nations General Assembly on October 14, 1968, Prime Minister Indira Gandhi summarized very well India's basic approach to the great international issues of today. Her address is therefore worthy of close examination. After deploring the actions of the U.S.S.R. in Czechoslovakia during the summer, Mrs. Gandhi declared:

> If the use of force in international affairs is not renounced, and the rights of nations and the equality of races are not respected, how can tensions be reduced or the danger of conflicts avoided? The world is caught in a vicious circle, because of which any viable international machinery to regulate relations between states is

being progressively undermined and faces the danger of eventual collapse.

Nuclear weapons today represent the ultimate in force. Thus any effort to eliminate force as the determining factor in international relations must begin with practical steps towards disarmament. But the nuclear menace has become such an accepted fact of life that the world has developed a certain insensitivity to the nature of the threat. Despite every solemn resolution adopted by this Assembly, States continue to enlarge their capacity for nuclear war. The arms race and the search for more sophisticated weapons have rendered meaningless the concept of balance of power. Yet, every advance in military technology is accompanied by an effort to maintain a balance of terror. This encourages local wars and undermines the established political authority in States which are struggling to protect their freedom.

It is by restricting, reducing and eventually eliminating the growing nuclear menace that firm foundations of peace can be laid. The limited achievement of the partial test ban treaty has been offset by the refusal of States to halt the testing of nuclear weapons. The problems of insecurity cannot be solved by imposing arbitrary restrictions on those who do not possess nuclear weapons, without any corresponding steps to deal with the basic problem of limiting the stockpiles of these weapons of mass destruction in the hands of a few powers. How can the urge to acquire nuclear status be controlled, so long as this imbalance persists? Unless the powers which possess these weapons are prepared to exercise some self-restraint, collective efforts to rid the world of the nuclear menace cannot bear fruit.

Although the government of India basically stands for peace, the United Nations, and nuclear disarmament, it has incurred criticism from other nations, notably the United States, for its reluctance to arrive at an agreement with Pakistan about the most serious and most enduring conflict it has had with another nation since the achievement of independence — the conflict over Kashmir, which remains unresolved in spite of the efforts of many nations, notably the U.S.S.R. at the Tashkent Conference, where Premier Kosygin sought to bring about an agreement on this issue between Marshal Ayub Khan, President of Pakistan, and Prime Minister Lal Bahadur Shastri, who died of a heart attack immediately after the conference. Throughout the Kashmir controversy, India has opposed every attempt by Pakistan to lay claim to that area, on the ground that self-determination as a principle cannot be applied internally to specific parts of a sovereign country. As of 1968, this single most important issue between India and Pakistan remained unresolved, although it no longer appeared that President Ayub Khan would seek its settlement by force. Meanwhile, the U.S.S.R. maintained friendly relations with both Pakistan and India, and gave various forms of aid to both nations. It is conceivable that, at a future time, the U.S.S.R. may seek again to persuade India and Pakistan to accept some form of accommodation in Kashmir.

Disturbing as Pakistan's moves to obtain possession of Muslim-occupied areas of Kashmir have proved to New Delhi, a more formidable danger for India has been the prospect that, sooner or later, Communist China may attempt again to use military force against the Indian Republic, as it did in the early 1960's. As of 1968, New Delhi and Peking remained poles apart in their internal policies, with India's democracy in sharp contrast to China's Communist dictatorship, and the fear persisted in India that, at some time or other, the Chinese Communists, frustrated at home and abroad, might again strike at the Indian Republic. Although the danger of such an attack did not appear imminent as of 1968, Peking's close relations with Pakistan caused anxiety in New Delhi.

To sum up, two decades after the achievement of independence, India, contradicting predictions that it would disintegrate into a congeries of independent states, has proved capable of developing modern technology and of providing modest but increasing improvements in living conditions for its vast population; has succeeded in avoiding serious internal conflicts among its wide variety of racial, religious, linguistic, and economic groups; and has kept its secularism alive. For a country which had experienced one of history's worst communal blood baths at the time of its transformation from a colony of Britain and a congeries of 562 princely states into an independent nation, it was truly remarkable that in 1968 India, whose population is 60 per cent Hindu, had a Muslim President, a Muslim Chief Justice, a Muslim Cabinet Minister, and many other Muslims in high government posts, including a Muslim Ambassador to the United States.

And, in spite of its limited experience with democratic institutions before 1945, India has surprised itself — as well as the rest of the world — by maintaining its new patterns of democracy under the rule of law and within a free society. It is gradually welding the widely diverse religious and linguistic groups within its borders into a united nation; and it is continuing to develop an economy which, although still very backward in the field of agriculture, has already acquired a broad and firm base for modern industrialization. At the same time India is effecting a social transition from a population divided primarily into a minority of the wealthy and the powerful and a vast majority of the poor and the weak to an increasingly strong social order marked, on the one hand, by the rise of a new, technologically oriented middle class, and, on the other hand, by an expanding measure of social justice. Meanwhile, by forging a foreign policy which has made possible increasing cooperation on the world scene with a wide spectrum of both developed and developing nations, and by strongly emphasizing the use of the United Nations and other international organizations, Indian leaders hope to help the world community achieve a stable and lasting peace.

Selected Bibliography

Alexandrowicz, C. H. *Constitutional Developments in India.* Bombay: Oxford University Press, 1957.

Anstey, Vera. *Economic Development of India,* 2nd ed. New York: Longmans, 1932.

Appleby, Paul H. *Public Administration in India: Report of a Survey.* New Delhi: Manager of Publications, 1953.

———— *Re-examination of India's Administrative System.* New Delhi: Manager of Publications, 1956.

Archer, W. G. *India and Modern Art.* London: Allen and Unwin, 1959.

Austin, Granville. *The Indian Constitution: Cornerstone of a Nation.* Oxford: The Clarendon Press, 1966; New York: Oxford University Press, 1966.

Bailey, F. G. *Caste and the Economic Frontier.* Manchester: Manchester University Press, 1957.

Basham, A. L. *The Wonder That Was India.* London: Sidgwick and Jackson, 1954; New York: Hawthorn, 1963. (rev.).

Berkes, Ross N., and Mohinder S. Bedi. *The Diplomacy of India.* Stanford: Stanford University Press, 1958.

Bouquet, A. C. *Hinduism.* New York: Hutchinson's University Library, 1948.

Bowles, Chester. *Ambassador's Report.* New York: Harper, 1954.

Braibanti, Ralph, and J. J. Spenger, eds. *Administration and Economic Development in India.* Durham, N. C.: Duke University Press, 1963.

Brecher, Michael. *Nehru: A Political Biography.* New York and London: Oxford University Press, 1959.

———— *Nehru's Mantle: The Politics of Succession in India.* New York: Frederick A. Praeger, 1966.

———— *The Struggle for Kashmir.* New York: Oxford University Press, 1953.

Brown, D. Mackenzie. *Indian Political Thought From Ranade to Bhave: The Nationalist Movement.* Berkeley: University of California Press, 1961.

―――― *The White Umbrella: Indian Political Thought from Manu to Gandhi.* Berkeley and Los Angeles: University of California Press, 1953.

Brown, W. Norman. *The United States and India and Pakistan.* Cambridge, Mass.: Harvard University Press, 1953.

Chakravarty, P. C. *India's China Policy.* Bloomington, Ind.: Indiana University Press, 1962.

Chaudhuri, Nirad C. *The Continent of Circe: An Essay on the Peoples of India.* London: Chatto and Windus, 1965; New York: Oxford University Press, 1966.

Choubey, Jagdish Narain. *Problems of National Integration.* Delhi: National Integration Council, 1961.

Coale, Ansley J., and Edgar M. Hoover. *Population Growth and Economic Development in Low-Income Countries: A Case Study of India's Prospects.* Princeton: Princeton University Press, 1958.

Congressional Record, 85th Congress, 2nd Session, June 6, 1958. Senate Debate on Section 2 of the Mutual Security Act of 1952 as amended (Kennedy-Cooper proposal "to assist India to complete successfully its current programs for economic development").

Constitution of India, The. New Delhi: Manager of Publications, 1956.

Cormack, Margaret. *The Hindu Woman.* Bombay: Asia Publishing House, 1961.

Cressey, George B. *Asia's Lands and Peoples.* New York: McGraw-Hill, 1951.

Davis, Kingsley. *The Population of India and Pakistan.* Princeton: Princeton University Press, 1951.

Douglas, William O. *We the Judges: Studies in American and Indian Constitutional Law from Marshall to Mukerji.* Garden City, New York: Doubleday, 1956.

Dube, S. C. *Indian Village*. London: Routledge and Kegan Paul, 1955.

———*India's Changing Villages: Human Factors in Community Development*. London: Routledge and Kegan Paul, 1958.

Embree, Ainslie T., ed. *The Hindu Tradition*. New York: Modern Library, 1966.

Fischer, Louis. *Gandhi*. New York: Signet, 1954. Paperback.

Fisher, Margaret W., and Joan V. Bondurant. *Indian Views of Sino-Indian Relations*. Berkeley: University of California Press, 1956.

Gadgil, D. R. *Economic Policy and Development*. Poona: Gokhale Institute, 1955.

——— *The Industrial Evolution of India*, 4th ed. Bombay: Oxford University Press, 1942.

Garratt, Geoffrey Theodore, ed. *The Legacy of India*. Oxford: The Clarendon Press, 1937.

Gibb, H. A. R. *Mohammedanism*. Mentor, 1955. Paperback.

Gorwala, A. D. *Not in Our Stars: Through the Eyes of An Indian Critic*. Bombay: Jaico Publishing House, 1958. Paperback.

——— *Of Matters Administrative*. Bombay: Popular Book Depot, 1958.

Government of India. *Report on India's Food Crisis and Steps to Meet It*, by the Agricultural Production Team sponsored by the Ford Foundation (Ministry of Food and Agriculture and Ministry of Community Development and Cooperation, April 1959).

Griffiths, Percival Joseph. *Modern India*. New York: Frederick A. Praeger, 1957.

Harrison, Selig S., ed. *India and the United States*. New York: Macmillan, 1961.

Harrison, Selig S. *India: The Most Dangerous Decades*. Princeton: Princeton University Press, 1960.

Hart, Henry C. *New India's Rivers*. Bombay: Orient Longmans, 1956.

Hutton, J. H. *Caste in India,* 4th ed. New York: Oxford University Press, 1963.

Isaacs, Harold Robert. *Scratches on Our Minds: American Images of China and India.* New York: John Day, 1958.

Isherwood, Christopher, and Swami Prabhavananda, trans. *The Song of God: Bhagavad-Gita.* N.Y.: Mentor, 1954. Paperback.

Kabir, Humayun. *Education in New India.* London: Allen and Unwin, 1956.

————— *The Indian Heritage.* London: Meridian Books, 1947; Bombay: Asia Publishing House, 1955.

Kālidāsa. *Shakuntala,* trans. Arthur W. Ryder. New York: E. P. Dutton, 1928.

Kautsky, John H. *Moscow and the Communist Party of India.* New York: Wiley, 1956.

Kidron, Michael. *Foreign Investments in India.* New York and London: Oxford University Press, 1965.

Kogekar, S. V., and Richard L. Park, eds. *Reports on the Indian General Elections, 1951–52.* Bombay: Popular Book Depot, 1956. Distributed in the United States by the Institute of Pacific Relations.

Korbel, Josef. *Danger in Kashmir.* Princeton: Princeton University Press, 1954.

Kramrisch, Stella. *The Art of India: Traditions of Indian Sculpture, Painting and Architecture.* New York: Phaidon, 1954.

Lamb, Beatrice Pitney. *India: A World in Transition,* 3rd ed. New York: Frederick A. Praeger, 1968. Paperback.

Levi, Werner. *Free India in Asia.* Minneapolis: University of Minnesota Press, 1952.

Malenbaum, Wilfred. *East and West in India's Development.* Reports on the Economics of Competitive Coexistence (National Planning Association, April 1959).

————— *Prospects for Indian Development.* London: Allen and Unwin, 1962; New York: The Free Press of Glencoe, 1962.

Masani, M. R. *The Communist Party of India*. New York: Macmillan, 1954.

Mayer, Albert, and Associates, in collaboration with McKim Marriott and Richard L. Park. *Pilot Project, India*. Berkeley: University of California Press, 1958.

Mehta, Asoka, "The Political Mind of India," *Foreign Affairs* (July 1957).

Mehta, G. L., "As Others See Us," *Foreign Affairs* (October 1958).

Menon, V. P. *The Story of the Integration of the Indian States*. New York: Macmillan, 1956.

Morgan, Kenneth W. *Islam: The Straight Path*. New York: The Ronald Press, 1958.

Morris-Jones, W. H. *Parliament in India*. London: Longmans, 1952.

Myers, Charles A. *Labor Problems in the Industrialization of India*. Cambridge, Mass.: Harvard University Press, 1958.

Nanda, B. R. *The Nehrus: Motilal and Jawaharlal*. New York: John Day, 1963.

Natarajan, S. *A Century of Social Reform in India*. Bombay: Asia Publishing House, 1959.

Nehru, Jawaharlal. *The Discovery of India*. New York: John Day, 1946; Anchor Books, 1960 (paperback).

———— *Glimpses of World History*. New York: L. Drummond, 1949.

———— *India's Foreign Policy*. Publication Division, Ministry of Information and Broadcasting, Government of India, 1961.

Overstreet, Gene D., and Marshall Windmiller. *Communism in India*. Berkeley: University of California Press, 1959.

Palmer, Norman D. "India," in George McT. Kahin, *Major Governments of Asia*. Ithaca: Cornell University Press, 1958.

———— *South Asia and United States Policy*. Boston: Houghton Mifflin, 1966.

—— *The Indian Political System.* Boston: Houghton Mifflin, 1961.

Pannikar, K. M. *Asia and Western Dominance: A Survey of the Vasco da Gama Epoch of Asian History, 1498–1945,* rev. ed. New York: Hillary House, 1959.

Park, Richard L., and Irene Tinker, eds. *Leadership and Political Institutions in India.* Princeton: Princeton University Press, 1959.

Parton, Margaret. *The Leaf and the Flame.* New York: Knopf, 1959.

Planning Commission, Government of India. *First Five Year Plan.* New Delhi, December 1952.

Planning Commission, Government of India. *The New India: Progress Through Democracy.* New York: Macmillan, 1958.

Planning Commission, Government of India. *Report of the Indian Delegation to China on Agrarian Co-operatives.* New Delhi, May 1957.

Planning Commission, Government of India. *Second Five Year Plan.* New Delhi, 1956.

Rau, Benegal N. *India's Constitution in the Making.* Bombay: Orient Longmans, 1960; New York: Paragon Book Reprint Corporation, 1964 (2nd ed.).

Rawlinson, Hugh George. *India: A Short Cultural History.* New York: Frederick A. Praeger, 1952.

Rosen, George. *Democracy and Economic Change in India.* Berkeley: University of California Press, 1966.

Ross, Nancy Wilson. *Three Ways of Asian Wisdom.* New York: Simon and Schuster, 1966.

Rostow, Walt W. Testimony; U.S. Senate, Committee on Foreign affairs, 85th Congress, 2nd Session, Hearings: "Review of Foreign Policy, 1958."

Rowland, Benjamin. *The Art and Architecture of India.* London and Baltimore: Penguin Books, 1953.

Rudolph, Lloyd I., and Suzanne H. Rudolph. *The Modernity of Tradition: Political Development in India.* Chicago: University of Chicago Press, 1967.

Singer, Milton, ed. *Traditional India: Structure and Change.* Austin: University of Texas Press, 1959.

Smith, Donald E. *India as a Secular State.* Princeton: Princeton University Press, 1963.

Smith, Wilfred Cantwell. *Modern Islam in India: A Social Analysis.* Lahore: Ripon Printing Press, 1947.

Spear, Percival. *India: A Modern History.* Ann Arbor: University of Michigan Press, 1961.

———*India, Pakistan and the West,* 3rd ed. London: Oxford University Press, Home University Library, 1958.

Stein, Arthur. "India and the USSR: The Post-Nehru Period," *Asian Survey* (Berkeley, California), vol. VII, no. 3 (March 1967).

Tagore, Rabindranath. *Nationalism.* London: Macmillan, 1917.

Talbot, Phillips. "The Second General Elections: Voting in the States." American Universities Field Staff, India, PT–6–1957.

Talbot, Phillips, and S. L. Poplai. *India and America: A Study of Their Relations.* New York: Harper, 1958.

Tennyson, Hallam. *India's Walking Saint: The Story of Vinoba Bhave.* Garden City, New York: Doubleday, 1955.

Thompson, Edward John, and Geoffrey Theodore Garratt. *Rise and Fulfilment of British Rule in India.* London: Macmillan, 1934.

Thorner, Daniel, and Alice Thorner. *Land and Labor in India.* Bombay and New York: Asia Publishing House, 1962.

Tinker, Hugh. *India and Pakistan: A Political Analysis,* rev. ed. New York: Frederick A. Praeger, 1968.

Turner, Roy. *India's Urban Future.* Berkeley: University of California Press, 1962.

UNESCO, *India: Paintings from Ajanta Caves.* New York Graphic Society by arrangement with UNESCO, 1954.

Useem, John, and Ruth Hill. *The Western-Educated Man in India.* New York: Dryden Press, 1955.

Ward, Barbara. *India and the West,* rev. ed. New York: W. W. Norton, 1964.

Weber, Max. *The Religion of India*. Glencoe, Illinois: Free Press, 1958.

Weiner, Myron. *Party Building in a New Nation*. Chicago: University of Chicago Press, 1967.

—— *Party Politics in India*. Princeton: Princeton University Press, 1957.

Wiser, William, and Charlotte Wiser. *Behind Mud Walls, 1930–1960*. Berkeley: University of California Press, 1963.

Woodruff, Philip. *The Men Who Ruled India*, 2 vols. New York: St. Martin's Press, 1954.

Zimmer, Heinrich. *The Art of Indian Asia, its Mythology and Transformations*, completed and edited by Joseph Campbell, 2 vols. New York: Pantheon Books, 1955.

Zinkin, Taya. *Challenges in India*. New York: Walker, 1967.

NOVELS AND PERSONAL MEMOIRS

Anand, Mulk Raj. *Coolie*. London and New York: Hutchinson International Authors, 1947.

—— *The Village*. Toronto: Nelson, 1939.

Chaudhuri, Nirad C. *The Autobiography of an Unknown Indian*. New York: Macmillan, 1951.

Forster, E. M. *A Passage to India*. New York: Harcourt Brace, 1924.

Gandhi, Mohandas K. *An Autobiography: The Story of My Experiments with Truth*. Boston: Beacon Press, 1957. Paperback.

Markandaya, Kamala. *Nectar in a Sieve*. New York: John Day, 1954.

Masters, John. *Bhowani Junction*. New York: Viking Press, 1954.

Mukerji, Dhan Gopal. *My Brother's Face*. London: Thornton Butterworth, 1935.

Narayan, R. K. *The Financial Expert*. East Lansing: Michigan State College Press, 1953.

—— *The Guide*. New York: Viking Press, 1958.

Nehru, Jawaharlal. *Toward Freedom: The Autobiography of Jawaharlal Nehru.* Boston: Beacon Press, 1958. Paperback.

Rajan, Balachandra. *The Dark Dancer.* New York: Simon and Schuster, 1958.

Rama Rau, Santha. *Remember the House.* New York: Harper, 1956.

·

Index